THE BLACK
AND THE BLUE

A COP REVEALS THE CRIMES, RACISM, AND INJUSTICE IN AMERICA'S LAW ENFORCEMENT

MATTHEW HORACE

and Ron Harris

hachette

BOOKS

NEW YORK BOSTON

Hachette Books
Hachette Book Group
1290 Avenue of the Americas, New York, NY 10104
hachettebooks.com
twitter.com/hachettebooks

First Edition: August 2018

Hachette Books is a division of Hachette Book Group, Inc. The Hachette Books name and logo are trademarks of Hachette Book Group, Inc.

The publisher is not responsible for websites (or their content) that are not owned by the publisher.

The Hachette Speakers Bureau provides a wide range of authors for speaking events. To find out more, go to www.hachettespeakersbureau.com or call (866) 376-6591.

LCCN: 2018938061

ISBNs: 978-0-316-44008-0 (hardcover), 978-0-316-44007-3 (ebook)

Printed in the United States of America

LSC-C

10 9 8 7 6 5 4 3 2 1

In memory of Delaware State Trooper Stephen Ballard and ATF Special Agent Gregory Holley, who proudly embodied the black and the blue.

CONTENTS

A NOTE ON INTERVIEWS AND

ATTRIBUTIONS

While researching this book, my co-author, Ron Harris, and I conducted interviews with close to one hundred law enforcement professionals, elected officials, community advocates, and survivors of police shootings. These individuals represented every race, color, gender, age, profession, and political affiliation. The law enforcement and police interviewees represented every rank of service from patrol officer to detective to chief of police. For a year, we spent long hours on the road driving or on the trains and planes from Boston to Chicago to Los Angeles to New York City to St. Louis to Newark to Baltimore and Seattle to St. Petersburg with the goal of collecting a real profile or representation of urban, suburban, and rural policing environments.

Some people we sought out because of their many years of dedicated service to the noble profession; some we sought out because of their knowledge of criminal justice reform; some we wanted to hear from because their approach ran counter to my views as a black officer—they believed that everything is fine. If I wanted to hear all sides of the issue, I had to be open to all perspectives.

While many of the interviewees agreed to be identified by their real names, some did not. This is primarily because many of these people are still actively working in law enforcement. Among the many courageous individuals who let us talk to them and come into their homes are

Trooper Tony April, Detective Brian Mallory, Chief Kathleen O'Toole, Commander Crystal King-Smith, Chief Chris Magnus, and Chief Philip Banks. We've included firsthand accounts from each of them.

Within the ranks of law enforcement lurks the dated and dangerous concept that "Cops don't tell on cops." This is why I decided to take on this project. If not me, then who else, to help figure out what is really going on in law enforcement? I've included my own personal experiences.

The majority of the interviews I conducted took place between 2015 and 2017. My process revealed many experiences similar to mine, particularly among minority police and law enforcement officers, and were generally corroborated by white police officers, albeit from different police environments and departments.

Finally, I am a champion of wholesale police reform in the United States. And like the brothers and sisters in blue I interviewed, I am proud of my own personal contribution and the contribution of all law enforcement officers who put their lives on the line to serve our country.

For 27 years, I depended on law enforcement professionals—both black and white—to protect me from harm, danger, or death. We do things that many could never do, go into places where many would never go, and confront situations that many could never face. We routinely place ourselves in harm's way to protect the liberties of people we will never know or see. I never felt that any officers I ever worked with would not have risked their own safety to ensure mine or that of other members of the public. For this I am eternally grateful.

But, as leaders, we understand that to address a problem, we have to acknowledge the problem. I don't know that most Americans even understand that we have a problem. I hope and trust that *The Black and the Blue* awakens Americans to the problem of racial injustice in our law enforcement community—and our society—and helps address the problem.

—*Matthew Horace*

INTRODUCTION

I am a cop. Make no mistake about it. I've been part of the best and the worst that my noble profession represents. I've worked hard and played hard, true to cop culture. I've been in sports leagues with cops, I have eaten, drunk, and worshiped with cops. I have picnicked, partied, and celebrated with cops. I have cried with cops and when some of us have died, a part of me has died with them. I have pursued bad guys and protected communities in every state in the country, even Guam, and at nearly every level of law enforcement. I've held lots of titles. I was a police officer in Arlington, Virginia, before I joined the Bureau of Alcohol, Tobacco and Firearms, where I started as a special agent and progressed to become an ATF senior executive. I've headed task forces, conducted trainings, overseen high-risk operations, coordinated multistate investigations, and more.

Still, at my core, I'm just a cop, one of the hundreds of thousands of men and women who have at some point taken an oath to protect and serve the people of this great nation.

I'm the guy who responds to the pleas for help; the guy who breaks up family fights; who pushes through the bolted door, knowing that danger and death may lurk on the other side. The guy who goes on that "routine call," aware that it could be my last; who comforts crime victims; who finds missing children and talks down irate lovers. I'm the officer on that dimly lit road trying to figure out whether the object in a person's hand is a cell phone or a handgun, who in a split second must decide whether a motorist reaching for the glove box is nervously searching for his registration and insurance card or making a dangerous lunge for a weapon.

I am Officers Gabriel Figueroa and Paul Abel in Pittsburgh, who rescued a child from the back seat of an SUV as it teetered precariously on the edge of a steep hillside while the unconscious driver and front-seat passenger sat slumped over, overdosed on heroin.

I am Officer Katrina Culbreath in Dothan, Alabama, who, after listening in on a trial where an 18-year-old mother pleaded guilty to shoplifting in order to feed her 17-month-old daughter, drove the woman to a local grocery store and bought her food.

I am a man who has shed too many tears and stood at attention too many times as the mournful wail of bagpipes, signaling the final goodbye to a fallen comrade, washed over me.

I am Officers Jose Gilbert Vega, 63, a father of eight and two months from retirement, and Lesley Zerebny, 27, a rookie just returning from maternity leave after the birth of her 4-month-old daughter, both gunned down as they responded to a domestic disturbance call in Palm Springs, California.

I am the five Dallas officers killed by an insane gunman as they protected the constitutional rights of Black Lives Matters supporters to march in protest against shootings involving police—Brent Thompson, Patrick Zamarripa, Michael Krol, Lorne Ahrens, and Michael Smith.

I am also a "male black," shorthand for the millions of African-American men who, because of the decades of myths and prejudices, are inherently viewed as suspicious and dangerous. Our presence prompts women to hold their purses just a little tighter, families to click their car doors shut, store clerks to phone in about a "suspicious black man." We are always a threat, always "strapped." The scary weapon we carry is the very skin we're in. We are "armed" with it everywhere we go.

Like other black men, I feel the frustration, the humiliation, the fear, and the rage just knowing I am at risk for doing nothing more than breathing. As a black man, I brace myself through every police encounter, whether I am a corporate executive, cafeteria worker, or computer geek, schoolteacher or United States senator, professional athlete or architect, or cop.

So, even as a cop, I am the black child who was told by loving parents that no matter how absurd the reason for the stop by police, no matter what insults are hurled my way, no matter what degradation I'm subjected to, submit so you can make it home alive.

I am filmmaker and Harvard University professor Henry Louis Gates Jr., arrested at his home in Cambridge, Massachusetts, after someone telephoned to say they thought a suspicious black man had broken into Gates's home.

I am Gregory Gunn, the son of a respected Montgomery, Alabama, police officer, who was walking home after a late night of work and playing cards. Gunn was unarmed when he was stopped by the police, because the officer said Gunn looked "suspicious." The officer shot and killed him.

I am Tamir Rice, a 12-year-old boy playing a decades-old game of imaginary cops and robbers with a toy gun. It was given to him by a relative. The police were called and Rice was shot dead within two seconds of the officers' arrival.

I am DeJuan Guillory, a 27-year-old father of three and the son of a former police officer. He was riding his ATV four-wheeler with girlfriend when an officer stopped him and asked them for their IDs after just responding to a call about an ATV theft. Guillory's ATV had not been stolen. However, the officer shot and killed him and later charged his girlfriend with attempted first-degree murder of a police officer.

As a career African-American law enforcement officer, I've literally lived on both sides of the barrel, my finger on the trigger, one second away from using deadly force in one case and, in the next, as a black man with a police officer's gun pointed at my face, a blink away from being killed.

In writing *The Black and the Blue*, I entered this discussion from both sides. Consequently, I found that the crimes and injustices in law enforcement are about race, and are also about more than race.

We cannot pretend that the racism, prejudices, and biases we—black, white, men, women, native born, or immigrant—all carry are not issues within our society and, hence, law enforcement. But the issues go much deeper. Cases of police misconduct, inappropriate police shootings, racial profiling, and police "mistakes" point to much broader, systemic issues, rather than just a few bad apples. Too often, they reflect a culture of disregard among police for the people they are paid to serve, an us-against-them mentality that affects us all. In many cases, unacceptable tactics and procedures are woven into the fabric of local policing by our elected officials, who provide tacit and, in some cases, explicit approval of discriminatory, unconstitutional police conduct. Practices that are ingrained in most of our departments lead to encounters that put the public and police officers at risk.

Too often, police officers aren't adequately trained in the real day-to-day requirements of the job. Additionally, we send officers into the nation's cultural and racial divide without the proper tools. Consequently, they make errors in judgment. They chase a suspect down an alley when they shouldn't, and somebody ends up getting shot. Officers use force that wouldn't have been necessary if they had used their heads. What should have been routine results in tragedy.

We welcome men and women into law enforcement who should never be there. I've worked with men and women we all knew were time bombs waiting to explode. Then there are scores of officers who, despite their track records of misconduct and malfeasance, manage to go from one law enforcement agency to the next.

Too often, misconduct by officers at every level of the police hierarchy is tolerated or condoned by a cop culture that places loyalty between cops ahead of our sworn oath to serve and protect the public. This is often referred to as the "blue line." Officers fear the dangerous consequences of being ostracized by other officers. Most frustrating: When officers' bad acts are revealed, rarely are those officers held accountable.

Unfortunately, we are so acculturated by police mythology embedded in movies and television shows (one-quarter of the top 100 television shows are law enforcement dramas) that we rarely find fault in what officers do. Even when police departments want to get rid of bad cops, when they decide an officer should be prosecuted in the death of a civilian, the public rarely places blame on the police, regardless of the brutality, regardless of who gets killed.

When I started writing this book, I told a friend, a former chief of the New York City Police Department, that I didn't want to minimize the risks officers face. While I understand the frustrations of African-Americans and others, I want to make sure they understand how difficult the job can be. My friend turned to me and said, "Black people know how hard the job is. What they don't understand is how it is that we, the police, are *never* wrong. They don't understand how, in case after case, a person is shot and killed by police, but the police never are at fault. They never do wrong."

The need to address the subject of police and race has been brought into sharper focus recently by the Black Lives Matter movement. Capitalizing on the lightning speed of social media, Black Lives Matter has shone a beacon on instances of questionable shootings of black men by police. BLM's efforts stirred hundreds of thousands of people across America into action.

Despite claims to the contrary, Black Lives Matter is not anticop, just as the women's movement is not antimen, and the civil rights movement was not antiwhite. Black Lives Matter generated improvements in a handful of police departments around the country. More police departments are seeking different use-of-force tactics and have adopted body cameras to better monitor their officers' interactions with the public.

Some, like the Cleveland Police Department, have instituted new hiring procedures to better screen out possible problem officers. Some have increased training to focus more on how to handle complex human interactions, such as with the mentally ill and the homeless, two groups who now account for a very large share of police departments' enforcement load.

Fewer have followed the lead of the Seattle Police Department, which is training officers to recognize and handle the biases that we all have. Meanwhile, the New Jersey attorney general has mandated that every police department begin bias and use-of-force training.

Most people know that something is wrong, but we are poles apart on what it is. Study after study shows that white and black Americans see this issue dramatically differently. In Minnesota, the home of two of the most high-profile shootings of black men, more than 90 percent of black Minnesotans hold a favorable opinion of Black Lives Matter, according to a local poll. However, only 6 percent of their white neighbors share that view. Visualize that for a minute. The question is asked and 90 black people out of 100 move to one side of the room and only 6 white people out of 100 join them in agreement. Everybody else is in opposition.

Conversely, virtually all the white respondents to the poll had a positive view of law enforcement while only about 1 in 4 of the black respondents did. Let's try our visualization again, this time with 98 white people on one side of the room and 26 black people joining them in agreement.

That's not a gap. That's a chasm.

1.

THE BOOGEYMAN

Implicit bias lives in our police departments, just as it exists among our coworkers, families, friends, and associates. It affects us all and consumes some of us. Thirty years ago, however, the term *implicit bias* hadn't entered the lexicon, and it was the last thing on my mind as a young rookie on a domestic abuse call when I entered an apartment building in Arlington, Virginia. I was just praying I wouldn't have to shoot the person standing in front of me.

The textbook definition of *implicit bias* says it is the attitudes or stereotypes that we all have. They, in turn, affect our encounters with people, and influence our actions and decisions in an unconscious manner. In other words, we internalize repeated messages from our family, our friends, our neighbors, our community, and the stereotypes and images we see on television, and in movies, magazines, and other media.

Bias is different from racism and sexism. Racism and sexism affect the conscious prejudice, discrimination, or antagonism directed against someone of a different race or sex based on the belief that one's own race or sex is superior. Implicit biases are attitudes and assumptions ingrained in our subconscious. Our implicit biases explain why tall men are almost invariably asked if they played basketball and why, if I say, "peanut butter," you are likely to respond, "jelly." They explain why studies show that European standards of beauty are widely accepted as the norm, even among Asians, African-Americans, and Hispanics. Those same studies show that, across the board, regardless of race, Americans have a pro-white bias. African-Americans and Latinos are less pro-white-biased, but the overall culture apparently pushes us in that direction as well. Implicit bias also explains why wealth and power are most often associated with white men. Unfortunately, it also explains why black men are inherently felt to be dangerous by much of America, even by many African-Americans.

We all have these biases. They don't necessarily make us bad people. They just make us people. Unfortunately, when they are held by someone with a badge and a gun, and the power to take a life, those biases can play out negatively and people who shouldn't be, end up dead.

I first learned about my own bias as a rookie cop while on a domestic dispute call that evening in Arlington. I was working a DUI assignment when I got the call to assist another officer. So, I hurried over. I met with the primary officer, a woman who was from a nearby police force who was my partner on this call. She brought me up to speed and we walked over to the residence. Since it was a domestic violence call, I assumed we would be meeting a distraught woman, probably crying, possibly injured.

Wrong.

The complainant was a man, average build, about 5-foot-10, possibly Hispanic. He said he had been assaulted by his lover, Leslie, and he wanted Leslie out of the apartment. We both felt it was weird, a man being beaten up by a woman. Still, I'm thinking, *This will be simple. Handling a woman is a lot easier than dealing with an adrenaline-charged, probably irate, possibly drunk man.* It was dusk when I got the call. By now, it was getting dark. As we headed upstairs to the apartment, my partner and I agreed that she would take the lead for a woman-to-woman conversation. *Good plan*, I said to myself.

Wrong again.

When we entered the apartment, Leslie was sitting on the sofa. Leslie was a large black man, as wide as a La-Z-Boy. Trust me, Leslie was *big*. Now, I'm concerned, but not overly so. Back then, I was 6-foot-2 and weighed a well-muscled 260 pounds. Still, I'm mentally rehearsing my training for situations like this, in case of resistance. Leslie was polite. He said he was sorry that he and his lover had created the disturbance that had brought us to his door. Everybody was amiable, and things were going fine until we told Leslie something we knew he didn't want to hear.

"Sir, your roommate wants you to leave the apartment," my partner said. "Please stand up so we can go downstairs." Our reference to Leslie's partner as his *roommate* was further evidence of our bias at the time. If it had been a heterosexual relationship, we most assuredly would have referred to the other individual as *boyfriend* or *girlfriend*.

"I don't want to leave," Leslie responded. "This is my apartment, too."

He was passionate, but not threatening.

"Sir, you have to leave," my partner said. "Please come with us downstairs, and I'm sure we can work this out."

We needed Leslie out of the apartment because it would have been extremely difficult to handle a big guy like him in that small space. Again he said he didn't want to leave and refused to stand up. My partner asked again. Same reaction. We went back and forth with Leslie for a minute or so about standing up and he told us repeatedly that he didn't want to leave and how he loved his partner. This was not good. Noncompliance is cause to notch things up a bit. We were now getting close to possibly having to use force, which is always dangerous. Then without warning, Leslie did exactly what we asked him to do. He stood up, and that was when things really got scary.

———

To be honest, I never really wanted to be a cop. I joined the Arlington County (Virginia) Police Department in 1986, not long after graduating from Delaware State University, a historically black public university in

Dover, Delaware. Representatives from the department visited our campus in my senior year and recruited me to join the department. I liked them, but I didn't immediately commit. Still, I thought, depending on how my initial plans panned out, it could be a good fit.

My goal after graduating college was to become a starting offensive lineman in the National Football League. I played left and right guards and filled in at tackle from time to time. I was big, and I was fast. People, including me, thought I was pretty good. I made the All-Mid-Eastern Atlantic Conference team one year. So, I figured I'd give the NFL a try. That dream, however, was set back significantly when I was cut during tryouts with the New York Giants the summer after my graduation.

I had thought about following the typical career trajectory of guys trying to break into the NFL. You spend the year eating and lifting and running, trying to get bigger, stronger, and faster while working security at clubs and concerts to make ends meet until the next training camp. Some guys make it and others do it for as long as five years before giving in to the reality that they just weren't good enough. I considered it, but my father, an electrician, and my mother, a secretary, took me aside and suggested it was time to move on with my life and start a career. The offer from the Arlington County Police Department was available and sounding better by the day. So I took it.

Arlington's was one of the very few accredited police departments in the nation, which made them special. One of the requirements for all accredited police forces is that their officers must all be college graduates. I liked that. I thought it would make any organization much more professional and would mean fewer guys just looking to play cops and robbers. Arlington was also a very affluent area, a lot more than the neighborhood I grew up in. The median household income in Arlington is almost double the median household income for the rest of the nation. Consequently, it was also the highest-paying police department in the

Washington, D.C. area, even higher than the police department in the nation's capital. That particular fact really attracted me to the job.

———

Which is a roundabout way of explaining how I had come to this moment in time where I might have to shoot someone.

If I thought Leslie was big sitting down, he was a mountain standing up, at least 6-foot-8 and well over 300 pounds. I thought I was buff, but I was nothing compared to him. At this point, my partner and I were at an extreme disadvantage. Somebody could get hurt or worse. The only thing that I had that could really handle him without me or my partner getting hurt was my weapon. In 1986, tasers weren't as readily available as they are now. So, to collect ourselves and manage a potentially volatile situation, we reversed our instructions.

"Sir, could you please sit down?" I said.

Leslie looked at me, confused. "I don't want to sit down," he responded. "She asked me to stand up, so I'm standing up."

Now, we have this huge, possibly violent man standing in front of us and not following our command for him to sit down. Things were not good, and then Leslie heightened the tension. He said he needed to see his lover downstairs. Now that was not going to happen. We certainly weren't going to allow a person who is accused of assaulting someone back into close proximity to the alleged victim. So, again we asked Leslie to sit down. He ignored us. We asked again. He refused. We asked again. He refused again.

My partner and I knew that we would be hard-pressed to arrest Leslie without additional support, based solely on his size. I had resigned myself to the fact that once we put hands on this very large man, if his noncompliance continued, lethal force might be necessary. We had choices to make. If we tried to handle him physically, we could both be hurt badly. If we had pulled our weapons at this point, our actions likely would have been defensible, and if, at some point in a struggle, we had shot Leslie, we probably would have been justified.

"I feared for my life" would have been my defense, and it would have been reasonable, though not completely accurate. That's what the higher-ups tell officers to say when something goes awry. You learn it in the police academy and it becomes the mantra of every officer when any shootings occur. And who can prove that you weren't in fear for your life, even if the fear was caused by something improper that you yourself did.

Here's an example from a true story. On a winter afternoon in New York, an 18-year-old black male was seen leaving a local store. A police officer radioed in that he saw the teenager tugging at something in his waistband, possibly a gun. The teenager, however, was unarmed. Other police began to follow the man. The suspect didn't know he was being followed. As the teenager neared his apartment building, police say they told him to stop but he ran into the apartment building. Video of the incident, however, shows the man casually walking into his home as though he never heard a command. The officers then tried to kick down the front door of the apartment building so they could get to the kid's apartment. Remember, this was a teenager who might or might not have a gun, but police were trying to kick down a door to an entire apartment building.

When that didn't work, two officers went to the back of the building, where they were let in by a first-floor tenant. They located the teenager's apartment. The teenager was living with his grandmother. Officers went to her apartment, and she let them in. When the teenager saw the police, he ran into the bathroom and tried to flush a small bag of marijuana down the toilet. When he turned around, an officer shot him in the chest. The cop said, "I feared for my life." We all agreed that at that point he may have actually feared for his life. Who could say otherwise? But here's the other side. He created the situation that caused him to fear for his life and shoot that youngster. There was no reason to chase that kid into his house. The kid hadn't committed a crime. There was no need to try to break down the door of the apartment building, home to numerous residents. Also, why did the officer go into the bathroom? The suspect had already been cornered. He was trapped in the bathroom, so why not wait outside? What if the kid did have a gun and was waiting for the officer to come in? Then the officer might have been killed, or there might have been a shootout and the grandmother might have been inadvertently killed. Now an unarmed man was dead, a family was grieving, and the officer was facing a disciplinary hearing, possibly a trial, possibly loss of his job. And for what? A few bags of marijuana?

My partner and I were trying to avoid a similar stupid mistake. So we were at a stalemate. We really didn't want this encounter to go awry. We didn't want to shoot an unarmed man over a lovers' quarrel. The man who called us didn't want his lover shot. But we were very, very close to some kind of force being used.

So I was standing at the ready. So was my partner. I could see her widening her stance almost imperceptibly in preparation for a struggle. Leslie was just looking at us, confused and frustrated. Then, right before we started taking things up a notch, Leslie began to weep. He put his face in his hands, tears running down his cheeks, and sat down. Inside, I breathed a deep sigh of relief and my sphincter muscle relaxed. We eventually convinced Leslie to walk out on his own, where we arrested him without incident.

The point of the story is this: Leslie was big, and he was black, but did that make him bad? I am big and I am black. Does that make me bad? I ask that question, because *bad* was the term a Tulsa, Oklahoma, police officer used to describe Terence Crutcher, an unarmed African-American man and father of four on September 17, 2016, just seconds before another Tulsa officer shot and killed him. The video of the incident has been seen by millions around the world.

Crutcher had stopped his vehicle on a Tulsa street when police received a 911 call a little after 7 p.m. about an abandoned vehicle in the middle of 36th Street North just west of Lewis Avenue. One caller said:

"Somebody left their vehicle running in the middle of the street with the doors wide open. The vehicle is still running. It's an SUV. It's like in the middle of the street. It's blocking traffic. There was a guy running from it, saying it was going to blow up. But I think he's smoking something. I got out and was like, 'Do you need help?' He was like, 'Come here, come here, I think it's going to blow up.'"

The other caller said: "There is a car that looks like somebody just jumped out of it and left it in the center of the road on 36th Street North and North Lewis Avenue. It's dead in the middle of the street. Nobody in the car."

Judging by the 911 calls, police clearly knew something was wrong, even if they didn't know exactly what. They had a car blocking traffic and possibly either a confused or high or disturbed man in the vicinity. None of the callers, however, mentioned a weapon or a threat of violence.

Officer Betty Shelby arrived on the scene first. Crutcher was standing in the road outside his car. Shelby exited her vehicle and almost immediately pulled her weapon. She gave Crutcher a series of verbal commands. At one point, he had his hands in his pockets. She told him to take them out. He did. Crutcher, however, didn't say a word. Shelby had called for backup. Crutcher put his hands in the air in a surrender pose and began to walk back to his car. By now, at least four officers were at the scene in addition to a police helicopter overhead. Shelby drew her gun and she and another officer followed Crutcher as he walked to his car with his hands in the air. The other officer had his taser out. Shelby was the only officer with a gun drawn.

Officers in the helicopter overhead, which included Shelby's husband, filmed the incident. With tensions high, an officer in the helicopter looked down at the scene and made this assessment: "That looks like a bad dude." Two seconds later, Crutcher was shot dead—with one hand in the air and the other by his side. He was unarmed and there was no weapon in his car. When I saw the video footage, the comment from the cop in the helicopter really stuck in my head. It made me question everything that had happened.

What evidence made the officer conclude that Crutcher, 40, was a "bad dude"? He had never seen the man before, so he had no previous encounters on which to base his claim. He had not run the license plates on the car. If he had, he would have found that the car had not been stolen. He would have also found that Terence Crutcher, who was the registered owner of the car, was not wanted for any crime. Additionally, Crutcher had made no verbal or physical threats to anyone, not to the people who made the 911 calls, nor to any of the officers on the ground. Crutcher had no visible prison or gang tattoos, nor other visible markings that might indicate he was dangerous. He wasn't wearing biker gear or clothing that glorified crime or violence. So, what made him a "bad dude"?

For the officer in that helicopter, Crutcher did have one telltale marking. He was a "male black." Crutcher, like so many black men, was dead because too many of us view an African-American man as the real-life boogeyman. We are imbued with diabolical attributes and devious motives. Consequently, black men are suspected of wrongdoing, locked away, or gunned down.

In the court proceedings that followed, Shelby testified that she shot Crutcher because she feared for her life. There's that ubiquitous phrase again. "I thought he was going to kill me," she told a court. How did she come to that conclusion? For what reason would Crutcher want to harm Shelby? He was not an escaped fugitive. He was not wanted for any crime. He was not trying to escape or elude arrest. There were no signs that he was armed. He had not made any threatening gestures toward Shelby or the other officers. If anyone should have been in fear for his life, it was Crutcher. Shelby had her gun trained on him. He was surrounded by armed police. What reason could Crutcher possibly have had to want to harm Shelby? It strains credulity.

So, where did things go wrong? Let's review the Crutcher shooting through a law enforcement lens. The goal of every law enforcement confrontation with a citizen should be to gain compliance in a situation that is safe for the person and safe for the officer. As an ATF agent and an agent training instructor at the Federal Law Enforcement Training Center in Brunswick, Georgia, I've taught hundreds of officers how to handle themselves in these situations. In every encounter, officers should go through what we call a use-of-force continuum. There are five steps in the continuum. The officer's first step is to establish *presence*. This is in some ways the most important step in the interaction between the officer and the people he or she is addressing. It's sometimes called command presence. If officers present themselves well, no force is required in most cases. Presence encompasses the officer's appearance and attitude. It should be professional and nonthreatening. It's the way you look, the way you dress, the way you stand, the way you walk and carry yourself. You should exude confidence, but not arrogance. You need to look like you're in command of yourself and you can handle whatever situation arises. You can be friendly and engaging, but you cannot appear to be someone who is not in control.

The next step is *verbalization*, which refers to the officer establishing verbal contact with the individual. The officer should give very clear, concise, nonthreatening instructions. If the officers have not established command presence, however, verbalization may not work. The guys on the corner or the couple in a domestic squabble have already dismissed you as out of touch or ineffective. So, nothing you say matters. That's why I say command presence is so important. As you talk with people, your tone should be polite but authoritative. People need to know you mean business. "Good morning. I am Officer Matthew Horace. We are responding to a request for help. What seems to be the problem? You, sir. I need you to take 10 steps back and stand there. You, miss. Please go to that corner and my partner will talk to you." Sometimes you must shorten commands or raise your voice. Unfortunately, some cops arrive on the scene and immediately start shouting commands, addressing people disrespectfully, and treating victims like suspects. African-Americans and Latinos know this response all too well.

The next step up is *empty hand control*. Now, you are using bodily contact to control the subject in a way that protects the individual and you. You may need to place one hand on the person's back and grab the person's arm with the other. You may be using that to move him to a different place temporarily or to put the person in a posture that is more secure for you and the person.

Now, if there is resistance, we start moving to the next level, which is stuff that doesn't look good on video. We are now using *intermediate force*. Officers may have to use punches and kicks to restrain an individual. They can use batons or chemical sprays or Tasers to get the person under control. In some of our tactical takedowns, such as SWAT or special response teams, we've fired a bean bag round from a shotgun. It's not lethal, but if you get hit with one, you're going down. Under intermediate force, you may need to swarm an individual and take the person down to the ground. I've used this tactic numerous times. None of this stuff looks pretty, but the person is alive. The infamous beating of Rodney King in Los Angeles in 1992, which ultimately set off the worst riot in the nation's history, was shocking to watch. It was excessive, horrific, and criminal, but in the end King was still alive.

In Crutcher's case, Betty Shelby skipped the use of intermediate force and went from *verbalization* immediately to the last step on the continuum—the *lethal force* that took Crutcher's life. They did use a taser, but he was shot almost simultaneously. With so many officers on the scene, they could have rushed him and taken him to the ground. But they didn't. If they feared he was going into the car to get a weapon, they could have retreated to a safe distance and fired on him the moment his hands disappeared into the car. They didn't do that, either. Again, there was no evidence that Crutcher had a gun or that he was violent.

None of these situations are as simple as my textbook explanation. These encounters can take place over 30 minutes or longer, during which the officer has time to go through the continuum at a methodical pace, or they can happen in an explosion of less than 60 seconds. I've had it happen to me. You are trying to guide someone with an empty hand and the person pulls away. You then decide to make a hard grab and be more forceful, and *boom*, the individual swings at you. Now, you may have to use your baton across the femoral artery on the person's thigh or the brachial artery on the person's arm or kick the person in the back of the knee to bring the individual down.

But these are tactics I'm telling you about, when the real problem is the perception of African-American men, and, to some degree, African-American women, as inherent threats by their mere presence. In police parlance, it initially comes across the police radio with these three words: "suspicious black male." I have heard this term too many times throughout my years in law enforcement, spoken as if the two last words in the phrase automatically prompted the first word in the description.

When I was on the police department in Virginia, I was often dispatched to calls of a "suspicious black male" and, in response, I would ask via the radio, "What is he doing?" My question was simple. Just what is he doing that makes him suspicious, other than being a black male? Generally, when I did this, my mostly white fellow officers would key the radio microphone to make a clicking sound in a show of sarcastic disapproval at my question, and a supervisor might call me to ensure that I was responding to the call. Most times these calls involved nothing more than a black man waiting for a bus; he was just waiting for the bus in the "wrong" neighborhood. Another time, a black guy was passing out flyers. Another time, a kid and his girlfriend had a tryst planned in a secret meeting place during the day. It was always innocuous stuff. It's not that we shouldn't investigate "suspicious" people, but what makes them suspicious?

For example, I was called to investigate a report of a suspicious white male. In this case, the call said, "suspicious white male, no shoes, no shirt, dirty blond hair." What made him suspicious was not that he was a white male, but that he was shoeless and shirtless in the middle of December, a sign that he might have been high on PCP, because PCP users were always hot.

I approached him and told him I needed to speak with him. He replied, "Fuck you, nigger." I immediately called for backup because PCP imbues users with extraordinary strength when they are high.

If we have an inherent fear of or bias against blacks, they are always going to be suspicious. Even as a federal agent, I have been on surveillance or supporting an operation and have had an officer approach me and say that neighbors called about a "suspicious" vehicle, which meant it was a black guy driving a car. I've been the man in that suspicious vehicle.

When I was assigned to Seattle, Washington, as assistant special agent in charge of other ATF agents and police officers in seven northwestern states and Guam in 2002, I lived in a golf course community in Mill Creek. It was a great little community just north of Seattle. The community had about 1,000 homes developed in manicured clusters that centered around a world-class golf course. My subdivision had 103 homes and there were two African-American men in this neighborhood. There may have been a total of six black men in the entire community.

I had been living in Mill Creek for a little over a year when I was driving my newer-model Mercedes-Benz through the development and noticed flashing lights behind me. The way the community was engineered really didn't allow you to speed. So, I was confused and concerned. Why was a sheriff's deputy stopping me? The officer asked me for my driver's license and registration. I gave it to him and asked what I had done.

I also presented my federal ATF credentials, to which he responded that he didn't recognize my vehicle as one with which he was familiar. At this point, I'm thinking, *Is he familiar with every car and every person in the development?* He could have followed me, had my tag run, and realized that I lived in the community and that both my license and registration were current. But let's assume that I didn't live in the community. Let's assume that I was lost or visiting a friend or admiring the homes or checking out the neighborhood because I might want to move there. That's not probable cause to stop me. None of those activities make me "suspicious." And, just for argument's sake, what crime would a guy in a newer-model Mercedes be up to in this neighborhood? A burglary? A robbery? A drive-by shooting? My car was worth more than anything I could steal. What rational reason could he give for stopping me?

None.

I subsequently made an appointment with a commander in the Snohomish County Sheriff's Department and explained who I was and what had happened. I also told him which vehicles my wife and I drove, including my federal undercover vehicle, and advised him that I never expected to be stopped by anyone in his department ever again unless I had committed a violation. And I wasn't.

Not once have any of my white friends and colleagues told me they have been stopped under similar situations. Why not? Because African-Americans live with a double standard and our actions are interpreted differently than those of our white counterparts.

Not long ago, I was walking into a hardware store in my suburban Pennsylvania community and stood in line behind a white man with a holstered firearm. He was clean-shaven and well-dressed, in khaki pants and a polo shirt. I assumed that he was a local police officer. Nobody was alarmed or anxious by his presence. I thought to myself, even if he were a cop, how could every person in the hardware store know that he was? Perhaps the employees, but certainly not all the customers.

Here's the other side. In 28 years of dutifully carrying a firearm as part of my job, I've never walked into a commercial establishment with my weapon openly displayed. Scores of black law enforcement officers

I have known for years do the same. We would never want that call to go into dispatch that a black man with a gun was in the store. Even if we were wearing khaki pants, penny loafers, and a tennis sweater, I would fear that the law enforcement response would not be a positive one. There is a boogeyman effect when radio traffic says, "black man with a gun" that escalates the response, no matter what the conditions.

John Crawford, for example, was casually shopping in a Walmart in Beavercreek, Ohio, on August 13, 2014, with his pregnant girlfriend. As Crawford's girlfriend wandered off to one part of the store, he headed toward the other and the two began a conversation via cell phone. At some point in their conversation, Crawford, 22, casually picked up a toy gun from a store shelf with his left hand while still talking on the phone with his right. A white shopper, Ronald T. Ritchie, saw him with the toy rifle and called the police. He told the dispatcher a black man was armed with a rifle and was menacing customers in Walmart.

"He's pointing it at people," Ritchie said.

Ritchie then told the police dispatcher he was watching as it appeared Crawford was trying to load the gun. He also told police Crawford was pointing the rifle at children. With Ritchie on the telephone continually describing a situation to the dispatcher, police rushed to the store. They made their way into Walmart, down the aisle, and within one second of their approaching Crawford, he was shot dead. After the shooting, Ritchie's wife, who was with him in Walmart, posted on Facebook how she saw Crawford load the weapon and menace people.

Tragically, the entire incident was built on a lie and the fear of a black man with a gun. Walmart surveillance footage showed Crawford never pointed the toy rifle at anyone, never waved it around in a menacing manner, never even pretended he was going to shoot it. Instead, it was by his side as he walked the aisles and talked on the phone with his girlfriend. In fact, footage showed Crawford was pointing the rifle to the floor and was on the phone when Ritchie told the dispatcher, "He just pointed it at, like, two children." Crawford encountered two sets of parents and their children. Neither showed alarm or even excitement in response to Crawford's presence. The second parent, Angela Williams, a 37-year-old white woman, however, died of a heart attack as she tried to pull her two children to safety in the chaos of the shooting. The local coroner ruled her death a homicide because the panic of the shooting caused her heart to go into arrhythmia. Her teenage son blamed her death on Ritchie. "I hope that he's happy with himself," he said after the incident.

Afterward, a special prosecutor was appointed to review the case, and presented evidence to a grand jury that the officers who shot Crawford had done nothing wrong. The same special prosecutor declined to prosecute Ritchie after a local judge later found there were grounds for Ritchie to be charged with a crime for the erroneous statements that led to Crawford's death.

Three months later, 12-year-old Tamir Rice was playing cops and robbers 200 miles upstate in Cleveland with a toy gun a relative had given him. He had been inside a local community center for a while until officials there shooed him outside into the November cold and snow of a local park. Rice walked around the park pointing his toy weapon at imaginary villains. Someone saw him and called the police to report a black man in the park pointing a pistol at random people. The caller twice told the police, "It's probably fake," referring to the pistol. Toward the end of the two-minute call, the caller said, "He is probably a juvenile." The dispatcher, however, never relayed that information in the request for officers to respond.

Instead, police were told via radio only "of a male black sitting on a swing and pointing a gun at people." Two police officers, Timothy Loehmann, 26, and Frank Garmback, 46, heard the information and sped to the park. Garmback drove the car recklessly within six feet of Rice, clearly bad tactical procedure. If Rice had been an actual shooting threat, Garmback would have put the officers at risk of being shot by placing them directly in the line of fire with no protection. As the car came to a halt, Loehmann immediately exited the vehicle, gun drawn, and shot Rice within seconds of leaving the car while shouting directions for him to drop the gun.

Rice died a day later.

As in the case of Crawford and hundreds of others, an unarmed black male was dead, and nobody was at fault. Following a grand jury hearing, police officers were not indicted for any criminal conduct.

Ironically, a year later just 45 miles away in Akron, Ohio, a white male, Daniel Kovacevic, strolled through black neighborhoods with an assault rifle slung across his back. Kovacevic wore a black ski cap pulled far down on his head that covered his hair and sunglasses that hid his eyes. Residents called the police. He was not shot. Instead, officers can be seen on a video explaining to black residents that Kovacevic was just exercising his constitutional right in Ohio to openly carry a weapon without threat of violence from others or the police, just as any person in Ohio does... except for John Crawford and Tamir Rice.

As jury after judge after jury has refused to find officers guilty of anything, including misdemeanor charges, in deaths of unarmed black men and boys, America is saying to us that it is officially reasonable to be afraid of a person just because he is black. And because you fear him, it is okay to kill him.

For me, the most startling example of the boogeyman effect was illustrated in a recent study on justifiable homicide. Only 2 out of every 100 homicides in America are ruled justifiable by law enforcement. For a homicide to be justified, it must be a "homicide that is committed in self-defense, in defense of another and especially a member of one's family or sometimes in defense of a residence, in preventing a felony especially involving great bodily harm, or in performing a legal duty and that is justified under the law," according to Merriam-Webster's dictionary.

That 2 percent figure holds true virtually for every racial scenario except for when a white person shoots a black person. For instance, when Hispanics killed black men, 5.5 percent were ruled justifiable. When whites killed Hispanics, 3.1 percent, or 3 out of 100, were justified. When blacks killed blacks, the number was 2 percent, and when blacks killed whites, less than 1 percent were found to be justifiable.

But when a white male killed a black man, the number sky-rocketed; 16 percent were deemed lawful, eight times the rate for African-Americans.

By now, most of us have seen the statistics that show the disproportionate stops of African-Americans on highways, streets, and in neighborhoods. We have seen the statistics that also show that stops of white drivers are 30 percent more likely than stops of African-Americans to reveal drugs and contraband. Yet police still suspect African-Americans at double, triple, even five times the rate of white Americans. And the race of the officer doesn't seem to matter. In Baltimore, where black cops make up 52 percent of the police department, one man was stopped and questioned more than 20 times without any charges ever being filed. Each specious stop deepens the divisions between the African-American community and the police. And each encounter creates a possibility that somebody—police officers and/or citizens—will be harmed.

I've had this discussion with lots of my white friends, and most nod their heads in acknowledgment, but I can tell many of them don't truly believe it, even coming from me, a cop. One person told me that when hearing of these encounters, he has always assumed the person did something wrong to cause the police officer to respond in a deadly manner. A friend's wife told me, during a discussion of the shooting of a black man, that she simply rejected all this talk that these incidents were somehow related to race. "How can you say it had anything to do with race unless the policeman said something racist or he was wearing a KKK shirt or something?" she asked.

I understand that, for most of my white friends, it just isn't part of their reality. However, when one African-American they know—a friend, a colleague, a coworker, a celebrity, even a United States senator—states this is a reality, why is it so hard to believe? I point to US Senator Tim Scott (R-South Carolina), a staunchly conservative black Republican and one of only three African-American members of the Senate. Scott and I have never met. We are as different as cornbread and Kool-Aid.

He is from a small Southern town. I grew up in urban northwest Philadelphia. He was raised by a single mom who struggled mightily and successfully to raise him and his two brothers. I had the good fortune of two parents who both worked good-paying jobs. He graduated from a private, mostly white religious college, steeped in the teachings of the Southern Baptist Convention. My higher education was at a public, historically black university that was formed because for years African-Americans were not permitted to attend most white colleges and universities.

He is a strong and outspoken supporter of Attorney General Jeff Sessions, who wanted to bring back the days of harsh sentencing and police tactics initiated during the war on drugs that devastated black communities. As I will discuss in the next chapter, I was in the forefront of that mistaken policy with the Bureau of Alcohol and Firearms and helped lock up hundreds of thousands of black men and women as the nation marched off in the wrong direction. I never want to go there again. Scott is staunchly to the right. I am more middle of the road.

Despite our differences, we are bound together by the threat of law enforcement because of the color of our skin and our gender.

Scott passionately told his own story on the US Senate floor in 2016, following a series of highly publicized police shootings. He talked about the fear, anxiety, and shame he felt the very first time he was stopped by an officer. "The cop came up to my car, hand on his gun, and said, 'Boy, don't you know your headlight is not working properly?'" He said that, even as an elected official, he had been stopped seven times in one year, on one of those occasions because the officer said he thought Scott was driving a stolen car. Yes, he said, he was speeding twice, "but the vast majority of the times, I was pulled over for nothing more than driving a new car in the wrong neighborhood or some other reason just as trivial."

He recounted how his brother, who had achieved the highest rank in the US Army for an enlisted man, was stopped during a trip from Texas to visit family in Charleston. The police officer told his brother he stopped him because he was driving a Volvo, and black people don't usually drive Volvos. For that reason, the officer told him, he thought the car might be stolen. Scott told of a young black man who worked in his office and drove a "nice car," a Chrysler 300. He had been pulled over so many times that he sold the car to stop the harassment. Near the end of his speech, Scott, a black man far to the right politically of the vast majority of other black men in America, uttered words that spoke for all of us.

"I do not know many African-American men who do not have a very similar story to tell, no matter their profession, no matter their income, no matter their disposition in life," he said. "Imagine the frustration, the irritation, the sense of a loss of dignity that accompanies each of those stops. I have felt the anger, the frustration, the sadness, and the humiliation that comes with feeling like you're being targeted for nothing more than being just yourself."

As part of my effort to further explore this issue, I traveled to St. Louis and Ferguson, Missouri, where the police shooting of 18-year-old Michael Brown in 2014 sparked rioting and reignited the decades-old conversation about the shootings of African-Americans by police. Brown's death was followed quickly by the killings of other African-Americans by police. They galvanized this new discussion. I wanted to understand what sparked the incident in Ferguson. What had been happening in a town of only 21,000 people that has pushed us to where we are now? What I soon discovered was that, for black residents in Ferguson and in St. Louis, the relationships between African-Americans and the police were nearly identical.

As I met people, I encountered a wonderful young woman named Amy Hunter. She gave me a deeper understanding of just how personal and deep the fear, the anguish, and the anxiety about police stops goes for African-American parents.

She is the manager of diversity and inclusion at St. Louis Children's Hospital, one of the city's major medical institutions. Hunter lives in the upscale University City neighborhood of St. Louis, where median incomes run about $100,000 and where crime is largely an afterthought. There are no drug houses on the corner, no drive-by shootings, no gang bangers at every turn. Still, she and her then-husband made a pact that they would give them "the talk," the conversation many black parents have with their children about the special procedures they must follow when they are invariably stopped by police.

"We sat them down and told them how to behave if the police should stop them," Hunter told me over the dining room table of a friend in an even wealthier St. Louis suburb. "We told them, don't smart off, regardless of what they say. Do exactly what they tell you to do. We just want you to come home safe. We will handle whatever happens. We don't want to have to identify your body because you've been shot by a police officer."

Hunter was also one of the hundreds of protesters who lined the streets of Ferguson night after night following the shooting of Michael Brown. By her count, she was on the street nearly every day following the shooting, including the freezing-cold nights when they protested against the backdrop of the city's Christmas decorations that read SEASON'S GREETINGS. She was tear-gassed and held at gunpoint with M-16 rifles pointed at her chest.

I asked her why an upper-middle-class woman who didn't live in Ferguson and who had not experienced what its residents endured at the hands of police would be so dedicated to the Ferguson protest. I reminded her that she had told me her sons were now grown and doing quite well. It certainly must not have sat well with her employers that she was out there every day, putting herself at risk, I observed. Why would she do something like that? She looked at me with a kind, almost patronizing look, and then she told me a story.

When her sons were 12, she dropped one off to hang out with his friends in an area in University City called the Delmar Loop. The Loop is a popular entertainment district filled with specialty shops, restaurants, and music venues. Unless he was touring, local resident and rock-and-roll pioneer Chuck Berry performed there almost weekly until his death in 2017. When Hunter's son arrived in the Loop, his friends were drinking. He knew that was a no-no, so he decided to walk home. He lived less than a mile away. When her son was about five houses away from home, he would later tell his mother, he saw police following him. Ultimately, he said, he was stopped, questioned, and searched. The police told him they stopped him because he matched the description of a man carrying a machete. "He was 12," Hunter said. "He was 5 feet tall." She recalled how flustered her son was when he arrived home, frustrated and trying to make sense of it all.

"He was asking all these questions because he was trying to understand it," she said. Her son told her he had done as she instructed, but he still couldn't understand why the officer stopped him.

"He said, 'But, Mom, I'm wearing khaki pants and a polo shirt and a belt and it's tucked in, and I have on Sperry Top-Siders.' It was as if he thought his clothes could save him from the experience. But there's nothing he could wear that would save him from that, and I knew it. So, he said, 'Mom, I want to know, is it because I'm black?'

"I said, 'I don't know. Maybe.'" Her son continued to ask questions, she said. She could tell that he was troubled by the experience—the fear of being stopped by men with guns, the uncertainty of the outcome, the vulnerability. And as he talked, she could see that he was trying to hold back the tears that were welling up in his eyes.

"He looked at me and said, 'Mommy, I just want to know how long this will last.' And then I looked at my 12-year-old son, now with tears rolling down my face, and I said to him, 'For the rest of your life.'"

She looked down for a few seconds and then back up at me. Now, she had tears in her eyes.

"That's why I went to Ferguson," she said. "I want this to stop."

Tony April

Captain, Alaska State Trooper

When I was growing up, I couldn't stand cops. I would see a cop and they would come into my neighborhood and treat everybody like criminals. Cops would call us niggers or boy. "Get off my street, boy," "Nigger, get out of here." They were always insulting us, saying something to demean us. It was like being on a plantation; the neighborhood was all black and almost all the cops were white. They liked to wear these mirror sunglasses, and they wore their shirts tight. Everybody hated them. Their profanity: "Fuck this, fuck that." Our perception was that if you were a cop, you killed black people to get promoted. That's the way we looked at it, because that's what it seemed like was happening.

In 1979, they beat a black man to death. He was on a motorcycle and they chased him. So, when I was a kid, there were two things I said I would never do. I would never join the military and I would never be a cop. I ended up doing both.

I grew up in Miami in a neighborhood called the Goulds, right down the street from a housing project called Cutler Manor. We had a big family. There were 10 of us—6 girls and 4 boys. I was sixth out of the bunch. We had two loving parents. My mother, Jimmie April, stayed home and looked after us. My father, Robert Claude April, was a no-nonsense guy. He'd kill you in a minute if you messed with his family.

I finished basic training in Fort Jackson, South Carolina, and where do you think they stationed me, a kid from the Goulds? Anchorage, Alaska! They sent a Florida boy who had never even seen snow to Anchorage, Alaska, the coldest place in America. That was crazy. The only good thing about it was that I met my wife there.

In 1991, I joined the Alaska National Guard and in 1994, I started working for the Alaska Department of Corrections. That was a tough job. I worked in the segregation unit where inmates were locked down 23 of 24 hours a day, where they could not come out of their cells. The prisoners were mostly whites and Alaskan natives. There were lots of skinheads and white supremacists—and me.

I had one inmate, every day he'd say, "Hey, nigger, bring me my food" or "Nigger, bring me my paper." I'd walk by and he'd spit on my shoes. My biggest thing was to avoid reading their [criminal histories]. It revealed what crimes they were in for. I didn't want to read their jackets so I wouldn't develop a bias against them. I wanted to see them as human beings.

I joined the Alaska State Troopers in 1997. As a trooper, you spend 15½ weeks in the academy and then you go through 3½ months of field training. When I was in the academy, everybody told me, whatever you do, you don't want to go to Palmer, Alaska, for field training. They had a reputation for [terminating recruits]. Of course, I was sent to Palmer.

One day, I came back to the station and saw a trooper who I later learned was completing an application background check on another applicant. I asked, "What are you doing?"

"Trying to keep people like you off the force," he shot back.

Near the end of my probation period, my evaluation read so bad that it seemed like I didn't know how to walk and chew gum at the same time. The sergeant in charge threatened me: "I'm going to fire your ass in two weeks." I thought about quitting right then and went home to tell my wife that I was done! But a fellow trooper who was white said, "Don't quit. That's just what they want you to do." So, I stayed.

They assigned me to Bubba Cox, who was the hardest FTO (training officer) that we had. He was a no-nonsense, no-soft-spots, straight-shooter guy. Bubba and I went on a call one day. He told me to handle it. But this white guy began talking to Bubba and totally ignored me. Bubba interrupted him, "Sir, this is the officer you should be talking with. He is handling this call." The guy ignored the comment and just kept talking to Bubba. Finally, Bubba said, "Okay, we're done. If you don't want to talk to him, we're out of here." And we left.

The last day of my training, Bubba and I pulled up at the station. I didn't know if I had passed or failed. "Before you get out," Bubba said, "I want to let you know, I didn't give you a damn thing. Everything you got you earned." I'll never forget, Bubba had a little tear that streamed down his face.

Two years later I was chosen as Trooper of the Year.

2.

BEING BLACK IN BLUE

I was 28 years old and hadn't done a damn thing wrong, but there I stood in fear for my life on a hot afternoon on a Providence, Rhode Island, street. A white man in blue jeans, a T-shirt, and sneakers was pointing a very large gun at me and threatening to turn my head into a canoe.

"Get your ass on the ground right now," he said. "Don't you move a fucking inch."

He didn't say "nigger," but he might as well have. The barrel of his gun looked as wide as New York City's Lincoln Tunnel. From the nature of his commands, I figured he was probably a cop. If not, I was in real trouble. Bad guys don't give commands. They just shoot. The probability of him being a police officer, however, just made things worse. On this afternoon, I was a federal law enforcement officer in the middle of a case, and I was about to be shot by another law enforcement officer who thought that since I was the only black man around, I must be the criminal.

It was the summer of 1990. George H. W. Bush was president, Iraqi dictator Saddam Hussein had invaded Kuwait, and HIV/AIDS was so new that contracting the disease was considered a death sentence. The Honda Accord and the Ford Taurus were the top-selling cars. Hip-hop and rap music had taken hold; so, as part of my job, I was dressed in a

Coca-Cola T-shirt, some cool jeans, and my Fila sneakers, doing my best to look like a cross between Ice Cube and LL Cool J.

America was in the midst of the infamous war on drugs, and as a special agent with the Bureau of Alcohol, Tobacco and Firearms, I was at its center. Making things right, or so I thought.

Like most African-Americans, I had no idea then that this "war" would devastate black communities as much as, if not more than, the narcotics. By the early 1990s, however, cocaine use had reached epidemic proportions. The industry was driven by sales and consumption in white America. White Americans made up 80 percent of the users and sellers, but cocaine's most visible and devastating effects were seen in African-American communities, where cheap crack cocaine reigned.

Twenty-four-hour violence washed over black neighborhoods as drug dealers and addicts put down roots. Addicted women—mothers, young teenagers, professionals, and nonprofessionals—were reduced to trading oral sex for meager sums to feed their addictions. Families were ripped apart. Neighborhoods, including the one where I grew up, were ravaged. I was reminded of the impact of the crack epidemic every time I visited my mother and father in our North Philadelphia row house. A community of once neatly trimmed lawns now included boarded-up houses that were used for sex and getting high. There were three drug houses on my parents' block. Street corners where some of us idled away parts of our adolescence were now controlled by dealers and their runners and lookouts. Crack zombies, adults searching aimlessly for their next high, meandered down vacant twilight streets. My mom sometimes couldn't sleep because she feared what might happen. Every time I visited my parents and saw what cocaine had done to my neighborhood, I knew I was definitely doing the right thing. Get the drugs. Get the dealers. Get the guns.

Part of my new job with ATF was working undercover, which is always dangerous and always tricky. My assignment on this particular day was to purchase a gun and drugs from a Latino man we had been tracking for a while. He wasn't Colombian drug kingpin Pablo Escobar, but he was a major player on the local drug scene. A conviction on drugs alone could result in significant prison time, but under the new federal sentencing guidelines, possession of a weapon brought enhanced, longer sentences. So, we wanted both.

In our strategy meeting before the bust, we had gone over the plan. After I purchased the drugs and the weapon, I would walk a safe distance away and give the arrest signal through a microphone wired to my body. Everything went as planned. I had the guns and the drugs. I was walking away. "Move in now," I said into my microphone. Mission completed. It's time for a beer. But as my team members made the arrest, a plainclothes Providence police officer, not involved in the operation, heard the radio traffic—"Move in, move in. Suspect on the move"—and descended on me.

The suspect's description and mine couldn't have been more different. I was the wrong color, the wrong size, and the wrong ethnicity. The cop, however, had apparently heard all he needed. There was a suspect, and, me being a black guy under 30, I was him. Fortunately, another Providence police officer who was part of the undercover operation intervened. The officer apologized, though, I admit, I wasn't in the mood for offering forgiveness after coming that close to possibly losing my life. My guys had to pull me back to keep me from punching him out.

What I experienced that day in a 10-second, near-death exchange encapsulates what it is like to be "black in blue" in America, the dichotomy, the fragility, and even the peculiar dangers of being an African-American law enforcement officer. You are part of the law enforcement team, but not so much so that there aren't risks. Like your white colleagues, you are sworn to protect and serve, but soon after taking the oath, you discover that your duties include protecting the minority communities you serve from racist, bigoted, or biased actions of fellow police officers—black and white.

You wear a uniform that represents decades of inequity, insensitivity, and brutality imposed on African-Americans. Consequently, your own communities often eye you with suspicion and distrust, even disregard. Yet, nowhere is your presence more desperately needed than in disenfranchised black communities that are misunderstood and devalued by the rest of society. Where your white or even Latino counterparts often see fear and potential criminals at every turn, you see a historical African-American narrative of people struggling against the odds to create a better life for their families. You differentiate between the teenagers who just want to play basketball and the real predators. You know the financial and environmental pressures of that single mother who is doing her damnedest to raise her children on a meager income in a community with an indifferent education system, dramatically limited services, and few recreational opportunities. She doesn't always succeed, but she's trying. You see grandmothers and aunts and uncles and cousins and fathers, where some just see suspects. These circumstances may mirror the reality of officers of all races and ethnicities, but in America, skin tone tends to color our vision, no matter what our background.

As a black cop, it becomes part of your job to navigate this maze, and serve differing cultures for the sake of the greater good. And, while doing so, you know that missteps allowed for your brethren and fellow officers are not allowed for you. Your mistake could end your life.

That may sound like an exaggeration, but Natalia Harding knows this story all too well. Harding lives in Brooklyn, New York. She is a slight woman, regally adorned with carefully coiffed gray hair. We sat in her neat, compact living room and she told me how her son, Omar Edwards, had wanted to be a cop since he was 5 years old. "I don't know where it came from," she said as she showed me photos from his youth. "Nobody in our family ever had much to do with police," Harding recalled. She said that when he was 10, he began hanging around the 73rd Precinct station house on East New York Avenue in Brooklyn. He would help out and ask officers what the codes on the police radio meant. In 2007, he graduated from the New York Police Academy at age 23 and became "one of New York's finest." He was so proud of his achievement that he wore his badge around his apartment the whole day. "He loved the job," she said. "He was so proud of what he was doing. He felt like he was making a difference."

Two years later, Omar, now a newlywed of only three weeks and the father of two small children, was dead. He was shot and killed by a white police officer who saw Omar chasing a man who had broken into Omar's car, and assumed he was the bad guy. Omar had wrestled with the thief, but he broke free, and Omar, his gun drawn, gave chase. Not until officers tore open Omar's shirt as he lay handcuffed and dying on the street, did they see his police academy T-shirt and realize that the black man they had shot three times, once in the back, was one of their own.

What happened to Omar is a painful reminder to every black law enforcement officer that we are different. We live by different rules.

The truth is, it's amazing that so many African-American men and women are cops, considering our collective and personal history with police. The gulf between our communities is as old as the racist laws and mores that police officers have been called on to enforce against African-Americans, Asians, and Latinos in America for more than 100 years, from Alabama to Arizona, California to Connecticut, Maryland to Montana, Texas to Tennessee, West Virginia to Washington state, and not just in the South.

Police officers were on the front lines, the daily enforcers of racial segregation and discrimination. It was their duty to arrest African-Americans for being in white neighborhoods or being downtown after dark, for attempting to drink from whites-only water fountains, using whites-only restrooms, entering whites-only restaurants and other public establishments, sitting in the whites-only section on public transportation, talking too loud in the presence of white women, and for not getting off the sidewalks when whites walked by. In 35 states, they were required to arrest citizens for marrying someone outside their race.

Police forces across the South would arrest thousands of black men and women, most often for the false crime of vagrancy (not having a job), to support a system of forced labor. Under an arrangement that didn't end until just before World War II, those black men and women were then leased as cheap labor to states, local governments, white farmers, and corporations, including U.S. Steel, then the largest company in the world.

In some cases, as in the public lynching of Thomas Shipp and Abram Smith on August 7, 1930, in Marion, Indiana, police were participants in meting out "justice."

In 2016, the International Association of Chiefs of Police, America's largest police management organization, recognized the historical role police have played as enforcers of racist and discriminatory policies by issuing a formal apology to the nation's minority population "for the actions of the past and the role that our profession has played in society's historical mistreatment of communities of color." Terrence Cunningham, then-president of IACP, said on behalf of the organization's 23,000 members at the association's annual convention, "There have been times when law enforcement officers, because of the laws enacted by federal, state, and local governments, have been the face of oppression for far too many of our fellow citizens."

Because of cops' historical role in perpetrating brutality against black communities, almost none of my family or friends were thrilled about my decision to enter law enforcement. I grew up in Philadelphia during a time when a high school dropout named Frank Rizzo ran the Philadelphia Police Department, which viewed all African-American residents of Philly as criminals. A racist, a bigot, and a bully, Rizzo would later become mayor and appoint his brother to run the fire department. Before his ascent to top cop, Rizzo once told a reporter that he would be so vicious as police commissioner that "I'm going to make Attila the Hun look like a faggot."

Several times during his career, Rizzo was charged with beating suspects in his custody with a blackjack. But the charges were always dismissed. He personally led Saturday night roundups of gays and staged a series of raids on coffeehouses and cafés. He claimed they were drug dens. Not one person was ever charged with a crime as a result of those raids. In 1972, shortly before Rizzo resigned as police commissioner to run for mayor, he ordered police to raid the Black Panthers headquarters, herd its members into the street, and force them to strip naked. That left a bad taste in the mouth of African-American residents of Philly. Even now, some still spit at the mention of his name.

My personal encounters with police had been mundane until 1983, in large part because of my parents. They barred me from street corners and other innocent locations that might draw police attention. They wouldn't even let me go to the Parliament/Funkadelic concert that e-v-e-r-y-b-o-d-y was planning to attend for fear that something might happen and police would be called. But in 1983, our beloved Philadelphia 76ers, led by Julius "Dr. J." Erving and Moses Malone, won the National Basketball Association Championship after six long years of coming so torturously close. That year, I was a sophomore at Delaware State University, home for the summer, and there was no way I was going to miss the celebration in downtown Philly.

When I came out of the subway staircase on the east side of City Hall, however, I was met by a snarling German shepherd followed by four or five cops, coming right at me. I turned to head back into the subway, but I didn't move fast enough. Next thing I knew, I was holding on to a traffic-light pole and screaming as a police K-9 dog ripped off my right sneaker and began gnawing on my foot. A police officer finally pulled the dog off me and told me to "get the fuck out of here." The dogs and the officer disappeared into the crowd, but I wasn't in shape to go anywhere. Some people helped me hobble a few blocks to 13th and Market streets and turned me over to two other police officers.

I told them I had been bitten by a police dog, and they drove me to Hahnemann University Hospital. I was there for a week, long enough to be pissed. My irate father called a black editor he knew at the *Philadelphia*

Inquirer, the city's daily newspaper. The editor, Acel Moore, assigned the story to a white reporter named Bill Marimow, who later earned two Pulitzer Prizes, one for his work on this story. Marimow wrote 40 stories on how a corps of K-9 officers and their dogs, who were out of control, routinely used their dogs to attack people. His report changed the way the Philadelphia K-9 units worked.

Once out of the hospital, I did my own investigation. I found the report that the officers turned in after dropping me off at the hospital. Under the section that asked for an explanation of my injuries, they had written "unknown," even though I told them I had been bitten by a police dog. That stunned me.

So, it doesn't take much more to explain why being a law enforcement officer wasn't at the top of my list of desired professions. Most of the African-American cops I know have a story like mine or had a similar initial ambivalence about becoming a cop.

Lisa Montague is retired now from the Baltimore City Police Department after 19 years. She had a good career, rose to the rank of sergeant, and has one of the best minds I've ever met when it comes to day-to-day law enforcement and how to deal with the myriad of problems police face as they go about their jobs. I loved hearing Montague explain how she and so many women officers worked through various situations by using brainpower instead of brawn. There were some scary stories, but one of my favorites was a simple shoplifting case.

"I get to the store and I see a guy taking off down the street with the can of pork and beans in his hand," Montague said. "The store manager is chasing behind him. The manager turns to me and says, 'Aren't you going to go after him?'

"I said, 'For a can of pork and beans? No, sir. He's a local. I will see him later and arrest him then.' Now, some young male cop might have chased him to settle it 'mano a mano.' But that's just macho stuff. It may look good, but it's not effective policing. I couldn't believe it, but when I got back to the squad room, I found out the store manager had reported me to my sergeant."

"What did your sergeant say?" I asked.

"He asked if that's what happened. I said, 'Yes it did. There were no bodies, nobody was injured, no broken windows. So, no, I'm not chasing down a suspect for a can of beans.' He just laughed."

For all Montague's skill, achievements, and love for her job, like me, she never wanted to be a police officer. Never.

"I didn't look at them as people," she told me, "because they didn't treat us like people when I was growing up. As I got older, I'd watch the way they dealt with blacks. It was a power thing. *You do what I tell you to do.* They come into your home, *You shut up and you sit down.* They were supposed to be there to protect us, but that's not what happened. We had a saying in my neighborhood, 'Be careful when you call 911, because you don't know who is coming.'"

After graduating from high school, Montague completed two years of college and began looking for employment. "I knew I needed a job, and I didn't want a regular job. I wanted a city, state, or federal job. That's what we were always taught by our family. Those were the good jobs. So, I applied everywhere, the post office, social security, and the police department.

"The police department was the first one to call. I didn't want to be a police officer, but I needed a job. Even when I started at the police academy, I was always hoping that some other [agency] would call, and I could get out, because I did not want to be a police officer."

In interviewing many African-American officers around the country for this book, I found that a lot of them did not like cops growing up and never intended to become one. Carl Williams didn't want to be a police officer, either. Williams had a distinguished career as an officer in the nation's capital until he was shot by a neighborhood hoodlum during a 1974 Christmas party that he and other officers were throwing for the children in southeast Washington. He was shot in the arm and stomach and left the service a year later.

Williams is a Vietnam veteran who was also injured during one of the war's most brutal battles. He grew up poor in West Baltimore, which was the major reason he enlisted in the military. As a kid, he said, there were so many people in the house, not only did he not have a bedroom, he didn't even have a permanent bed. "I slept where I could find a place every night," he told me as we sat in the den of his home in Gwynn Oak, Maryland. From Williams's home, we could see the site of a former "whites-only" park, Gwynn Oak Amusement Park. During an eight-year campaign to desegregate the facility, Williams's future wife, Lydia, unofficially integrated the park in 1963 by walking right in. Her skin complexion was so light that park officials thought she was white. Her bold move and continued protests from blacks in the area led to the park's official desegregation on August 23, 1963, when an 11-year-old black girl rode the park's "whites-only" carousel on the same day the Reverend Martin Luther King Jr. gave his famous "I Have a Dream" speech in the nation's capital. That very same carousel now sits in the center of the Smithsonian Museums on the National Mall in Washington, where hundreds of thousands of children and adults from around the world ride it annually.

Williams became a D.C. police officer following his time in the US Air Force, where he was assigned to the military police. He rose to the rank of sergeant in the District of Columbia Police Department at age 24. He couldn't assume the position, however, until a year later, in part because he had completed all the requirements before the traditional age when officers are made sergeants.

That was ironic, because Williams joined the military to get away from Baltimore and its racist police, he told me. One of the things he wanted as an adolescent was a pair of shoes popular with him and his friends. They were only sold downtown at a shoe store called

Manchester's. Downtown Baltimore in the 1960s was a place where segregation in restaurants, stores, and other facilities was vigorously enforced.

"There was separate everything. My grandmother had told me repeatedly not to go downtown by myself, because everything was segregated, and you were pretty much at the mercy of the police and other white folks when you went there. But I wanted those shoes," he said with a smile. "You know how it is when you're young."

So, one day he slipped downtown and not long afterward, emerged from Manchester's with his prized possession under his arm. Not long after he came out of the store, he was stopped by two Baltimore cops.

"They were red-faced, and I could smell the alcohol on them," he recalled. "They stopped me and said, 'What you got in that bag, nigger?'

"I told them it was shoes. They took the bag and opened the box and started making fun of the shoes because they had these pointed toes, which was the style back then. One of them said, 'Yeah, nigger, you can use these shoes to kill the roaches in the corner.'

"Then they asked me for a receipt. Being young, I had left it at the store. I definitely didn't want to lose my shoes, so I said, 'Sir, the store is still open. We can go back to the store and they can tell you I just bought them.' They didn't want to do that. They slapped me and pushed me around some and then gave me back the shoes. They said, 'Get the hell out of here, nigger,' and I left. I never told my grandmother, because she would have beat my ass for going down there in the first place. Everybody in our neighborhood already didn't like police because of the way they treated us. They would just come into your house—no warrant, no nothing—and talk to you like you weren't even human. But after that incident, being a cop was the last thing I wanted to do."

Even as African-Americans became cops, we were segregated and discriminated against at every turn. Initially, black police officers only patrolled black neighborhoods. They weren't allowed to arrest white residents. They also weren't allowed to ride in police cars and, during roll call, white officers sat while they stood.

One of the permanent, though unintentional, reminders of the racism black officers endured early on is on display at the police academy of the Miami-Dade Police Department. It's a photo of the 1960 graduating class, the first class in which an African-American officer was allowed to attend. Clarence Dickson was standing at a bus stop in the wee hours of the morning on the way to his job, when a white officer passing by saw him and thought he might have a good work ethic.

There were black police officers in Miami beginning in 1944, but none had been allowed to attend the academy. They were separate and unequal. In the early years in Miami, black cops had no headquarters, no cars, and no radio contact. They policed by walking or riding bicycles. They used the office of a black dentist as their headquarters. Later, they used a one-bedroom apartment in the "Central Negro District." There are many stories of arrested prisoners being taken to jail on bicycle handlebars, or by walking, and sometimes by hailing a black citizen's car as it was driving by. A real station was built for them in 1950; it was named the Black Police Precinct. It provided a station house for African-American police officers and a courtroom for African-American judges to hear cases involving black defendants. It existed until 1963.

Dickson said he used to hear whispers about him being the "first one," but he never understood the significance until one day during roll call one of the black officers walked over to him and said, "Some of us lost our jobs fighting to get blacks into the academy. Don't let us down." The other black officer didn't know it when he made his remark, but Dickson was flunking out of the academy at the time. "When he told me that, I felt a great responsibility to those guys," Dickson said. "I went back and I rose from being almost kicked out of the academy to graduating number two in my class. Out of about 40 of us, only 13 graduated. On graduation day, our academy class took a picture, all 13 of us standing up in our uniforms, relieved and proud. And there I was, the only black guy in that class."

Dickson would later become Miami's first black police chief. But, today, if you go back and look at that picture of his class hanging in the Miami-Dade Police Department Training Academy, you won't see him in it. What Dickson didn't know then was that the department had called his classmates back later to take a picture without him.

Twenty years later, Lisa Montague was still feeling the same discrimination as the second black woman in her Baltimore police district when she joined the force in 1979.

"All of the white officers made it clear they didn't want me there. One particular white male officer who bordered my section—say, I was patrolling section 832, he would be in section 831—he came out and said that he had a problem with me as a black woman and that I had no business on the job. He said this to my face. He said I was going to get one of them hurt, and if I ever needed backup, he said, 'Don't look for me.' We were in roll call when he said it. Other guys heard it. Some of the guys came up and told me not to worry about him, but it was clear that a lot of them felt the same way," Montague said.

I've felt the sting of that racism while being black in blue, as has just about every other black officer I've met. David Lomax and I were ATF agents together for nearly 30 years. We primarily worked in different cities, but we met often and swapped stories about what it's like to be black in blue. Before Lomax joined the department, he had been a police officer in St. Louis, and *man*, did he have some stories about his earlier days before he joined ATF.

"So, one of my first weekends on the job, I was paired with another African-American officer," he began. "We get a call to report at a house in South St. Louis in the Carondelet area. We get to the house, knock, and a lady comes to the door. First thing she said was 'Where are the police officers?' We're both dressed in our uniforms, big as day. So, my lead officer says, 'Miss, we're right here.' She said, 'I asked for police officers, not niggers.' I'm thinking, *Damn, that's messed up* because I'm just out of the academy. So, we contacted the sergeant, and he told us to leave. A little later, we get a call to the same house. The same lady answers the door. She looks at us and says the exact same thing."

David is incredulous, and so am I, but the story is so ridiculous and I've heard so many like it, deep inside I'm chuckling a bit. We order another drink and David starts up again.

"The next weekend, they partner me with this white guy. We're riding around, and I swear, the only word that came out of his mouth was *nigger*. We're riding through a black neighborhood near downtown, and he said, 'I'm so tired of riding around protecting these niggers.'

"He looked at me and I said, 'What's up? What are you saying to me?'

"You know what he said? He said, 'I'm not talking about you. Your color is blue.'

"So, I went back to the sergeant, who was Latino. He said, 'Your job is to keep your eyes and ears open and your mouth shut.' That's how he addressed my concerns. So, from that point on, I just kept my mouth closed and did what I had to do to advance."

After he graduated, the racist behavior continued, he said. "So, now I'm an officer and I'm out with this white officer and he pulls over this black family because their turning signal doesn't work. The man is in the car with his wife and his kids. I step out of the car, so I can watch my fellow officer's back. The cop walks up to the car and says, 'Hey, nigger, did you know your taillight is out?'

"This is 1981. I'm thinking, 'If this was me, and I was in the car with my wife and my children, I'm going to react a certain way.' And sure enough, the guy said to the officer, 'Sir, tell me what I'm doing wrong, but I don't appreciate you talking to me like this with my wife and family in the car.'

" 'Well,' the white cop started again, 'I don't give a shit what you think.'

"Next thing you know the white guy was on the ground. The black guy had knocked him on his ass, because another N-word had come out of his mouth. So, I go up to the guy and I say, 'I understand why you did what you did, but I'm going to have to arrest you because you assaulted a police officer.'

"So, the officer goes into the station and tells the captain I wasn't out there helping him. I tell the captain, 'If this guy is going to be out there calling somebody a nigger, and then he needs a "nigger" to get somebody off his ass, maybe he shouldn't be doing what he's doing.' The captain, a white guy, started laughing. All he had to do was tell the man why he got stopped and give him a ticket and let him go on his way. I would have reacted the same way, if he had talked to me like that."

I had my own encounter with a fellow law enforcement officer and the N-word. Ironically, my incident brings us to where we started, in Providence, Rhode Island. I am now an ATF officer, and this is about two years after I was nearly shot by the white cop while undercover. As part of our duties, we frequently worked surveillance in conjunction with other agencies. One night, we were working a joint case with the Providence Police Department's Special Investigations Bureau. I can't remember the particular case, but it was dangerous enough for me to wear my ballistic vest and bring a tactical rifle. At the police department, I was teamed up with another ATF agent. We left and decided we'd better grab a bite to eat. Once you get rolling on these operations, you never know what is going to happen. You may not eat until you're done. You may end up following a suspect to another state. So, we stopped at Burger King. We went through the drive-through window and were heading out onto the street. I was driving. As I was pulling onto Broad Street, a carload of black guys zoomed past, almost hitting us.

My partner yells out at the car, "Fucking niggers." He quickly remembers who is sitting right next to him and says, "Oops."

I don't say a word, but I am steaming. I'm trying to decide how to respond. So, I come up with a plan. I drive us to a really rough area in South Providence, a known hangout for gang members and drug dealers. I place the car in park and turn to him, "John, get out." He refuses and I tell him again. "Get out." People are starting to gather now and look at the Crown Victoria parked in the middle of the intersection.

I then exit the vehicle and go around to the driver's side with my tactical gear—big ATF letters on my ballistic vest, firearm in holster—and yell, "John, get the fuck out of my car before I drag you out!" He's not moving, so I unhook his seat belt. By now, his face is turning red. I yell once more for him to get out. By now, people are really beginning to take notice. I was about to drag John out of the car, which could have been bad for me, but, fortunately, he got out, and I drove off. What happened next? Let's just say our surveillance was not compromised, John got back to the office safely, and the issue was resolved to my satisfaction. I just knew one thing when I left that scene. That was the last time I wanted to hear a cop call a black person "nigger."

Brian Mallory

Former New York Police Department Detective

The things we did in the early '80s, we would be in jail for today. Back then, there were no cell phones, no social media, no cameras on every street corner. If anybody was going to make a complaint, it was their word against the cop's, and the cop always won. I had a very short temper back then. If I stopped a guy and a guy opened his mouth, he'd learn very quickly not to fuck with me. It might be a slap in the face, might be a jack, it might be a nightstick. If you opened your mouth, you would get it.

Back then, the ends justified the means. We had roll call one day, and the captain comes down. Our captain never came out of his office. So, this was unusual. He says, "Who's got sector Adam?" My partner and I raise our hands. He says, "The community council is complaining about kids selling pot on this corner. I'm coming by at 5 p.m. with some community council members. I don't want to see anybody on the corner at 5 o'clock."

We're two young cops from Long Island. Lots of the cops came from Long Island then and a lot still do. Long Island was like a different world compared to the neighborhoods in New York City. It was like a different country. On Long Island, there are towns that are predominantly white and towns that are predominantly black. Not very integrated. I went to a high school that had no black students. None. My college was somewhat mixed, but I didn't have any black friends. I wasn't discriminating against them. I just didn't have any interaction with African-Americans. I didn't have any interaction with African-Americans until I joined the police department. I didn't have black friends until I was a cop, and those were fellow cops. A lot of white cops were like me. They didn't have any interaction with minorities until they became cops.

Anyway, we go out. About 20 minutes to 5 p.m., we pull up to the corner. There are five or six Puerto Rican kids selling pot. I yell, "Guys, off this corner until after 6 p.m. Don't come back until after then."

One of the kids yells back, "Fuck you. This is a public street. We have a right to be here."

I look at my partner: "What did he say?" I'm a New York City police officer and he's talking to me? His friends are there, and they are smirking. It's 1983. I'm fresh, one year in the department and I've got this 16-year-old kid mouthing off. I get out of the car with my nightstick and club him until he drops. "Pick him up," I yell to his friends, "and I don't want anybody here for the rest of the fucking night."

You could never ever do that now. That would be problematic. At the very least, you would be fired. But the captain didn't give a fuck what I did to keep the corner clean. He's not saying break the law, but he doesn't want to be embarrassed in front of the council members. He would have called us into the office and chewed our asses. Back then, it was a different city. If you let somebody talk to you like that in that environment, it wasn't going to be the last time.

I started as a uniform cop in Midtown. I did less than two years in uniform, because, early on, I effected a bribery arrest. I had arrested this pimp and while I was booking him, he offered me $500 to let him go and $400 a week to let him and his girls operate. I wore a wire and set up a meeting and got him on tape. I don't know what happened to him. I know he went to trial, but the big thing was I got a bribery arrest.

Back then, a bribery was the best arrest you could have. That was better even than a murder collar. That showed you had integrity. The police department had so much bad press over the years that they were looking for stuff like that.

Then, I got into a shootout in 1986 in Midtown Manhattan and that put me on the fast track. A couple of days before Christmas, we got a call about a possible robbery in a jewelry store. We went in the store and two armed guys were robbing the store. So, there was a shootout. There were customers and employees working. One of the robbers walked out without any injuries. I shot the second one twice. They were both convicted and sent away. An employee in the store was hit in the crossfire and killed. I don't want to say my bullet hit him, but there's a saying we had as police officers: "The most important thing is to sign out and go home." So, after that shooting, I pretty much had a free pass to go wherever I wanted to go. That put me on the fast track to detective.

Back then, 42nd Street was a sewer. There was nothing there but porn theaters, drug dealers, prostitutes, pimps, and johns. I was very hard on pimps. I hated them. I had more respect for thieves than I did pimps. These guys would turn young girls out. You see a new one out and in a matter of weeks, she's hooked on heroin. We were hard on them. Yes, we would beat them up.

It was hard arresting a pimp, because they knew how to skirt the law. So, we would take it out on them with their cars. We would slice their interiors up with box cutters, use slappers or nightsticks to break the glass and the dashboards. If they had soda or beer in the car, we'd pour it over the interior. We might lock their keys in the trunk of their cars. The vast majority of pimps were black, but that didn't have anything to do with it. A pimp was a pimp. If you were a pimp, I didn't like you, and you were going to have a problem with me and my partner.

The customers crossed every nationality and every industry or job title. To slow down the traffic, we would take the girls' wigs. When they dressed up for the night, all of them put on wigs. So, we would take their wigs so they couldn't work. In the winter, we would take their shoes. You can't walk around the streets with no shoes. Then, we would take the wigs and stick them under the turret lights on the top of our police vehicle and we would put the shoes on the hood of the car and we would drive slowly through the area so they could see us.

One day, we got called in by Internal Affairs for a G.O. 15. That's where you have to go before Internal Affairs to answer to complaints. They told us we had been under observation: "We've been following you for 30 days."

The first thing that went through my mind is, *I'm going to get fired*, because they have seen all the stuff that we've been doing. I'll remember what they said until the day I die. "You two are very unconventional in what you do, but you're extremely effective." That was it.

When I was put on the track to become detective, I was first transferred to the Organized Crime Control Bureau. That was 1986. I was in the Narcotics Division. Crack was the drug. Crack hit around '85, and that is when everything went off the rails. Assaults were up, shootings were up, murders were up. You had these internal fights among dealers. So, you had a lot of shootings, and you had a population of people addicted to crack who had no income. So, what were they doing? They were committing burglaries, robberies, grand larcenies.

That was a dangerous time—2,300 homicides in a city of 8 million people, and they were harder to solve. Most homicides are committed by someone who knows the assailant. Back then it was drive-by shootings or it was gang-related or a robbery that goes bad. That makes it harder to solve. Precincts 75, 77 in Brooklyn, or Precincts 32, 34 in Manhattan. They were looking at 100 homicides a year. You couldn't even investigate them all, because they were coming so fast.

It was a grind. Every day I did undercover work. You go out and either buy drugs or arrest people for selling drugs. It was so lucrative, they made so much money selling drugs, you couldn't stem the tide. We would execute a warrant in the morning, knock the door down with the battering ram, arrest three or four people, and seize the drugs and the money. You would go back to the precinct, process the prisoners, voucher the drugs, stamp every bill as evidence, and then take them down to Central Booking. You would drive by the location on the way to Central Booking, and the door you knocked down would be up and the place would be back up and running. At some point, you got to realize it was a losing battle.

You were making your arrest numbers for the month and you were getting lots of overtime but nobody was under the illusion that they were making the community any better. As a young cop coming into narcotics, it felt like I was in a war zone. We were cops from Long Island, now in Brooklyn, and it got to be an us-against-them mentality.

From the day officers got on the scene, we were told, "Get your overtime, keep your head down, get promoted. It's a shithole. It's the fucking ghetto." You would lose those wide eyes the longer you worked there. It was like shoveling sand into the tide. So, the attitude was "I'm going to come in, do my cases, do my time, and get out and that's going to be it." None of us were under the illusion we were helping anybody.

As a young cop, most of what I saw didn't make sense. Sometimes, it was clear the blacks were giving a heads-up to the drug dealers about us and I'm left thinking, *Isn't this their neighborhood?* This is where they live. This is where their kids go to school, and we're trying to clean it up. Why would they do that? Why are they helping drug dealers and not helping us? And the answer for us was, *That's just the way it is.* Because for us it didn't make any sense. They're killing your kids and they are bringing this blight on the neighborhood and we're the cavalry coming to help and you're not helping us.

But actually, we weren't the cavalry. We were more like an occupying force. There were times we would go in and things would get physical. There were certainly times when there was collateral damage. People were in the building, they were in front of the building. We just came in to take doors down and arrest everybody. There was no connection between us and them. Sometimes you go in and knock down the wrong door. That was too bad. If a civilian was in the wrong place at the wrong time, "Sorry, pal." It's just another number. Let the judge figure it out.

So, even though they weren't selling, there were times when honest civilians who had never had negative interactions with the drug dealers were having them with the cops. Cop tosses him and searches him. The black guy says something. Now, you expect that guy to look up to the cop and give you information. But he's thinking, *That's the guy who frisked me and made me look like an asshole in front of my girlfriend. That's the guy who called me "nigger." That's the guy who kicked me in the ass.*

It was like the end of the Vietnam War—they are telling us to take out a complete village to save the village. I didn't see it then, but it's much clearer to me now. At the time, certain things were embedded in us in the police academy. The first day I was in the police academy, the instructor came up and we're all 21, 22, 23 years old, and for a lot of us, it's our first job. He looks out and he writes on the board, CYA, and he says, "If you don't remember anything, remember this. Everything you do, every time you engage, every time you go out there, cover your ass." That puts you on the defensive the first day. It's us against them. That was the first message in the police department: Cover your ass.

Lots of stuff started in the academy. You learned that even if a cop did something bad, you didn't report him. Again, it's us against them. You learned very early on, the Internal Affairs Department and everybody in it is an enemy. Internal Affairs was only going to hurt you. Nothing good was going to come out of that. That's the golden rule. You're never going to call Internal Affairs. If you do, now you're a rat. In the police department, you'd rather be called a coward or a racist than a rat.

If the shit hits the fan and you call for help, and everybody knows you're a rat who reported another cop, are they all going to come help you? Are they going to come as fast? As an active cop, those were all things you thought about. There's nothing scarier than if you chase somebody into a building and you have no idea who's on the other side of the door. The last thing you want to worry about, when you call for backup, is whether they were coming.

Internal Affairs is a much more accepted part of the police department now. Some people look at it as a necessary evil. Now, going to Internal Affairs is almost part of a career path. In the old days, why would guys fucking volunteer to be assigned to Internal Affairs when you know you're going to be investigating cops, or you got fucking jammed up for something you did and you got transferred to Internal Affairs, and you are going to fuck other cops over because of something you did?

I wasn't naive to think cops weren't doing things wrong. Like doctors or lawyers or anybody else, there are always going to be bad guys. I can't tell you that I never worked with anybody who was taking money and doing something wrong. Some guys are just criminals and they just use the badge as a way to make money. Other guys are what I call "situational."

I worked with this one guy. He was a great guy. I didn't know it, but he had two families. He had a wife and a kid on Long Island and a girlfriend and a kid in New Jersey. When I started, we got paid $17,900. I was a young single guy, so I was fine, but I would think, *How do you survive on fucking $17,900 with two kids and two women?*

Anyway, this guy worked the red-light detail [high prostitution area]. He had to write a certain amount of traffic summonses. You had to do 25 summonses a month as a uniform cop. That was your quota. My partner and I were very active. So, we each wrote 100 summonses a month. This is when I was trying to make detective and get into anticrime. This guy was making his quota, but he started taking $50 from cabbies when he pulled them over for red-light summonses. It worked for the cabbies because it wasn't on their record and he needed the money.

But he got caught. One of the cabbies complained, and he lost everything—his job, his pension, his benefits, his reputation. It's stupid. I understand the pressure and the temptation, but it's stupid. I've been collecting my pension for 20 years tax-free. I've collected $1 million. I have full medical coverage for my wife, my kids. How many $50 do you have to collect to make up for that?

3.

WHO MATTERS MOST?

"I wonder if because it is blacks getting shot down, because it is blacks who are going to jail in massive numbers, whether we—the total we, black and white—care as much. If we started to put white America in jail at the same rate that we're putting black America in jail, I wonder whether our collective feelings would be the same, or would we be putting pressure on the president and our elected officials not to lock up America, but to save America?"

—Former Atlanta police chief Eldrin Bell in 1990
at the height of the war on drugs

During the war on drugs campaign, when I was up and down the streets and ghettos of the United States, busting down the homes of black and brown people, I never questioned that although we were tearing up these neighborhoods, we had not touched the homes and hoods of white users and dealers in this cleanup of America. I was too busy locking up folks, granted, but what we saw in the media and what most Americans—white, black, Hispanic, Asian, and me—had come to believe, was that most of the nation's cocaine users and dealers were white. Furthermore, they were white people who lived in nice neighborhoods and had decent jobs.

The nation's first drug czar, William J. Bennett, was appointed the director of the Office of National Drug Control Policy under President George H. W. Bush. His job was to rid the country of the cocaine menace. He explained, "The typical cocaine user is white, male, a high school graduate employed full time, and living in a small metropolitan area or suburb." Yet, the article claimed, it was black people who were disproportionately being imprisoned under harsh laws that we had designed, with the full support of most black lawmakers, to send them to jail for longer sentences.

We did this because we believed, erroneously, that the drug epidemic was rooted in African-American neighborhoods and to protect those communities, we needed harsher sentences, broader police powers, and, if need be, the lawful ability to violate some people's constitutional rights. Everyone on every level of justice was involved: local cops, police chiefs, federal law enforcement agents, prosecuting attorneys. African-American mayors and black congressional leaders, educators, and hard-core law-and-order Republicans, had come together to battle the scourge of cocaine. We needed to come down hard on anyone connected with crack cocaine. Everybody had bought into the cause. And when it came to that fight, nobody was clearer or more focused on ridding the streets of drug dealers and addicts than Special Agent Matthew Horace.

When I hit the streets, I was merciless. I was big and badass, and my goal was to unleash my personal fury on anything in my path connected with dope. I wanted to rain down pain and suffering on them the same way they had unleashed this plague upon America. I cursed them silently and to their faces, and I helped send thousands to prison. I was relentless. I worked undercover, buying drugs and guns. I busted down doors, sometimes it seemed almost daily. I dragged scum downstairs, pulled them out of their cars, and cornered them in the alleys. You didn't want to see me coming. I grilled them during interrogations, called them liars and thieves and punks and sissies and anything else until they broke. And, yes, I did things that I'm not proud of, because I knew the hurt heroin and crack can bring. It was not something I read about in newspapers, books, and magazines, or saw on television or in the movies. It was personal, as much of policing is—whether my brothers in blue want to admit it or not.

A cousin on my father's side, Maurice, sold cocaine and crack. Crack was a low-cost version of cocaine popular in poor black neighborhoods because it was cheap and a small quantity could get you high. Maurice earned a bullet in the back for his dealings and was paralyzed for life.

My mother's sister, Aunt Joan, was a heroin addict who was in and out of jail. When drugs made her an unfit mother, my grandparents raised her three children. I recall brief encounters with her when she showed up at my grandmother's home. Her hands were always swollen, which I later found out was indicative of heroin users. My mother ultimately banned her from our home to protect my brother and me.

My mother's brother, Uncle Jerome, was also barred from our house. As a teenager, he was a star. He was a smart, enterprising kid who always made the family proud. He held down two paper routes and later landed a job at the *Philadelphia Inquirer*. It was a big thing at that time, a black kid working for the *Inquirer*. After high school graduation, he went into the Air Force. He came back to Philly after he was discharged and got hooked on heroin. He was in and out of jail.

At some point, he crossed the wrong person and was stuffed into a cardboard box and thrown in the Delaware River. My family thinks the perpetrator was a drug dealer he owed money. He survived and showed up dripping wet at my grandmother's house. She gave him enough money to flee the city and he landed in Baltimore, where he died. Years after he left, the people he apparently stiffed still came around asking for him.

Most of my childhood buddies were not sucked into the abyss until after I went away to college. Every time I came home for a visit, I would see someone who knew me but whom I could barely recognize—a former classmate, a fellow high school football player, a girl I had dreamed of dating. Their bodies and faces had been shrunken and twisted from cocaine use. My childhood friend Kenny, who lived a few doors down from my family, began using and was in and out of prison for many years, mostly for nuisance crimes to support his habit.

John lived on the street right behind our house. He was a few years older than me, but we played together as kids. He volunteered for the Navy to escape the gangs that by my senior year had permeated parts of the city. He returned home and got involved in the drug game. He was murdered, execution-style, on a street corner in West Philly. People from the neighborhood say he was killed by the Junior Black Mafia, a notorious street gang that terrorized inner-city Philadelphia in the mid-1980s through the early 1990s. My friend Thomas lived six doors down from us. He and I used to walk to high school together. Thomas was very talented. I always thought he would be a famous artist one day, but he also got involved with drugs and began hanging with the Junior Black Mafia. He was killed in a shootout with Philadelphia police.

Meanwhile, I could see how crack houses—three on my parents' block alone—had transformed our neighborhood. Too many yards were now unkempt. Trash littered once-clean streets. Teenage drug dealers and their juvenile couriers controlled the corners. Addiction destroyed families as husbands and wives, locked in its deadly embrace, lost jobs, and could no longer support or raise their children. Young men and women, crippled by cocaine, abandoned their dreams and became lost souls, transfixed by an unquenchable thirst for another hit. So, you're damned right. I was there to kick ass and take names. It didn't register with me that I was making war on the very people the whole country and I claimed we were trying to save, until I was on the outside looking in on another drug epidemic.

Fast-forward 30 years. America is experiencing the deadliest drug crisis in its history: opioids. Heroin and opiates are killing our friends, family, and neighbors in record numbers, the vast majority of them white. In 2014, for example, 47,055 Americans died from heroin and other opium-related drugs. That is more than 3,900 people a month, more than died in the September 11 terrorist attacks, more than the highest number of murders in any year in the nation's history. In subsequent years, the numbers have remained virtually unchanged. By April 2016, the current opioid epidemic had claimed 200,000 lives, more than all the Americans who died in World War I, three times the number of US military deaths in the Vietnam War, five times the number in the Korean War.

By any measure, the current death toll and the family destruction associated with the illegal heroin and opiate trade dwarf what we were dealing with in the crack days. At the height of crack and powder cocaine from 1984 to 1996, America averaged about 8,000 drug-related murders a year. Add to that number about 7,000 cocaine-related overdose deaths annually and the total is less than half the number of people dying each year now from opiates. The problem is magnified by the other crime that comes with it. Addicts need to get high, and they will do anything to get their fix—theft, burglary, robbery, prostitution. Additionally, dealers are lacing their drugs with Fentanyl, a synthetic opiate so powerful that it is a near-death sentence for any heroin addict who unknowingly uses it. Consequently, the number of heroin- and opiate-related deaths keeps climbing.

The accounts of all these colliding forces are painful. In Baldwinsville, New York, firefighters responded to overdose victims on three separate occasions at the same house. In each instance, the person had stopped breathing. Firefighters used the drug Narcan to save them. The victims were 21, 22, and 23. To the west in Parma, Ohio, a fire department rescue unit also responded to three overdose calls in the same house on the same day—the mother in the morning, the son in the afternoon, the daughter in the evening. The mother died.

To the north in Warren, Michigan, Peggy and Edward Babinski came home to discover their two children, 41-year-old son Edward Jr. and daughter Heather, 28, dead from a heroin overdose. A little over an hour away in Monroe County, Michigan, rescue units also responded to three heroin overdose deaths on the same day. Two of them were found in separate rooms of the same motel. The other was in a mobile home park. All of them were under the age of 35.

Same story in Seattle. Beginning at 11:18 a.m. one morning, fire department medics responded to an overdose call in the 7800 block of Aurora Avenue North. They found two people who could not be saved; the heroin had been mixed with Fentanyl. Two hours later, firefighters responded to another overdose in the 900 block of North 80th Street. This time it was a woman. She also died. Less than 20 minutes later, firefighters rolled on another overdose call, this time in the 900 block of North 102nd Street. They found two men unconscious. Fortunately, they survived.

Back in the Midwest, in Crestline, Ohio, the Hess family lost two loved ones to heroin on the same day. Jason Hess, 35, died of an overdose. A few hours later, his distraught mother, Barbara Fultz, took a pillow and a blanket to a cemetery behind the house, lay down on a headstone, and swallowed a bottle of Valium. "Please don't weep for me," her suicide note said. "I am ready for this rest. Thank you, heroin, another victim."

It was her 60th birthday.

Finally, there is the heartbreaking photograph that went viral of a 4-year-old boy alone and bewildered in the back seat of an SUV on the side of a busy road in East Liverpool, Ohio. In the front seats were his mother and her male friend, slumped over and unconscious in a heroin overdose stupor. City officials posted the photo on Facebook to illustrate the plight of their city. One officer called it "a cry for help."

East Liverpool, a small suburban community of just under 11,000 people, exemplifies what heroin and opiates are doing to predominantly white communities across America. Unconscious addicts have been dumped so frequently in the East Liverpool hospital parking lot that administrators developed a special alert system to treat them. Paramedics have picked up overdose victims from the Walmart parking lot, from roadside ditches, and from apartments and homes across town. At one point, it had become routine for children to see a passed-out parent jolted to life with a dose of Narcan. Drug dealers from out of state flock to the desolate streets, selling highs for $10 or $15 a hit. For too many residents, there's little else: no jobs, no recreation. In some ways, the bleak scenario—particularly the street dealers—sounds eerily similar to my days on the streets dealing with the crack epidemic.

But the nation's response to this opioid drug epidemic, one in which most of the victims are white, is dramatically different.

There are no evening news reports, photographs, and headlines of law enforcement officers, dressed in tactical gear, cordoning off white neighborhoods, questioning and searching white people as they make their way home from work. There are no breaking news stories about scores of addicted white parents being marched off to jail and their children shuttled into foster care. There is no erroneous media coverage about "opiate babies," neurologically and psychologically damaged children born to white families, as there were about African-American children born to black female crack addicts.

In this new fight against heroin, doors aren't being kicked in. Civil liberties aren't being trampled, and victims and communities aren't being demonized by the public and the news media as they were in my day. Heroin and opiate addicts are not filling up jails and prisons in record numbers, as the millions of crack-addicted African-Americans in the mid-1980s and the 1990s did. During the height of the war on drugs, for instance, the number of white drug offenders in state prisons increased by 110 percent. The number of black drug offenders in state incarceration, on the other hand, exploded by 465 percent. African-Americans, 14 percent of the drug users during this period, made up 35 percent of those arrested, 55 percent of those convicted, and 74 percent of those sentenced to serve time.

These days, police interactions with mostly white heroin and opiate addicts are fueled by a kinder, gentler government and law enforcement policy. It's more like a police encounter not long ago in Manchester, New

Hampshire. New Hampshire is second to West Virginia as the state with the highest rate of overdose deaths.

Manchester Police Officer Ryan Boynton was eating a quick mid-shift dinner at the police station when an alert came over his radio to respond to a drug overdose. Boynton headed to a nearby housing complex where a young man, who appeared high, eventually opened the front door. Boynton glanced through the opening and asked the man about the call. "Oh, yeah, that's my fiancée," the man said.

Police already had visited the house previously on an overdose call so Boynton already suspected the man and his girlfriend were addicted to heroin and opiates. The man said his fiancée was okay and had left. Boynton talked to the woman by phone and confirmed that she was alive, for now. As he prepared to leave, Boynton offered two suspected illegal drug users this advice: "You guys gotta work on it," he said. "There's resources."

"I know," the man responded. "I'm trying, it's really tough with her. It's Russian roulette."

None of this is what suspected black crack addicts would have experienced in my day. Instead, we would have found a reason to search the house and arrest the people living there. That was common procedure.

When I read the following account, I chuckled. After paramedics in Seattle rolled up on three heroin-related deaths, police issued a statement to the local newspaper: "Anyone wishing to dispose of heroin or other drugs can call 911 or contact officers at one of the city's five precincts. Police also are encouraging people who feel they need to use heroin to be sure not to do so alone." Additionally, Sergeant Sean Whitcomb was interviewed by the paper, and offered this advice to heroin users: "From a practical standpoint, if you must use, if you're going to use, don't do it alone—and don't have the other person get high at the same time. Have someone who can call 911 and start CPR. We have Naloxone. We can save your life. We just need to be called."

That was certainly not American law enforcement's attitude during the days of crack cocaine. Local cops were locking up African-American addicts as fast as they could catch them. Consequently, four out of every five people arrested for drugs were charged with possession, not sales. Trust me, if you had shown up at a police station to turn in drugs, as that Seattle officer suggested, you were going to jail for possession. If you were caught on the street with five grams of crack, you were going to prison, because, back then, crack was the devil, and anything associated with it was tainted. Powdered cocaine, which most white people used, had one set of lower punishments. With crack, it was either rehabilitation, death, or incarceration, and since the first choice was unavailable to most black addicts, they were left with the remaining two outcomes.

I do not advocate we return to the failed drug policing practices we used during my days on the street. Despite efforts by Attorney General Jeff Sessions and President Donald Trump to reinstate those arcane policies, the nation is dealing smartly with the current drug crisis as a public health problem and a law enforcement concern, rather than allowing punishment and imprisonment to be our first response. But the idea of this more humane, effective approach is not new. It was offered when we were locking up black addicts and sending them off to prison at an astounding rate.

But the nation wouldn't listen.

Nobody was voicing that refrain more fervently than Kurt Schmoke, then the first black elected mayor of Baltimore. Schmoke served as mayor of Baltimore from 1987 to 1999. He notes that "Race still matters when it comes to dealing with criminal justice issues. Most elected officials are talking about [opioids] as a public health problem, because the race of the victims is different, versus the 1980s when the perception was that the victims were mostly black."

Schmoke pointed to his effort in the late 1980s to halt the spread of HIV among African-American heroin addicts as an example. Before the arrival of HIV/AIDS public officials were not treating drug addiction as a health issue, he said. Instead, addiction to heroin and crack cocaine was a crime, which lead to the acceleration of black incarceration during the mid 1980s into 2000. Public health officials, however, found early on that the deadly disease HIV/AIDS was being spread through those populations where infected addicts swapped needles. As mayor, Schmoke proposed a needle-exchange program, giving addicts clean syringes in exchange for their possibly HIV/AIDS-infected syringes to slow the spread of the disease and subsequent deaths. City and state leaders wouldn't hear of it. Those people, they said, belonged in jail. It took Schmoke four years to convince local officials to implement his needle-exchange program. Nobody wanted to treat heroin addiction among African-Americans as a public health concern then.

Baltimore is a microcosm in many ways of the disparity in how we—black and white—respond to crime regarding black America as opposed to white America. If there ever was a place in America that epitomized the idea that black lives don't matter, it is Baltimore by every measure of well-being.

The median income for white families in Baltimore is $60,550, compared to $33,610 for black families. Among black men between the ages 20 and 24, nearly 1 of every 3 is unemployed, as opposed to 1 in 10 among their white counterparts. The life expectancy in 15 predominantly black Baltimore neighborhoods is shorter than in North Korea. In 8 predominantly black Baltimore neighborhoods, the life expectancy is worse than in Syria. Baltimore teens between 15 and 19 years old face poorer health outcomes and a bleaker economic outlook than those in economically distressed cities in Nigeria, India, China, and South Africa. Teens in Baltimore, along with those in Johannesburg, South Africa, saw the highest prevalence of sexual violence, substance abuse, depression, and physically transmitted sexual diseases in the world.

The result has been crime. Murders in Baltimore have topped 300 for 10 straight years. The number of assaults, armed robberies, and burglaries in Baltimore per capita leads the nation.

Baltimore's response to the surge in crime has been primarily to ratchet up its law enforcement efforts and lock up offenders. African-American communities are targeted for arrests as part of the drive to "protect" the community. Consequently, African-Americans in Baltimore are first in the nation by one measure. Baltimore ranks number one for locking up the largest percentage of its residents. Nearly all those faces behind the bars at 401 East Eager Street are black.

Leonard Hamm was the police commissioner from 2004 to 2008 under Martin O'Malley, who served with a "zero tolerance" mantra. O'Malley was true to his word. Under him, cops were super aggressive in black neighborhoods. A grand jury concluded that too many arrests were being made in black neighborhoods without merit, and the city settled a lawsuit from residents who said they were wrongly arrested for minor offenses.

O'Malley picked Hamm to run the department during his second and last term as mayor. O'Malley went on to become Maryland's governor and to run for the Democratic nomination for president in 2016. Hamm joined the department in 1974 when the city's black police officers were not allowed to ride in police cars. Smart and creative, Hamm rose through the ranks under the tutelage of Eddie Woods, Baltimore's third black police commissioner. As a major, Hamm was the first black officer to head the department's prestigious Central District, the hub of the city's entertainment, financial, and political districts downtown.

Hamm's and my career paths overlapped, but we'd never met. I was group supervisor of the team that consisted of about 15 people, including ATF agents, some Baltimore city detectives, a few Baltimore Housing Police officers, and Housing and Urban Development officials who managed the city's federally funded housing. Our job was to go after higher-level drug dealers who were funneling cocaine and guns into Baltimore. Back then, Baltimore was like the Wild West. I had never been assigned to a city where you could work drug and gun cases literally 24 hours a day. We were everywhere. One minute my team was searching apartments, houses, and cars, and crashing through doors, and another minute we could be doing undercover drug buys. You could be in New Jersey arresting a drug dealer one day and in Virginia the next, tracking down guns flowing into Baltimore. We arrested hundreds of people. I loved my team—in particular, two Baltimore housing cops who were hell on wheels on the street, but who I trained to develop complex investigations.

A special bond was formed between us that still exists. I hesitate to mention their names because of their current work, but one is still on the force in Baltimore. The other is a cop in Las Vegas. They told me about Hamm and suggested I meet him.

"He is a stand-up guy who speaks his mind," one told me. "So, you need to be ready for some blunt conversation."

"Trust me," the other one said, "when he speaks, he doesn't stutter. What he says is what he means."

Hamm is now head of the police department at Coppin State University, a historically black university in Baltimore, founded in 1900, at what was then called Colored High School. Before leaving and coming back to the Baltimore Police Department, Hamm headed the police department at Morgan State University, another historically black university, and the department for the Baltimore city schools. Ironically, Hamm's son, Akil Hamm, whom the father hired when he held the job of chief of the Baltimore city's public schools' police department, has risen through the ranks to become chief of the department now. After briefly stumbling around Coppin State's campus, I finally found the right building and took an elevator to an expansive second floor. I made two rights and turned right into a suite of offices and rooms that house the university's police department.

At 68, Hamm is still an impressive presence. He strode into the meeting room immaculate, draped in a tailored three-piece suit sans jacket, reflective of his reputation as a smart dresser before and during his tenure as commissioner. On the day we met, somebody had been murdered in Baltimore. I don't know who was killed, but someone is murdered in Baltimore on average every day, and almost all of them are black.

Murders in Chicago, the nation's third-largest city, have grabbed all
the headlines based on their sheer numbers, over 900 a year recently—
again, nearly all of them black. Baltimore, however, accompanied by
St. Louis in the Midwest, consistently leads the nation's big cities in murders per capita. Many of those murders are still being driven by street-
level drug trafficking.

I didn't know until we met that Hamm had experienced a personal
drug tragedy. His stepdaughter became strung out on heroin in the
1990s and ended up stealing and selling sex to pay for food and drugs.
She was found murdered at age 39 in a Baltimore alley in 2008. It didn't
take much for me to see how deeply Hamm carries the pain of that loss.
"She wasn't my stepchild," he explained adamantly. "I raised her from
nothing. I walked her to her first day of kindergarten. I was the only
father she knew. I just wasn't her biological father." Even as Baltimore's
top cop, with all the officers and resources at his command, he had been
helpless to prevent her death.

Our conversation quickly turned to what had brought me to him
in the first place—how public policy and law enforcement seem to take
divergent tracks depending on who are the victims and who is committing
the crime. Hamm started right in.

"If more white people were being shot down in Baltimore and Chicago, everybody's response would be different. But these are black people, and they don't really matter. Right now, heroin is a big problem in
Maryland, and they want to put more money into prevention. We've
had a heroin problem in Baltimore forever and ever. When it was black
people, the answer was 'Lock them up.' It was never a prevention and
treatment problem before, because the right people weren't users."

As a black police commissioner, Hamm said he suggested all of this
to O'Malley, but the mayor refused to act on Hamm's suggestions. Officers were there to lock up people, not to solve problems. O'Malley said,
"I want my police to be warriors, not social workers."

"That's what he said," Hamm recalled. "So, that's what we did."

He paused for a moment. A sense of frustration settled across his face. It looked familiar to me. We talked some more, before I climbed back into my car for the three-hour drive home. As I made my way north up Interstate-95, I thought about deadly police interactions with African-Americans and the difference in the two drug crises—one perceived as black and the other as white. Whether unconsciously or intentionally, American society is suffused with a racial bias that must be eradicated. When it comes to ailments and needs in the black community, the response is punitive and lacking. The incidents we routinely encounter, which would be unacceptable in the white community, are shunted aside, ignored, or explained away, as if we were throwaway people, as if our lives didn't matter. Our lower life expectancy, higher infant mortality, higher rate of chronic diseases, lower income levels, and higher unemployment rates are all interrelated. These same dire statistics have been the underlying cause of black riots since the 1960s. Police are merely the flashpoint, the most immediate intersection between abrasive and discriminatory policies and the black public.

I thought about my fellow officers who are upset or feel betrayed about a movement that is directed at fighting against police. But my brothers in blue are wrong. The suspect has once again been misidentified. These protestors are not saying white lives don't matter or that police lives don't matter. Everything in America—from educational institutions to social networks, television, news, films, financial markets—says white lives do matter. Instead, the message is a demand and a plea for society to embrace African-Americans' humanity. Black lives matter—too.

Kathleen O'Toole

First Female Chief of Police, Seattle Police Department;
First Female Commissioner, Boston Police Department

I think my childhood is what shaped my career. I was the eldest child in my family. I had a younger brother and my sister was the youngest. My dad was a schoolteacher. He was a wonderful human being, but he used to work three jobs to make ends meet. My mother was a seriously abusive alcoholic. I loved my mother dearly. She didn't want to be what she was. Her dad was an abusive alcoholic. She had a horrible illness. So, I had to assume the role of mom when I was just a little kid. I don't remember ever being a kid, really. I can remember being about 5 years old and taking my brother, who was 2, and walking down to the corner store. We had to cross really busy streets to get what my mother needed at the store. Because I had to assume a lot of responsibility at an early age, I feel comfortable being in charge, and I feel a sense of responsibility. When people talk about all the negative effects of growing up in a dysfunctional family, I laugh and say, "I don't know. I don't have many friends who grew up in a functional family." I never complain about it, because, but for that experience, I might not be where I am today.

When I was in high school, [being a police officer] wasn't even an option available to me. Women could only work in the Boston Police Department as either a matron or a secretary, not a cop. I was a junior at Boston College in 1974 when the Boston Police Department hired the very first female patrol officers. In 1979, I was in my second year of law school, going to school at night, when I was offered a job with the Boston police. I never aspired to be a cop, but it was a cool opportunity to see the law from a different perspective. I thought I'd stick with the job a year or two, but soon realized it wasn't just a job: It's a vocation, a calling. It's really about helping people.

In the academy, I was given all kinds of statutes, so I could arrest people, and physical training, and then I went into the field and was shocked.

What do you mean I have to help people resolve their marital issues? But that's most of what we do. We deal with people's problems and try to solve them. I've loved every minute of it, even on the most difficult days. I've had the opportunity and the privilege to save some lives and deliver babies. My husband (a retired police officer) likes to remind me that he delivered seven and I only delivered two.

I think it's unfortunate that those [television] shows [and movies] depict policing the way they do. It's all about shootouts and car chases, but, in reality, that's just such a small percentage of what we do. Ordinary day-to-day police work is very satisfying, but it isn't that exciting or that dramatic. We respond to calls 24/7 from people with a wide variety of needs. Over a year and a half in Seattle, we answered 1.5 million calls for service. Force was only used in 0.3 percent of those instances. So, it's a fraction of 1 percent of the times that we use force. The same holds true for most police departments. That's why I always refer to our organizations as "police services" rather than "police forces," because *police force* implies that we do that a lot, and that's not accurate.

Unfortunately, as cops, we are at the tail end of failed systems. When our institutions fail to provide people with the things they need to survive— skills, jobs, resources—they become police problems. So, if a community's education system isn't good, the people are living in poverty, or not getting the mental health services they need, we are probably going to end up in an encounter with you.

Our biggest challenges are at the intersection of public services, health services, and public safety. We have people on our streets who are addicted, who are homeless, who are in mental health crisis. We did nearly 10,000 mental health interventions in the Seattle Police Department in one year. Consequently, we must now do an enormous amount of training of our officers in mental health crisis intervention.

We need to harness our resources and work with other disciplines, other government agencies, nonprofits, and the private sector to augment our resources. That's how we can solve some of these problems so it's not a revolving door, so the police are not going to the same call day after day, responding to the same people who are not getting the services they need to resolve their issues. We go on lots of calls of people with serious mental health issues, dealing with domestic violence situations, alcohol and drug issues. We can't solve their problems, but we can steer them in the direction of services.

For example, we have too many black children who are not getting the education they deserve, who are not getting the services they need. We need to rally and figure out a way to wrap our arms around these kids, to help them succeed. There is a disproportionate number of young black children who face huge challenges and we as a nation need to do something about that. We had a program, called Summer of Opportunity, in Seattle. We didn't just give kids a job, we worked with John Hancock and other private-sector companies to get the kids mentors, extra tutoring, and educational support. We taught them how to come in and interview for jobs. We gave them jobs every summer. It was the police department. It was the private sector. It was prevention and intervention. This is the work that people don't think of as police work. It is.

Just before I left the Boston Police Department [2006], we had lost a lot of officers. We didn't even have enough police to answer all the 911 calls. I knew it was going to be a long hot summer because I had seen an uptick in gang activity. So, in March or April, I instructed our gang unit to work together with all our partners—in education and social services—and compile a list of the 1,000 kids who are most likely to pull a trigger or get shot this summer.

All of us—social services, the police, the schools—are all dealing with the same families, the same kids, all the time. In over 800 cases we were able to get into the homes before the school year was over to ask families what they needed. "Hey, we know your kid could have some issues this summer. Does he need a job? Can we get him some tutoring? What about your younger kids? Can we get them into summer camp? Do you have enough food in your refrigerator?" The police department put it all together, but it was kind of a multidisciplinary operation.

We need to prepare our officers to deal with the more complicated issues that they are inevitably going to face. We're trying to give the cops the tools, the skills that they need to do their job and at the same time use the least force necessary in doing so. I used to go to the range once a year to train at a target and occasionally, we got [cardiac pulmonary resuscitation training]. That was the extent of in-service training. Now in the Seattle Police Department, we are doing five times the training we used to do. We're focusing on things like de-escalation in use-of-force situations, mental health crisis intervention, and bias-free policing.

We wield so much power in policing. We can deprive people of their liberty. We can take lives, we can send people to prison. We have to be so careful not to wield that power inappropriately or unfairly.

Policing is a messy business, and policing will always be a messy business because we are dealing with complicated issues. We will have tragedies and when we do, we need to stand up and tell the truth. We need to be transparent. We need to apologize when necessary. We need to hold our officers accountable. We need to have systems in place to address these complicated issues and these developments because we're cops, we're human beings. With training, I'm convinced we can do a lot better, but there will always be something. We can do 1,000 things right, but there will be that one cop who does something wrong.

4.

THE SYSTEM

It was 2004, and my family and I were in the midst of another of our cross-country excursions as I moved from one ATF assignment to another. I think this was our third trek across the United States. We had left Washington, D.C. just three years earlier on our way to Seattle, where I worked as the number two person in charge of the region. Now, we were headed back to D.C., where I would be chief of staff to an ATF assistant director, the person in charge of all field operations for the nation. It was a great opportunity. I was excited.

We loved Seattle, but I think my wife was ready for a more stable life and a more consistent working environment for me. In Seattle, I was constantly on the road. My second day on the job, I flew to Alaska, to oversee the arrest of about 30 people for drugs, guns, and gang activity as part of a joint operation. I think the next week I was in Idaho. Seattle was like that. It is geographically the Bureau's second-largest division behind Denver. It includes Washington state, Oregon, Idaho, Alaska, Hawaii, and Guam.

Consequently, there was never a "routine" day. Our mission ran the gamut from incidents on Native American reservations to organized crime and street gangs in Seattle and Portland, from bombings to white supremacist groups and antigovernment militias in rural Oregon and

Washington state to gun trafficking in Guam and Hawaii. The scariest guys we had to deal with were the white supremacists and the antigovernment militiamen. They were as bad as the thugs in Boston, career criminals who had pages and pages of felony convictions for armored-car robberies, arms dealing, and violent assaults as soldiers in organized crime. In one incident in Boston, one of my informants was murdered, burned, and his mouth was stuffed with a roll of dimes to indicate that he was a snitch. Members of white militias and white supremacist organizations were always openly armed with rifles, and had ammunition bandoliers strapped across the waist and chest of each one. Both groups would kill you just for looking at them the wrong way.

With my schedule, most of the rearing of our two young children, unfortunately, fell on my wife. So, now it was on to a new adventure. As we bumped along the road, the children, ages 7 and 5, played and argued. Scattered toys, books, and clothes turned the back seat into a miniature Romper Room. One thing I tried to do with all the moves from division to division was to make the trip a learning experience, which is why we drove instead of flying. We went through Yellowstone National Park, visited the Silverwood Amusement Park in Coeur d'Alene, Idaho, drove through the Rocky Mountains, the Grand Tetons, and a few other natural wonders. It can be a tedious and boring drive. The trip consisted mostly of me driving while everyone else slept. Still, we got in some pretty good stops and saw a lot of the nation along the way.

After spending the night in Hays, Kansas, we made our way east along Interstate-70, past Russell, past Wilson, past Salina, past Abilene, until I began to see signs for Topeka, Kansas. Topeka public schools were the impetus for the famous 1954 *Brown v. Board of Education* decision by the US Supreme Court that outlawed segregation in public schools. The parents of Linda Brown, a third-grade student at a Topeka public elementary school, filed a lawsuit against the Board of Education after Linda was denied admission to a nearby, all-white school. Instead, she was bused to a segregated all-black school. The case was taken up by the NAACP, who advanced the argument that segregated schools were not equal, and therefore unconstitutional.

I made a mental check and realized we would be arriving in Topeka during the 50th anniversary of that decision. I said to my wife, "I would be very surprised if there is not a museum there." Just as the sun was rising over the horizon, we saw a sign that said, "Brown v. Board of Education National Historic Site." We got to the site before it opened, so we slept in the car for a while and then went to a nearby diner. The site is a former public school that has been turned into museum. It opened at 9 a.m. and we stayed until about 2 p.m. It wasn't a big museum, but it was well curated. We got pictures; we got posters. It was very interactive.

There was a replica of the bus Linda Brown and other black children rode to school because they couldn't attend the school just blocks away. The rule, barring young Linda and her fellow black children from attending their neighborhood school, was the impetus for the landmark case. We saw photos of Linda Brown, her parents, the harsh differences in the schools black and white students attended. The kids saw photos of Thurgood Marshall, the young civil rights lawyer for the NAACP who presented the *Brown v. Board of Education* case to the Supreme Court. Marshall later became a Supreme Court justice. It was a spiritual awakening for me and my wife. For the kids, it was informative and fun.

The next stop was Kansas City. If you're in Kansas City, you must tour the American Jazz Museum, go through the Negro Leagues Baseball Hall of Fame, and sample some of the city's famous barbecue. So, we did. Our next stop was St. Louis. In all my travels across the country, it would be my first visit to St. Louis. We saw the Arch, because when you're visiting St. Louis, that's what you do, but I was looking forward to seeing an old friend and colleague.

Jeff Fulton was my supervisor when I had been in D.C. He is a great guy and was very helpful to my career. We're politically poles apart, but that never mattered to Jeff or me. He helped me by exposing me to things I wouldn't have otherwise been exposed to, involved me in conversations that I wouldn't normally hear, shared with me information that I wouldn't normally come across. One of the biggest things he did for me was to recommend me for an audit team. I did it and it was a great move for me. The Bureau has teams of agents who audit the field divisions like mine in Seattle. The purpose of the audits is to assess their use of our prime information systems to ensure they are not being abused by officers.

Our key information system is the FBI's National Criminal Information Center, which everybody in law enforcement refers to as NCIC. NCIC is a database filled with millions of records about criminal offenses, dangerous people, and unsolved crimes. For instance, NCIC contains a huge database just on property crimes, including stolen guns, boats, cars, license plates, car parts, and securities. It also has tons of personal information. Any US citizen who has had contact with law enforcement, whether they were local cops, state troopers, or federal agents, probably has had his or her information logged into the system. The data on people might include whether they are on the National Sex Offender Registry, whether they are on supervised release from custody, or if they are foreign fugitives. The database lists missing persons, known gang members, suspected terrorists, and people who may be wanted for crimes or just for informational purposes.

Thousands of law enforcement agencies—local, state, and federal— are constantly adding information to the system, based on their encounters with the public. At the same time, thousands of individual law enforcement officers are accessing the system as they do their jobs, from checking on a person's priors while making a traffic stop to researching individuals during high-level surveillance. Access to this powerful database has made law enforcement much more effective. It's like having the keys to the castle. But it's not a given. Agencies from sheriff's departments to state police to local law enforcement can lose their access to NCIC. If your officers are using it for frivolous reasons or they are violating the protocol, the FBI can kick you off the system.

Technically, any law enforcement officer could use NCIC to run a neighbor's information through the system to see who they are, but that's not what the system is for. You can't just say, I'm suspicious about my daughter's boyfriend because he has pink hair, tattoos, and a nose ring, and run him through the system. There have been rogue officers who ran a woman's license plate through the system and then used the information to call her for a date or to stalk her. You can go to jail or lose your job for doing that. Each agency is responsible for auditing the use of the system by its officers. That was my job as a member of the Bureau's auditing team. I'd travel to our different division offices—Philadelphia, New York, Seattle, Kansas City, Miami—to make sure that our use of the program was compliant. The job brought me in contact with people at some of the highest levels in the Bureau—assistant directors and the heads of our regional divisions. It also forced me to sharpen my analytical skills, verbal skills, and writing skills. Instead of doing widgets and digits as part of my job, I was interviewing possible future bosses and colleagues about their procedures. If they meet you and they are impressed, perhaps you are then a person they want on their team. I am forever grateful to Jeff for giving me that opportunity. So, I wanted to stop by and say hello, and thanks.

We were staying at the Embassy Suites in downtown St. Louis. It was August, and the humidity was so thick you could swim through it. I remember observing that almost everybody working in the hotel was black—the cleaning crew, the reservation clerk, the bellman, everybody in the restaurant, except for the hostess. By contrast, all the managers were white. It sort of had a plantation feel. We had breakfast, and before we got ready to leave, I went to the front desk and asked a young black woman for directions to my friend's house. In those days, there were no Google maps or GPS on smartphones. I explained that I was going to Wildwood.

She gave me directions and then asked, "What are you going out there for?" I thought it was an odd question. I explained to her I was going to visit a friend. She cautioned me to be careful. "Why?" I asked. "Is it a bad neighborhood?" I would learn later that day that it was an upscale community of single-family houses where the median household income was twice the national average. "No," she replied. "It's not bad. It's just, you know." Ten years later, I would learn what she meant by *you know*.

Like most Americans, prior to 2014, I had never heard of Ferguson, Missouri. When it erupted into protests and flames on August 9 following the shooting death of 18-year-old Michael Brown by a local police officer, I had to go look it up on a map. I discovered it was a small suburb of 21,000 people in northern St. Louis County, 10 miles north of downtown St. Louis. It was Ferguson and other communities in the same area that the receptionist was warning me about 10 years earlier. It was a small town where cops were white and black people weren't welcomed.

Like most Americans, I observed events unfold from the safety of my home hundreds of miles away. I monitored the TV channels and read the newspaper accounts on my laptop with dismay and disbelief. I made a few appearances on national television as a law enforcement analyst to give my perspective on the shooting. I was saddened by the shooting death of yet another unarmed black male and the destruction that followed it. I was stunned to learn that while two out of every three residents of Ferguson were black, the mayor was white, the police chief was white, as were nearly all the police officers. The city manager was white, the municipal judge was white, the prosecuting attorney was white, the court clerk was white, and all but one of the six city council members were white. It sounded like the description of a town in the Jim Crow South prior to the civil rights movement.

Imagine that in reverse. It is 2014 and you are a white person in a city where 67 percent of the residents are white, but every elected official and appointed official save one is black—mayor, city council, finance manager, city attorney, municipal judge, court clerk. And all but 4 of the city's 54 police officers are black.

As the demonstrations and violence in Ferguson continued, the media breathlessly reported events—the latest in a 50-year-long history of racial upheaval in America—as though they were somehow new. The contentious relationship between police and African-Americans and the resultant black backlash has been part of our nation's modern-day legacy, longer than most Americans have been alive.

The first revolt was in Cambridge, Maryland, a small community of 12,300 that sits on the eastern shore of Chesapeake Bay. Cambridge, one of Maryland's oldest cities, was founded in 1648. It later developed and grew, fueled by the canning industry, which canned oysters, tomatoes, and sweet potatoes. Its workforce and the city were financially centered around Phillips Packing Company, which once employed as many as 10,000 people. The city's economic base was so strong at one point that four teams in the old Eastern Shore Baseball League—the Canners, the Cardinals, the Clippers, and the Dodgers—were all located in Cambridge. But by the early 1960s, Phillips Packing Company had closed as the nation's food tastes changed. Unemployment shot up—7 percent among whites and 29 percent for blacks. The hard times began to exacerbate long-standing racial divisions that had lain dormant during a booming economy.

Long after the Supreme Court ruled public-school segregation unconstitutional, Cambridge staunchly maintained separate schools for blacks and whites. African-Americans were segregated into the all-black Second Ward, west of Race Street, which served as the unofficial dividing line between the black and white communities. Beginning in 1962, the city's African-American community, led by the Cambridge Non-Violent Action Committee, began pressing for greater access to employment, housing, and desegregated public schools. In 1963, the city exploded in fire, destruction, and death, following allegations of police brutality. Martial law was declared, the violence between blacks and whites subsided, and the unending history of black riots began. In 2014, Ferguson was just the latest in a steady historical drumbeat of African-American communities in revolt: Rochester, New York, 1964; New York City, 1964; Philadelphia, 1964; Jersey City, New Jersey, 1964; Paterson, New Jersey, 1964; Elizabeth, New Jersey, 1964; Newark, New Jersey, 1964; Chicago, 1964; Watts, Los Angeles, 1965; Cleveland, 1966; Chicago, 1966; Newark, 1967; Plainfield, New Jersey, 1967; Detroit, 1967; Harlem, New York City, 1967; Cambridge, Massachusetts, 1967; Rochester, New York, 1967; Pontiac, Michigan, 1967; Toledo, Ohio, 1967; Flint, Michigan, 1967; Grand Rapids, Michigan, 1967; Houston, 1967; Englewood, New Jersey, 1967; Milwaukee, 1967; Minneapolis, 1967; York, Pennsylvania, 1969; Hartford, Connecticut, 1969; Augusta, Georgia, 1970; Asbury Park, New Jersey, 1970; Dallas, 1973; Houston, 1980; Miami, 1980; Crown Heights, New York, 1988; Overton, Miami, 1991; Los Angeles, 1992; St. Petersburg, Florida, 1995; Cincinnati, 2001; Oakland, California, 2009; Anaheim, California, 2012; Baltimore, 2015; Milwaukee, 2016; Charlotte, 2016.

In response to these urban explosions, most of us—black and white—condemn the incidents as senseless violence. Radio commentator Larry Elder famously called the Ferguson demonstrators and rioters "monkeys." But long ago, many cautioned that we dismiss the motivation behind these events at our own peril. Nicholas Johnson, a University of Iowa law professor, was a Federal Communications Commissioner when he first began to fathom the meaning of the revolts.

During the late 1960s, when scores of US cities went up in flames, Johnson said, "A riot is somebody talking. A riot is a man crying out: 'Listen to me, Mister. There's something I've been trying to tell you, and you are not listening.'" The Reverend Martin Luther King Jr. abhorred violence, but he agreed. "A riot is the language of the unheard," he said. He then offered this prophetic observation 48 years before Ferguson:

"Riots do not develop out of thin air. Certain conditions continue to exist in our society which must be condemned as vigorously as we condemn riots. [America] has failed to hear that the promises of freedom and justice have not been met. And it has failed to hear that large segments of white society are more concerned about tranquility and the status quo than about justice, equality, and humanity. And as long as America postpones justice, we stand in the position of having these recurrences of violence and riots *over and over again*."

The accuracy of his prediction is frightening and damning. We have watched black angst convulse into violence in city after city, decade after decade.

Historically, the spark that invariably ignites each of these smoldering, impoverished communities is negative interactions with police. The encounters range from the all-too-familiar to the obscene. An unarmed black teenager is shot dead by Florida police; a 23-year-old Latino Vietnam War veteran is beaten to death by six Houston police officers and thrown into a nearby river; two Newark policemen, upset because a black cab driver signaled and then passed them while they were double-parked, beat and arrest him and then charge him with assaulting them.

A Dallas police officer, trying to force a handcuffed 12-year-old Latino to confess to a crime he didn't commit, plays Russian roulette with his service revolver and shoots him in the head, killing him. A black man is found beaten to death in his jail cell; police explain that he died after he fell from his bed. A black salesman, and former Marine, on a motorcycle dies of injuries sustained at the hands of Miami officers after he surrendered, following a high-speed chase.

While each of those incidents started with a police encounter, police officers aren't the only culprits. While police officers are complicit, they are just the most immediate and visible link in a chain that includes government officials, public priorities, and community consent. Unfortunately, when such incidents occur, we look for answers almost solely inside police departments, divorcing the officers' actions from the political, community, and societal norms that underlie their actions.

We point our fingers at police as though the wrongs within their departments or those committed by even the most racist or aberrant officers begin and end with them. They don't. Law enforcement does not operate in a vacuum.

First, officers are products of their communities, and have the same biases, prejudices, and assumptions that we all do. In the worst cases, those individuals must be weeded out of our departments or excluded through early employment screenings. Typically, large police agencies have multilayered hiring processes that include panel interviews, polygraph examinations, psychological examinations, and full-scope background investigations. These multilayered processes are supposed to eliminate unworthy candidates for employment into positions of public trust. They should, but recent history shows they don't. Additionally, most police agencies are small—less than 50 people—and may not have a robust screening process.

Second, police, particularly at their lowest ranks, are foot soldiers who are given targets and directives by higher-ups inside and outside the department who expect clearly defined results. Historically, these higher-ups haven't always cared how those expectations are met. Law enforcement did not create the Jim Crow laws in the South and discriminatory laws in the North and West or, afterward, designate which neighborhoods were unofficially off-limits to blacks, Latinos, and Asian-Americans. It was their jobs, however, to enforce those policies by arresting, jailing, and brutalizing anyone who violated them.

When heroin was rooted in African-American neighborhoods in the 1960s and 1970s, law enforcement did not decide that black addicts should be arrested and jailed, instead of being treated for their addiction. Government officials and the citizens they represented did. The mere possession of the paraphernalia used to administer the drug made someone subject to arrest.

Law enforcement did not create the war on drugs. Richard Nixon did in 1971 to avert Americans' attention from his administration's policies in Vietnam and in the nation's streets. Still, we were tasked with implementing it, which we did with extreme prejudice. We were the first cog in a process that rounded up addicts, tore apart families, and destroyed neighborhoods. We racked up thousands of arrests, and seized thousands of firearms and tons of drugs as we were ordered to show our superiors and the public that we were performing our jobs. We targeted black neighborhoods, though all the statistical evidence showed that white Americans were selling and consuming most of the cocaine. And when we used questionable, often coercive, and sometimes brutal tactics, few questioned our approach.

Then, as now, US senators and members of Congress, state representatives, mayors, and city council members were the ones pushing harsh law enforcement policies for political expediency, most often to the detriment of the poor and people of color.

Few cite pressure from the business community, for whom police protection is a priority, whether we're talking about liquor stores, football stadiums, flower shops, or shopping malls. Businesses cannot survive without customers and employees, and, as officers are told, neither will abide an area seen as unsafe. *Make it safe*, we are told.

No one points to civic leaders and city planners who impress upon law enforcement the importance of crime-free tourist and entertainment districts, from which cities derive vital tax dollars. The lifeblood of many American cities, these areas cannot be seen as unsafe. *Make them feel safe*, we are told.

Those imperatives come from government officials, civic and business leaders, and influential community groups, and they're pushed down to police departments with orders to carry them out. Police chiefs, supervisors, and commissioners relay those expectations to their deputy chiefs and commanders, who communicate them to captains, who explain them to lieutenants, who pass them along to the sergeants, who then tell patrol officers to hit the streets and make it happen.

I've attended roll calls when the sergeant made it clear that certain neighborhoods needed "closer attention," certain businesses had lodged complaints and needed to be attended to, certain neighborhoods had reported "undesirables" who needed to be removed. As patrol officers, armed with our orders and measured by the number of arrests we make and the number of traffic citations we issue, we hit the streets to uphold the law. As we do, we are mindful that job performance can lead to job advancement.

Along with our orders, we also take with us our personal biases, prejudices, and community norms, all of which inform our actions. Consequently, as we carry out our mission, some neighborhoods and people take precedence over others. Some people are seen almost immediately as suspects, instead of as law-abiding citizens. Some residents are treated with respect and some aren't. Property may take priority over people, like shooting someone in the back over a stolen vehicle.

Police procedures that are deemed offensive and inappropriate in some neighborhoods are okay in others. In a middle-class white neighborhood, it would be considered unacceptable for white 12-year-old boys walking home from playing basketball to be forced into a spread-eagle posture facedown on a concrete sidewalk, with three police officers' guns pointing at them—all due to a call about a man with a gun. But it happened to a group of black youth in Grand Rapids, Michigan. One of them lay on the ground, frightened and crying, "I don't want to get shot."

Ferguson, Missouri, and the death of Michael Brown are object lessons in how government policies and community consent can translate into police procedures that are oppressive, unconstitutional, and can have disastrous results. City officials may not envision negative law enforcement consequences as a result of their policies, but they occur. Ferguson officials wanted more money for downtown redevelopment and other city projects. So, to generate more revenue, police were ordered to ramp up enforcement of policies put in place by the city manager, the finance manager, the municipal court judge, the city prosecutor, and the municipal court clerk, and condoned by the mayor and the city council.

Police officers were encouraged to make up phony and excessive charges, to use arrests as a form of tax collection, and to violate the public's constitutional rights to fill the city's coffers with money from traffic tickets and arrest warrants.

Ferguson Police Officer Darren Wilson, a former cop at a nearby police department so bad that it was disbanded, fired the shot that ended Michael Brown's life. It was city leaders and their policies, however, that set in motion the tragic events that took place when Wilson encountered Brown.

5.

THE CONSPIRACY

Millions of people pass by or through Ferguson annually, though most would probably never notice it. They zoom by on Interstate-270, which borders Ferguson firmly to the north, or on Interstate-70, which slants diagonally near its southern border. When traveling along city streets, it is hard to know when you're inside the Ferguson city limits, or in nearby Berkeley or Kinloch or Dellwood. The towns are clustered together in St. Louis County and rub against each other like one big suburb of the city of St. Louis. Local residents, however, have a very clear understanding of the dividing lines. They understand how an interaction with police in one city could result in a warning or a ticket while in another city, the same violation could lead to jail.

Ferguson was founded in 1855 and named after William B. Ferguson, who, in exchange for naming rights, deeded 10 acres of land to the Wabash Railroad. The town's first schoolhouse was built in 1878 and 16 years later, Ferguson became incorporated as a city. By 1960, Ferguson had reached its current population of approximately 21,000 and hasn't grown much since then. The town's racial demographics remained virtually unchanged through 1990, when 74 percent of Ferguson's population was white, and 25 percent was black. Ten years later, however, African-Americans, mostly former residents of nearby North St. Louis, became the new majority, making up 52 percent of the city's population. By 2010, African-Americans had grown to two-thirds of the town's population.

From the outside, Ferguson is a sedate community of tree-filled neighborhoods, spread across six square miles. A quaint downtown is anchored by a True Value hardware store, a smattering of restaurants, including the Ferguson Brewing Company, the fire department, and the police station. The housing is primarily moderate-sized, single-family brick homes, a departure from the row houses that dominate much of neighboring St. Louis. There are some troubling areas, like Park Ridge, a low-income apartment complex where nearly half the city's annual homicides occur, and Canfield Apartments and the surrounding apartment units, where Michael Brown was shot and, until recently, a location for much of the city's low-level drug sales. Those communities are tucked away, off the main traffic corridors and obscured by tranquil thoroughfares, where you'll find the local Walmart and other chain stores.

The municipality is largely a town of haves and have-nots. There are some poor white neighborhoods, but African-Americans make up the largest share of the have-nots. Ferguson's median household income is $42,000; that's $8,000 below the state's median household income of $50,000. Four out of every 10 households earn less than $35,000, which is hard to get by on in the St. Louis area, or almost anywhere. White residents are mostly homeowners. Black residents are mostly renters, about 80 percent by some local estimates.

The dirty secret in Ferguson and the small municipalities surrounding it in northern St. Louis County was that for decades city officials used their police and court systems as a means of taxing residents to subsidize their governments. Local police pestered residents by aggressively handing out traffic tickets or housing code violations—missing trash can lids, unpainted fences, unkempt lawns, etc.—to rake in millions of extra dollars. If residents didn't have the money to pay the fines, off to jail they went, until a friend or family member could scrape together the money to bail them out and pay the charges and additional fines. Traffic tickets turned into arrest warrants, and people were carted off to jail. Some people lost jobs and careers were dashed as local municipalities used their jails as debtors' prisons. At its height, the police fed enough traffic tickets and municipal violations through the courts for the 89 municipalities in the county to pull in $52 million a year.

In 2014, St. Louis County, fueled by the excessive ticketing in cities like Ferguson, Jennings, Berkeley, Bellefontaine Neighbors, Pine Lawn, and Normandy, was handing out 34 percent of the state's traffic tickets and municipal fines, though it housed only 17 percent of the state's population. Those figures drove up the state's rate of traffic citations per person. Consequently, Missouri, with 36 citations for every 100 people, had the second-highest rate of traffic citations in the nation in 2014 after New Jersey. New Jersey's citations, however, unlike Missouri's, were largely parking tickets.

To keep their municipalities afloat, 55 city governments in St. Louis County ticketed their residents at an astounding rate. Thirty-seven of the cities issued 75 tickets for every 100 residents. Twenty-four handed out one ticket for every person in the city, and 17 municipalities, including Ferguson, gave out one and a half tickets for every man, woman, and child in the city, whether or not they could drive. All those tickets had to be handed out by somebody, and that somebody was police officers, under orders from their superiors.

Edmundson, a small municipality near St. Louis's major airport, sits along a stretch of Interstate-70 that is a known speed trap. Its mayor, John Gwaltney, sent a letter to his police officers in 2015, suggesting that they start writing more tickets to help pay for their salaries. In nearby Bellefontaine Neighbors, a police officer went to court to file a lawsuit against the city after he and other officers were demoted or fired because they didn't write enough tickets.

None of this is news to Stacey Owens, a man I met in Ferguson in 2017. Owens grew up in nearby Berkeley, Missouri, but he is intimately familiar with the Ferguson Police Department and its ticketing routine.

"Man, they've been stopping me since I was a teenager," he said, "and now I'm damn near 50." Owens and I were pushing food around our plates at Ferguson Brewing Company, a popular restaurant that also crafts its own beer. The restaurant is housed in repurposed two-story brick buildings on the main drag in downtown Ferguson, and gets a big lunch crowd of city employees and professionals. Cops also frequent it. Owens had eaten there on rare occasions, maybe three times, he said. On this day, he, a friend of his, and I were the only three black faces in the room in a city that is mostly black. I could tell that Owens wasn't very comfortable. I didn't know how uncomfortable until I excused myself and went to the bathroom. As I did, I took a shortcut past the open end of a large, U-shaped bar that separated two halves of the room. I passed next to the cash register. I did the same thing on the way back. When I sat down, Owens and his friend looked at me in amazement.

"Man, I thought you were going to be arrested," Owens said.

"What?" I asked.

"I thought the police were going to stop you because you went through that area behind the bar next to the cash register."

His friend, Tony Rice, turned and looked at him in astonishment.

"Man, I thought the same thing," Rice said. "I was holding my breath. We both thought the same thing and we hadn't even talked about it. I guess that's our mentality because we grew up here."

Owens is one of those rare people who latched onto a job and had the grit to remain there most of his adult life. At 19, he started at the local utility company, Ameren U.E., and has remained there for 30 years. He is responsible for moving the company's heavy equipment—transformers, big cable rolls—on a 22-wheel truck. When he first started out with Ameren, he went out and bought a 1978 Oldsmobile Cutlass. "It was gold with a burgundy vinyl top," he said proudly. "For a young dude with no kids, I had nothing to spend my money on but cars. That car used to get me stopped all the time. At least once or twice a week, I'd get stopped. Never got a ticket. It was so regular, that I would pull my license and registration out before I started the car to save time, because I knew I was going to get stopped. Sometimes they'd stop me, and it would make me run late for work. I would call my boss and tell him I'd been stopped again. He knew the deal. I even started leaving for work earlier because I knew I was going to get stopped.

"I never had problems in St. Ann, and Maryland Heights didn't mess with me. Jennings was known for [stopping you], too. I didn't go too far into Jennings, and Jennings was known for roughing you up. I stayed away from Florissant, too. My family warned me not to go to Florissant. My dad would have had a fit if he found out we were in Florissant."

After lunch, I drove six miles to the home of the Reverend Tommie Pierson. Pierson is the pastor of Greater St. Mark's Family Church in St. Louis County. Pierson's church was the meeting site and staging area for many of the Ferguson demonstrations in 2014. I had planned to talk with Pierson about the demonstrations, but the conversation turned to the long-standing practice of cities like his using police and courts as tax collectors. We sat in the dining room, which was just to the left after you enter the front door. Pierson sat at the head of the table. Behind him was a large portrait of his wife, Jo Ann. Pierson is a soft-spoken African-American man of 70, who with age has gotten rounder in the middle and balder on the top. His speech is gentle, his demeanor low-key and steady. He's also a man of action, having completed three terms as a Missouri state representative in 2016. He lives in Bellefontaine Neighbors, another of those towns notorious for stopping and ticketing African-Americans, and he has been fighting the practice since his church was founded there in 1996. Pierson's stories about stops and cops, however, go back to December 24, 1962, when he was a teenage transplant to St. Louis from Ripley, Tennessee. "I was living with my sister. She stayed in the 4200 block of Ashland. My other sister lived in the 4200 block of Lee. I didn't have a car, so I would walk every day between their houses. It was a straight shot down the street. And every day, the same police officer would stop me and ask me what was I doing and where was I going. Every day. Same officer. Neighborhood was about 70 percent white. Maybe that's why."

When Pierson landed a job at General Motors, he moved out, got his own apartment, and bought the car of many a young man's dream at that time, a brand-new 1965 canary-yellow Pontiac GTO, with a black convertible top. "I got stopped every day," he said. "One time, the cop said to me, 'When we see a black guy driving a car like this, we figure you stole it.' They stopped me with that car every time they saw me. One time, I had seven tickets in my pocket." When he opened his first church in Bellefontaine Neighbors, the practice of ticketing African-Americans was on the rise. "One time a lady came and got me out of the pulpit during service, because [police] had followed people onto the parking lot to give them tickets. I had to go out and run them off." While serving as a state representative, Pierson learned that his city's 33 police officers each had a quota of 30 tickets to fill each month.

While the practice of ticket writing as a revenue-raiser in Ferguson had been long-standing, beginning in 2010, a team began to emerge in Ferguson's government that would institute policies to dramatically accelerate its use. The key player was John Shaw. Shaw was hired in 2007 as the city manager, the most powerful position in Ferguson's government. He was 31 and earned $85,000, which would grow to $120,000 upon his departure eight years later. Shaw would hire the finance manager, the police chief, and the prosecuting attorney, and enlist the assistance of the presiding municipal court judge, creating a team that would wreak havoc on the black residents of Ferguson.

Shaw had absolute power to run Ferguson's day-to-day operations. Still, he and his team served at the pleasure of the mayor and the city council. Despite some misgivings, they offered him their unwavering support. Key was Mayor James Knowles, a license fee office manager, who became the face of Ferguson following the Michael Brown shooting, though he had little power. A polished public speaker, Knowles was elected to the Ferguson City Council at age 25, just a few years out of college. He was 31 when he won his first mayoral election in 2011, making him the youngest mayor in Ferguson's history, as well as one of the youngest mayors in the state. Knowles, who graduated with degrees in government from two local colleges, was also politically pliable. At one time, he was chairman of the Missouri Young Republicans. Later, he was a staff member of Democrat Ted House when House served as a Missouri state senator. Knowles became the face of Ferguson city government, but Shaw wielded the power.

When Shaw began looking to traffic violations and jail as revenue-enhancement strategies in 2010, traffic fines and collections accounted for $1.38 million, or 12 percent of the city's $11.07 million budget. By 2015, when Justice Department officials came in after Michael Brown's death, that proportion had more than doubled to $3.07 million, and then accounted for 24 percent of the city's budget.

For Shaw's efforts to increase revenue through greater ticketing, he needed a cooperative judge to enforce the fines and tickets. He found one in Judge Ronald Brockmeyer. Brockmeyer became municipal court judge seven years before Shaw was hired. Brockmeyer was part of the confusing judicial musical chairs that characterized the municipal court system in St. Louis County. While Brockmeyer served as a judge in Ferguson, he was also the prosecuting attorney 1½ miles to the east in Dellwood; the judge 7½ miles southwest in Breckenridge Hills; the prosecuting attorney in Florissant 3½ miles to the north; the prosecuting attorney in Vinita Park 14 miles to the south; and as a defense attorney 15 miles northwest in neighboring St. Charles County.

In Ferguson, Brockmeyer worked with the prosecuting attorney, the police chief, and the city manager to devise more ways to separate residents from their money. Brockmeyer bragged about creating new fees to bring in more money, increasing fines for repeat offenders, "especially in regard to housing violations, [which] have increased substantially and will continue to be increased upon subsequent violations," he wrote in an email to city officials. Fines would be doubled or tripled at his discretion.

He routinely added charges and additional fines when a defendant challenged a citation.

Assisting Brockmeyer was his court clerk, Mary Anne Twitty. Twitty had nearly the same power as the judge. She worked closely with him to increase the amount of fines, to collect them, and to order more defendants to jail when they couldn't pay. She even made some judicial decisions on her own. At one point, Twitty complained to the judge and the police chief that prosecutor Stephanie Karr's fines were too low. "We need to keep up our revenue," Twitty wrote. Karr, who also served as the Ferguson city attorney, raised her fine recommendations in response. Additionally, Karr said, "I have denied defendants' needless requests for continuance from the payment docket in an effort to aid in the court's efficient collection of its fines."

Twitty was fired after Ferguson's unrest when it was revealed that she had sent numerous racist emails to ranking Ferguson police officers and other government officials. One was a photo of dancing, bare-chested African women with the caption, "Michelle Obama's High School Reunion." Another said a black woman should be given an award for crime prevention for having an abortion. A third depicted President Barack Obama as a chimpanzee. Sergeant William Mudd, the police official who responded to Darren Wilson as his supervisor on the crime scene after Wilson killed Michael Brown, was part of Twitty's email chain. Mudd also testified in support of Wilson before the grand jury. He was fired for sending his own racist emails. Twitty and Brockmeyer kept the courtroom money train on track and the year Michael Brown was killed, 2014, it was running at full steam. That year, Brockmeyer issued 32,907 arrest warrants in Ferguson, a town of only 21,000 residents. The vast majority were for failure to pay traffic fines. It was by far the most warrants for any of the 90 municipalities in St. Louis County. By comparison, Florissant, with a population more than double Ferguson's, issued only 10,059 arrest warrants that year.

After a few years of watching Brockmeyer's abusive courtroom behavior, one unnamed Ferguson City Council member raised concerns with City Manager John Shaw about the judge's performance. The judge didn't listen to testimony, the council member told Shaw. He didn't review reports or examine the defendants' criminal history before ruling, she added. He didn't even allow witnesses to testify before rendering a verdict, she said. Perhaps, the council member suggested, it was time to get rid of the judge. Shaw listened, and then explained that, even though all those things might be true, there were more pressing matters.

"It goes without saying the city cannot afford to lose any efficiency in our courts, nor experience any decrease in our fines and forfeitures," Shaw explained. Ironically, while bludgeoning Ferguson residents with fines and jailing them when they couldn't pay, Brockmeyer was fixing traffic tickets for himself, a Ferguson police officer, and others in other courts. Helping him was Mary Ann Twitty, who would email other clerks on his behalf to have tickets quashed. Additionally, even as Brockmeyer piled debt upon debt on the poorest and financially most vulnerable, he was dodging $170,000 in unpaid taxes owed to the Internal Revenue Service.

At the beginning of the judicial pipeline to extract more money from residents were the police. They were headed by Thomas Jackson, a beefy, white-haired career cop Shaw hired in 2010 as Ferguson's police chief. Jackson had retired from the St. Louis County police after 31 years, where he had been a helicopter pilot and member of the county police department's tactical team. In 1991, he and a fellow St. Louis County police officer won a Medal of Valor for disarming a suicidal man. If Jackson didn't already know what his law enforcement priorities were before taking his new job, they were made crystal clear to him immediately after he was hired. Within days on the job, Jackson was informed by the city's finance director that "unless ticket writing ramps up significantly before the end of the year, it will be hard to significantly raise collections next year. Given that we are looking at a substantial sales tax shortfall, it's not an insignificant issue."

The chief responded that fines would increase once the city hired more officers and that he believed he could reach the city's projected budget of $1.5 million in fines. He considered incorporating a different shift schedule that would put more officers on the street to increase traffic enforcement. The following year, Jackson reported to Shaw that ticketing revenue for February 2011 was more than $179,000, the highest monthly total in four years. Shaw sent back his approval. "Wonderful!" he wrote. Later, Shaw and the city's finance director recommended that Jackson implement an "I-270 traffic enforcement initiative" in order to "begin to fill the revenue pipeline." The finance director's email came with an attached document showing how much additional money the initiative would generate. The plan would require paying five officers overtime for highway traffic enforcement for a four-hour shift. "There is nothing to keep us from running this initiative 1, 2, 3, 4, 5, 6, or even 7 days a week," he wrote. "Admittedly at 7 days per week, we would see diminishing returns." Jackson's patrol captain, Rick Henke, agreed and explained to his supervising police officers when the department initiated the program, "The plan behind this [initiative] is to *produce* traffic tickets, not provide easy [overtime]."

With the mission clearly defined, Ferguson's police began implementing the city's revenue plans. The number of tickets being issued skyrocketed from 24,000 traffic cases and 28,000 nontraffic cases in 2009 to 52,000 traffic cases and 50,000 nontraffic cases in 2014.

As captain of the Patrol Division, Henke constantly reminded his division commanders of the need to increase traffic "productivity." In response to his prodding, the Patrol Division supervisors closely monitored their officers' ticket writing and chastised them when they hadn't written enough. One month after Jackson became chief, for example, a patrol supervisor criticized a sergeant because his squad only issued

25 tickets one month. He particularly derided one officer who issued "a grand total" of 11 tickets to six people over three days "devoted to traffic stops." At one point, the same patrol supervisor wrote to his patrol lieutenants and sergeants that "monthly self-initiated activity totals [alluding to ticket writing] just came out," and they "may want to advise [their] officers who may be interested in the open detective position, that one of the categories to be considered when deciding on the eligibility list will be self-initiated activity."

A key factor in generating more revenue was to give out more tickets per stop. The Ferguson prosecuting attorney, Stephanie Karr, a lawyer for a private firm who also served as the city attorney, met with police officers during one session to give them a primer. For instance, she told them, "If a person is stopped for driving while intoxicated, police should make sure they also tacked on speeding, failure to maintain a single lane, no insurance, no seat belt, and a broken taillight." Karr, who would later be cited for helping fix a traffic ticket for Brockmeyer, told the officers they needed to add more cases per stop whenever possible to make sure "that the court is maintaining the correct volume for offenses occurring within the city." Police officers began diligently following her instructions. Officers sometimes wrote 6, 8, or, in at least one instance, 14 citations for a single stop. Some officers competed to see who could write the greatest number of tickets during one stop. To further make sure officers were "maintaining the correct volume of offenses," municipal court clerk Mary Ann Twitty each month gave Ferguson police supervisors a list of the number of tickets issued by each officer and each squad. Police supervisors put officers on notice by posting the list inside the police station. As part of an officer's performance evaluation, it was noted whether each of them had consistently shown "the ability to maintain an average of 28 tickets per month."

Under pressure, police officers issued more tickets, ticketing men, women, the young, the old, and whites. They particularly targeted

African-Americans, the most vulnerable of Ferguson's residents. According to the Ferguson Police Department's statistics, African-Americans accounted for 85 percent of all vehicle stops, 90 percent of all traffic citations, and 93 percent of arrests during those stops in a city where they comprised 67 percent of the population.

Cops were sure to hand out multiple citations per traffic stop, as per Ferguson City Attorney Stephanie Karr's instructions. Black residents were more likely to receive them. Ferguson's police records show that, from 2012 to 2014, African-Americans received four or more traffic citations on 73 occasions. Only twice did police issue four or more citations to anyone else.

Not all Ferguson police officers agreed with the abusive ticketing practice and the use of the municipal court as a debtors' prison. Several officers pointed out that what the department and the courts were doing was wrong. Their arguments were drowned out by their supervisors and their fellow officers. When one commander admonished an officer for writing too many tickets, the officer asked the commander if he was telling him not to do his job. When another commander tried to discipline a different officer for overticketing, Chief Jackson halted the supervisor and told him, "No discipline for doing your job."

As the number of charges initiated by FPD has increased in recent years, the size of the court's docket has also grown concomitantly. In fiscal year 2009, for instance, 16,178 new cases were filed, and 8,727 were resolved. In 2014, by contrast, 24,256 new offenses were filed, and 10,975 offenses were resolved. During its weekly court sessions, on average 500 people would overfill the courtroom and spill outside the building into the courtroom parking lot. Because of the tactic of imposing numerous charges with each traffic stop, the court heard, on average, 1,200–1,500 offenses in a single four-hour evening session.

With the stops and the ticketing came the harassment. African-Americans were more than twice as likely as white drivers to be searched during vehicle stops. Blacks were more likely to be cited and arrested following a stop, regardless of why the stop was initiated. Nearly 90 percent of the times Ferguson officers used force, it was used against African-Americans. In every dog bite incident by the police K-9 unit for which racial information was available, the person bitten was black. To drum up more money, officers began resorting to lodging even more charges. One was failure to comply, which they apparently also used for African-Americans who asked questions during a stop, whether they were walking or driving. Ninety-four percent of those "failure to comply" charges were issued to African-Americans. Fred Watson was one of them.

6.

WE CAN'T BE MADE WHOLE

Fred Watson was on top of the world in 2012. He was a young black man with a top-secret security clearance, earning six figures working in cybersecurity for the National Geospatial-Intelligence Agency, or NGA. He was a Navy veteran. He owned his home. He had neither personal nor police blemishes on his record. Like so many African-Americans in the region, Ferguson, in its greed and callousness, snatched it all away from him. On August 1, 2012, Watson went to Ferguson's Forestwood Park to play basketball. Growing up, Watson had often come to Ferguson to visit and hang out with relatives. So, he was as familiar with their neighborhood as he was his own in St. Louis. After five or six games, he sat in his car and cooled off. He changed into dry clothes, folded the others neatly and placed them on the back seat, and sat in his car to watch kids playing baseball.

As Watson explained in in a federal lawsuit and in interviews, from that day forward for the next five years, Ferguson police and its judicial system would strip him of the life he had built for himself and his family with a viciousness he could not imagine.

As Watson was relaxing that day, Ferguson police officer Eddie Boyd pulled into the park and nosed his cruiser in front of Watson's car. It was the first of the month, and Boyd needed to begin writing his monthly quota of traffic citations.

Boyd was bad news, and many people in and outside the department knew it. He had been a cop in St. Louis city, where he had faced multiple internal affairs investigations for roughing up arrestees. In 2006, he pistol-whipped a 12-year-old girl. A year later, he struck another child with a gun or handcuffs and then denied it in a report. The deputy director of the Missouri Department of Public Safety sent Boyd a letter on December 20, 2007, to tell him the department had concluded a 12-month investigation of claims and was preparing to discipline him. Fearing he could be fired or lose his state certification to be a police officer, Boyd resigned and signed onto Ferguson's department, where he fit right in.

Boyd parked his police cruiser in front of Watson's car and then walked over to the vehicle. Watson rolled down the window to see what the officer wanted. Before Watson could say a word, Boyd suddenly shouted, "Put your hand on the steering wheel!"

A stunned Watson complied. Boyd began again.

"Do you know why I'm stopping you? Do you know why I pulled you over?"

Now Watson was really perplexed. No one had pulled him over. He had been parked there for at least 10 minutes minding his own business. The officer then demanded Watson's driver's license, insurance, and social security number. For a police officer to ask for his driver's license and insurance was understandable, but why, Watson asked the officer, did he need his social security number? The officer responded that Watson might be a pedophile, for all he knew, because he was watching kids play baseball.

Watson told the officer his full name and gave him his address. He offered to provide his driver's license, which was in the back of his car, but he refused to provide his social security number. His response set Boyd off.

"Get out of the car," he demanded.

Watson placed his hands back on the wheel to avoid any sudden movement and asked the officer for his name and badge number.

"No, you don't need that," Boyd answered. "It'll be on your ticket."

"What ticket?" Watson asked. "I have not broken any law."

"Well, I think your [car window] tint is too dark, and I can give you a ticket for that," the cop shot back.

"Okay, sir, that's fine, Watson replied. Watson felt the officer was becoming unhinged and erratic, and he began to fear for his safety. So he picked up his cell phone from the center console of the car and told Boyd he was calling 911.

"Put your fucking phone down and put your hands on the steering wheel!" Boyd shouted.

Boyd then pulled his gun from the holster and pointed it at Watson. He radioed for backup. Tensions were mounting. A few minutes earlier Watson had been relaxing in his car, watching kids play baseball. Now he was trying to sit erect with a police officer's gun pointed at him and waiting for more police to arrive.

Watson put his hands back on the steering wheel. Boyd told him to cut the ignition and throw the keys out the window. Fearful a wrong move with his hands could get him shot, Watson refused and sat motionless, waiting for the other police officers.

After a few minutes, three more Ferguson police cars responded. They included a K-9 unit with a police dog. Boyd walked over to the K-9 officer and said, "We could let the K-9 out to sniff around his shit and tear it up." The K-9 officer responded, "It's your call. Whatever you want to do." One of the officers approached Watson's car.

"What's the problem?" he asked Watson. "Why don't you just do what he asked, so we don't have to take the dogs out, search your car, and take you to jail? If you don't, that's exactly what's going to happen."

Watson gave the officer his name and told him what had transpired. He told the officer he would get out of the car but that the police did not have his permission to search his car.

"Okay," the cop said.

Watson raised the car window and exited his vehicle. As he was getting out, Boyd hollered, "Get out slowly and put your hands behind your back!" While Boyd was squeezing the handcuffs on his wrist, Watson said, he pushed the door closed with his leg. He was placed in the back of Boyd's car and then watched as the officers searched his car without his permission.

Boyd opened the car door, and the other cops stuck their heads in and looked around. Then Boyd went into the car and started rummaging through Watson's possessions. He went through the glove box, the center console, Watson's backpack, and the pants he had left folded on the back seat. Boyd threw Watson's possessions around the vehicle as Watson sat helpless in the back of Boyd's police car. Before they left the scene and before the tow truck came, Boyd went through the car again.

Nothing illegal was found. Watson wasn't worried about police finding contraband in his car. He had led a squeaky-clean life to maintain his high-level security clearance. He was, however, concerned about the $2,000 in the center console. That was money to pay for his children's private school.

The other officer, the one who had spoken to Watson, retrieved Watson's cell phone from his car.

"Just be cool and do whatever the officer tells you to do and things will be okay," he told Watson. Things definitely would not be okay.

Watson was taken to the Ferguson Police station. All he had done was sit in his car and watch a baseball game and now he was going to jail. This certainly couldn't be how America was rewarding him for his military service. At the police station, another officer processed Watson into the jail. Watson asked the officer his name.

"Officer Hayden," he replied immediately. Watson asked Officer Hayden for the name of the officer who was arresting him. Boyd was standing nearby.

"Don't tell him that!" Boyd interrupted. "It will be on his tickets."

Watson asked Officer Hayden if the badge number of the officer would also be on the ticket.

"You are not privy to that information," Boyd interrupted again.

They took mug shots and put Watson in a cell. To get out of jail, he was ordered to pay a $700 bond. Boyd issued Watson seven tickets, as per Ferguson's policy of writing as many tickets as possible.

1. Driving without Operator's License in Possession, which he had on him;
2. No Insurance Card, which he also had;
3. Vision Reducing Materials Applied to Windshield or Windows, which was for a tint to the car's windows that was legal in Florida, where the car was registered;
4. Failure to Register Vehicle, even though the car's registration sticker was in clear view;
5. Safety and Emissions Testing—Inspection Sticker Required, which, because the car was registered in Florida, would not have been applicable in Missouri;
6. Seat Belts Required (but not for someone sitting in a parked vehicle);
7. Driving While License or Driving Privilege Revoked, though Watson wasn't actually driving, and he was in possession of a valid license.

As a police officer, I was always discouraged from issuing summonses for charges that would not stick in court. This procedure, called "stacking," is used most often to humiliate people when officers don't have a good case.

Watson looked for the name and badge number of the arresting officer on the tickets. Boyd's name was completely illegible on all of them. On five of the seven tickets, the space for his badge number was left blank, and on the other two tickets, his badge number had been written and then scratched out. So, at this point, Watson still didn't know the name of the man who had arrested him.

He wouldn't know that until later when he went to the tow yard to get his car. The documents he needed said Boyd was the arresting officer. When Watson finally got his car, his clothes had been thrown in the front seat, his papers had been pulled out of the glove compartment and thrown onto the seat and floor, and the $2,000 that he had in the center console to pay his kids' school tuition was gone.

The tow-yard attendant said the only person he had seen going through Watson's car was Boyd. Watson took pictures and then went down to the Ferguson Police Department to file a complaint. He asked for the chief. An assistant told him the chief wasn't there. Watson, angry and frustrated, registered a complaint about his treatment by Boyd. In response, Boyd added two more charges to his case:

8. False Declaration, because Watson had identified himself as Fred, but his driver's license, which he had seen when he went through Watson's car, gave his first name as Freddie; and
9. Failure to Comply, a charge apparently lodged against people who asked questions or protested their treatment by the police.

What Watson experienced was what thousands in and around Ferguson had endured for years. Like him, they have been cursed at, slapped with bogus tickets, jailed unfairly, and forced to pay a bail that many of them couldn't afford. Those who couldn't pay languished behind bars until family or friends cobbled together enough money to get them out. As they waited in jails, many have lost their jobs. Some have been made homeless. Watson could afford the bail, so he was out and able to resume his life. But the worst of Watson's experience hadn't come yet. Ferguson's machinery was intent on crushing him.

The next day, Watson told his bosses at NGA what had happened. He was undergoing a security clearance review, so any interaction with law enforcement had to be disclosed. He assured his supervisors that once all the facts were in, the charges would surely be dismissed. No security clearance meant no job. As a person who held a high-level security clearance for 25 years, I can tell you they are valuable, coveted, and to be protected at all costs. At one point, I was chief of the ATF

Personnel Security Branch, which evaluated all employees and contractors for security clearances and access to sensitive information. Two of the charges against Watson—false declaration and failure to comply—would have been serious for anyone holding a security clearance. The others were routine traffic violations. Those two, however, point to character and integrity. If people in ATF with similar charges didn't have them dismissed, it would have come before my division for evaluation to determine whether they could maintain their clearance and ultimately their job. So, I understand how anxious Watson might have felt. It was imperative that those charges be dismissed.

Watson was confident the charges would be dropped. As he said, he hadn't committed a crime. He went to prosecuting attorney Stephanie Karr to get the charges dropped, but she said no. He hired attorney Freeman Bosley Jr., formerly mayor of St. Louis. They showed Karr all Watson's information, his valid driver's license, his valid insurance policy, his Florida automobile registration. She still refused to drop the charges or come to any agreement. Watson stayed on his job, but because of the pending complaints from Ferguson, his security clearance was suspended temporarily.

A few months later, the court told his attorney the remainder of the money he had paid for bond, $670, had been used as payment for the fines in the first seven charges in the case, though Watson had never pleaded guilty and his trial was still pending.

The court then claimed Watson had failed to appear on the last two tickets he had received from Boyd, the ones that were most likely to result in his security clearance being revoked. On February 26, 2014, Karr sent a recommendation to Watson's attorney for him to pay various amounts of money for the pending charges: Failure to Appear, $152 fine; Failure to Comply, $542 fine; and False Declaration, $327 fine. Watson refused, and in April 2014, with the deadline quickly approaching for him to clear his legal matters so he could maintain his security clearance, he hired a second attorney, Bevis Schock. Karr sent Schock the same recommendation she had sent Bosley.

Schock found dealing with Karr and the Ferguson court just as infuriating as Bosley had. With his client's livelihood in the balance, Schock said, he encountered months of misdirection and intransigence from Karr and Ferguson.

"There then ensued endless maneuvering by the city back and forth, which...I interpreted as an unwillingness on the part of the city to either try the add-on cases or dismiss them," he said. "For example, I filed papers to transfer all the cases to the Circuit Court of St. Louis County, but the Ferguson municipal court only transferred those tickets against Mr. Watson that were for failure to appear. I tried other approaches to getting a resolution, but despite countless letters, phone calls, and in-person visits to Ms. Karr's office, I was unable to resolve the matters."

Twice Watson's cases were to be heard in St. Louis County Court outside of Ferguson, but each time, Karr would force them back to her jurisdiction. It was a common practice by the Ferguson court. Even though some matters should have been heard in a different court, Ferguson fought to keep them under its jurisdiction, so it would receive money from the adjudication.

Consequently, in August 2014, two years after his encounter with the Ferguson police, Watson was fired from the NGA. Without resolving the Ferguson charges, he couldn't regain his security clearance. Without his security clearance, he couldn't do his job. So, he was let go. Watson now felt the pain, the despair, the anger, the rage felt by so many people in the area. Watson was now without any source of income. He had two children in private school. That would have to end. He wouldn't be able to pay the mortgage on his house. How would he eat? His savings would be enough for now, but for how long?

———

In the same month Watson was fired, that first Saturday, an 18-year-old named Michael Brown and his friend, Dorian Johnson, strolled into the Ferguson Market. Brown was big—6-foot-4 and 292 pounds.

Johnson looked diminutive as they stood together. Brown was feeling good that day. He had just graduated from a program to get his high school diploma and the following Monday, he was scheduled to start a training program for heating and air-conditioning repair at Vatterott College technical school. For some reason, Brown pushed aside a clerk and grabbed a fistful of Swisher cigars that folks like to use to get high. And get high he did. He and Johnson headed to Canfield Drive toward the Canfield community. Just three minutes earlier, Ferguson officer Darren Wilson had responded to a call about a sick baby on Glenark Drive, just east of Canfield Drive. The call on the police radio said to be on the lookout for two black men who had robbed the Ferguson Market of a handful of cigars. Wilson had heard the call on the radio. He turned his car into the Canfield neighborhood on Canfield Drive, where he saw two black males walking. I went to Canfield Drive twice to understand what could have happened next. Canfield Drive is an inconsequential, two-lane, neighborhood street with little traffic, except for the residents in the apartment units surrounding it.

Wilson rolled down his windows and told Brown and Johnson to get on the sidewalk. Anyone who has been on that street knows that their presence was so inconsequential that it could have hardly mattered to motorists or passersby. I've never asked anyone walking under those conditions to walk on the sidewalk. Stopping black men as they walked was common practice among the city's police and a source of income for Ferguson. The charge is "manner of walking in roadway," and African-Americans accounted for 95 percent of all citations on that charge from 2011 to 2013. Johnson responded that they were almost where they were going, but Brown was confrontational. He was also high, twice the legal limit in Washington state, where marijuana is legal. "Fuck the police," he said.

Wilson had passed the two but rolled his car backwards toward them. He either didn't like Brown's comment, or he thought the two fit the description of the men suspected in the recent robbery. A fight ensued between Wilson and Brown, and Brown was shot and killed. It could have ended there. There would have been the mandatory investigation. Afterwards, a grand jury most likely would have declined to press charges, as it ultimately did. If it had, a jury most likely would have found Wilson not guilty, and Brown's name would have been added to the list of unarmed black males killed by police without much fanfare. But Ferguson police and city officials, either out of arrogance, ignorance, or lack of consideration, did something that heightened the tension that had already accumulated from years of abuse: They left Michael Brown's dead body in the street for four hours in plain sight of residents.

As Brown's body lay oozing blood toward the gutter, more police began arriving. The first officer was there 73 seconds after the shooting. At 12:07 p.m., an officer on scene radioed to dispatch for more units. St. Louis County police began arriving on scene at around 12:15 p.m. Ferguson police dispatched a dozen units to the scene by 1:00 p.m. St. Louis County detectives arrived about 1:30 p.m. with another dozen, including two canine units, by 2:00 p.m.

By now, Brown's body had been lying on the street for two hours, apartment buildings lining both sides of the street. A crowd had begun to gather. Children peeked from behind their mothers. Black men who knew Brown and those who didn't gathered and shook their heads. Few of them had seen death presented so raw. Neighbors called neighbors. Those neighbors called friends and friends notified as many people as they could. The crowd swelled, and minute after minute, hour after hour, those gathered wondered why the hell this 18-year-old boy's body hadn't been moved. Why hadn't they even covered him with a sheet? At 2:14 p.m., police sent another of 20 units from eight different municipal forces. At 2:45, four more canine units arrived on scene, and the SWAT team arrived at 3:20 p.m. Michael Brown's body remained on the street.

The medical examiner finally arrived and began his examination at around 3:30 p.m. At 4:00 p.m., Brown's body was taken away. By then, a community that had been incessantly prodded, insulted, harassed, and jailed—as part of a continuous city policy to raise money—had had enough.

"It's like something from slavery," the Reverend Pierson told me, "where they would gather the slaves to see the master beat one. That's what it felt like. It felt like they left his body out there as a warning so we all could see who was in charge."

And then Ferguson exploded. Days of riots and demonstrations evolved into weeks, weeks became months, until the months turned into a year.

———

From his home in nearby St. Louis, Fred Watson watched as Ferguson residents and people across the country rioted and demonstrated for months about Michael Brown's death. But he had his own problems. He felt as if Ferguson had killed him, too. Without his job, he had lost his footing. His place in the world, which he had worked so hard to attain, had been stripped away by a vengeful cop and a city that viewed him and others as cash cows.

Watson's case was highlighted in a 2015 report by the US Justice Department as an example of the systematic manner in which Ferguson had harassed and jailed black residents. Watson had been out of work now for a year. Surely, he reasoned, Ferguson would drop the charges now after being exposed and embarrassed by his case and the scathing Justice Department report. It wouldn't. Watson was beginning to run through the $58,000 he had saved for his first two years of law school. It was now being used to support himself and his children. As the money dwindled, he lived out of storage units, slept in basements and the back seat of his car. He sank into depression.

Desperate, and after law firm after law firm had turned him down, Watson enlisted the aid of Arch City Defenders, a nonprofit civil rights law firm in downtown St. Louis.

Possibly no one knows better the depth and breadth of abuse by police and the judicial system in St. Louis's surrounding suburbs than ArchCity Defenders. The law firm, with co-counsel Civil Rights Corps and Saint Louis University Law Clinic, has already won a $4.75 million settlement for residents of Jennings for the same tactics as employed by Ferguson. ArchCity has filed similar lawsuits against eighteen other municipalities, including Ferguson, for jailing people who are unable to pay court fines and fees. The organization works with the homeless, children, veterans, and the poor on a variety of issues. It was co-founded by Thomas Harvey, Michael-John Voss, and John McAnnar—three St. Louis University Law School graduates.

Harvey, who was executive director of the firm from 2009 to 2017, is a boyish-looking blond 30-something wearing eyeglasses. He is originally from Edwardsville, Illinois, which is about 20 miles east of Ferguson across the Mississippi River.

Harvey and his co-founders discovered the law enforcement and judicial abuses of Ferguson and the other municipalities while working on extralegal projects for the homeless as part of his studies for a law degree at St. Louis University. Homeless residents, desperately in need of shelter, couldn't get help because shelters did not accept clients with arrest warrants hanging over them. They could go to jail, but there was no telling when they would get out, because they didn't have the money for bail or to pay the fines. When he received his law degree in 2009, Harvey and the firm's two other graduates dedicated themselves to fighting the system.

Harvey has seen story after story of people terrorized by the prospect of being jailed in one of municipalities surrounding St. Louis. They are all poor and nearly all are black. He has seen the bail bond slips that some businesses paid to get their employees out of jail. At the Maternal Child Health Family Coalition, a nonprofit agency that helps poor, pregnant mothers, staff reported that women were afraid to drive into the area for fear of getting a ticket and being hauled off to jail. Those who had received tickets and didn't have the money to pay were so stressed, the staff told him, they were having problems with their pregnancies. Ultimately, they started paying for taxis for the women who were just too afraid to drive in Ferguson. He has met with the people who lost their jobs and lost their housing after being arrested and jailed. So, yes, he took Watson's case.

Finally, in September 2017, Watson returned to Ferguson's courtroom. Boyd was still working as a Ferguson police officer. All charges against him were dismissed. There was no explanation. There was no apology. But, for now, the worst part of his nightmare was over. Watson is far different from the man he was in 2012. He is no longer the person who was relaxing in that park in 2012—a self-assured, optimistic young man with the world on a string and a bright future ahead of him. Even in victory, he remains a victim of Ferguson.

"I will never be like I was," he said after being exonerated. "I can't get those five years back." His children will not be able to get back educational opportunities they missed during that period. They can't go back and redo the extracurricular activities they might have enjoyed. Gone is the Junior Olympics. Gone are the vacations, the trips to museums, plays, the swim parks they missed.

"We can't be made whole."

Crystal King-Smith

Commander Second District, Chicago Police Department

When I was in the 7th District, I was in this neighborhood, and women came up to me and they said, "Why do your officers call us out of our names?" I was a sergeant at the time. I had no idea what they were talking about. They told me the officers routinely rode through the neighborhood saying, "Bitch, come over here. I need to talk to you" or "Bitch, come over here to the car." This was the white and black [officers]. I went to roll call the next day, and after we went through the briefing, I wrote every negative epithet on the blackboard that I could think of—nigger, bitch, spick, ho, chink, porch monkey, honky, cracker, wet back.

I wrote it on the board, and I said, "Let me explain something to you. These are words that are offensive. Do not call somebody over to your car with these words or use this language when you are talking to people. You may think it in your brain—that's your business—but you can't say this." Whether we got a written complaint after that, I can't say, but nobody was stopping me on the streets talking about being called "bitches."

I don't think the public understands that not all the police officers are the same. Police officers are individuals, like everybody else. We just took the same oath. We are different people with different baggage, different hopes and aspirations, different ethnicities. We had different motivations for becoming police officers. Some people get on the job so they can beat black people. Yeah, really. Some come in because they want to have the gun and badge that gives them authority, so they can beat up everybody and order them around. They weren't weeded out by the psychological test. Some officers join because they want to solve crime. Some people want to make a difference. Some people get on because they just need a job.

I have officers who are racist. They have to leave the [Ku Klux Klan] hood in the car in the parking lot when they come to work.

When I first came on the force, there were still a lot of officers who didn't want to work with me [because I'm a woman]. You knew you would never work with certain officers, because it was well known they didn't work with women. First, you're upset. You're saying, "This is 1991, and I'm dealing with this?" It hurt at first, because they were judging me without even knowing me. Then I just felt, "Whatever. I'd rather work with someone who wants to work with me. That way I'm safer." In a small instance, it still exists, but I'm finding more officers who actually prefer to work with women. They say it balances the [police] car. It gives them more flexibility when they are in the field to deal with both men and women.

When it comes to the code of silence, every occupation has one. You can't get a doctor to testify against a doctor or a lawyer to testify against a lawyer. I'm not saying it's right, but we have it. Mostly what you have is officers policing themselves. Officers seeing something going wrong and they stop it, and it doesn't have to go no further. There was one incident where a lot of officers had chased down a stolen car. The guy crashed into an embankment. They pulled the guy out of the car and they beat him. When [my partner and I] got there, we jumped out of the car and ran over there. Five of them stopped, but the others continued. My partner and I had to say, "Hold on, let's cuff this guy and take him in."

Some cops are ignorant. They figure that's what they're supposed to do. They figure an ass whipping is what they are supposed to do. We intervened, but we didn't report it. If you did, on top of you being a black and a female, you would also be labeled a snitch. No one would work with you. You could have people not backing you up on your calls and assignments. When I first came on the force, if I got in the [police] car with people who had a reputation for doing [wrong] stuff, I would address it in advance. That's not snitching. We had a guy who had a reputation for taking money on traffic stops. It may have been true; it might not have been true. I told him, "If you take money, I am going to tell." I'm telling him up front.

I was 34. I was a rookie, but I had lived a life before the police department. That made me different from a 21-year-old. They told me the same thing they told all rookies coming out of the academy: "Throw out that academy stuff, because it's different on the street." A 21-year-old is still young and dumb. You put them in the police department, whoever gets them after the police academy is raising them. You could be raised to be ethically sound, or you could be raised to take money. It takes years to change the culture, because it's so ingrained with the people who are here, and they are teaching it down to the new officers.

We are in the process, in Chicago, of trying to turn this big boat around the way society wants us to police now. Before, society wanted us to be warriors. Now, they're telling us we don't want warriors; we want guardians. We want you to be more of a guardian. A warrior goes out and wants to get arrests, to protect the law. If there's a gray area, you fall on the side of the law and let the judicial system figure out how to handle it. We did an excellent job of that in the '90s. Cook County jail was filled to the brim. Now we still do arrests, but not everything is an arrest. We're supposed to get out on the streets and walk around and have more interaction with each community.

The [Chicago Police Department] superintendent has been putting people in position to make this change. He's trying to put people to make that change. [There is] one on the north side, [but] everybody else is part of the old network. To finish what he's started, he's going to have to be succeeded by someone with the same vision. I have lieutenants under the old regime, the old boys club. I have sergeants [in my department] who are from the old regime. I can't pick my people because of union constraints. It takes a long time to change that culture.

We're putting in new policies on use of force. We started after the Laquan McDonald shooting. (Laquan McDonald was a 17-year-old mentally disabled black teenager armed with a knife who was shot 16 times— 15 times while he lay on the ground—in 2014 by Chicago Police officer Jason Van Dyke. Van Dyke was on the scene for less than 30 seconds before opening fire and began shooting approximately six seconds after exiting his car. The first responding officer said that he did not see the need to use force, and none of at least eight other officers already on the scene before Van Dyke arrived fired their weapons.

We're taking common sense and writing it down for officers. You're not a coward if you use cover. You don't always shoot somebody with a knife: The law says you can do that—legally we can—but that doesn't make it right. People's lives have become more important. Now, we're trying to get officers more training. We have new use-of-force training that is scenario-based. We get a debriefing afterward of what we should or shouldn't have done.

That's been going on about a year and a half now. I love it. I get to hone my skills, see how I would react, and when we have the debriefing, there are some old ways that we can see don't work. Most of the officers like it, once they get into it. Officers don't like change. I remember how they complained about the automation of arrest reports. Now, they are saying, "I don't know why we didn't do this before." But people have to realize that everything changes. The ones that see the bigger picture, they realize it and go along with it. It's harder when you're older. Officers get real cynical. They say, "It's not going to make a difference."

Black people also need to be training officers on how they want to be policed. When I look at white officers, I know they might be afraid of black people. Their view of black people is what they see on TV and what they hear. We have neighborhoods in Chicago that are all white. Most of them are not used to seeing and interacting with black people or Latinos. If you watch us on television, most of what you see is black people as criminals. They have no morals. They have no culture, no self-respect, no compassion, no ambition. Now, I've worked with white officers who were much more understanding and gave black people more of a break than I would, and you have some black officers who were worse and more racist than the white officers. But I know I will have to teach a lot of [white officers] how to treat the people in that community.

That block can teach officers how to treat them, how to talk to them, how to communicate with them. We have a block club where I live, and we always invite the police to our events. The difficulty is: It's going to be hard for people who don't have community. The people who are being treated the worst are the people who don't have community. When you have community, you work as a collective and you can expect certain kinds of things. If the only time you come out is when the police do something you don't like, then you don't have a line of communication.

The police officer is a person, too. You can talk to them, you can engage them. You can go up and talk to an officer and draw them out of the car. Get the officer talking. They're pushing us to get out there and talk to them and engage, but if [an officer] keep[s] trying to talk to citizens and they don't want to talk to me, I may stop pushing. That's why [the rate of homicides we solve] is so low in some neighborhoods. The people won't tell police information they need to solve some of these murders. The officers say, "They are killing themselves. They don't want to help me. Fine. I'm still getting paid." Now, the detectives don't say that to me, but I can tell what's going on. The community has to push, too.

I can understand that some black people are afraid of police. When my three sons were teenagers, I was afraid of that stop by police. I had taught them what to say and I had told them the police are always right. Sure enough, they've been stopped. Even my dad has been stopped. He's been stopped several times. He was retired and in his 60s and living in Roselle. [Roselle, Illinois, is 3.4 percent black.] He had been stopped so many times that, one time, he told me, he rolled down the window and when the officer came up, he told him, "Officer, I know you're just checking on me and that's why you've stopped me so many times, but I can assure you that I'm alright."

Do police racially profile? Sure. It's not right, but we do it. One of my sons, my middle son, he was the passenger in a car when the police pulled them over. The police asked him for his ID, so they could check him for [arrest] warrants. Officers do that when they are looking for gang members. If you fit the profile—young black man—and you make a traffic violation, that could happen. Are we supposed to do that? No. Does it happen? Sure it does.

My oldest son was driving, and a Naperville (Illinois) officer pulled him over. The officer told him he stopped him because his taillight was out. My son said, "Sir, I don't think my light is out." They walked to the back of the car and, no, his taillight wasn't out. The officer said, "I'm sorry," and my son went on his way. They were racially profiling him. It was Naperville. My middle son got picked up by police while he walking to work in Hodgkins. It's a city right outside of Willow Springs. [Hodgkins, Illinois, is 1 percent African-American.] He was working at UPS. Every day he would make this long commute (from Chicago), and he walked part of the way. He was 19.

The police picked him up off the street because they said he looked like somebody that committed a crime. They took him back to the station and they put him in a police lineup. They held him for two and a half, maybe three hours. Then they said, "You're not the one." They took him back to where they picked him up. He didn't tell me about this until much later. When he told me, I was nearly ballistic. I'm saying to him, "No! No! That's not what they're supposed to do." They didn't harm him; they didn't hit him. He was okay with it. I said, "They just can't pick you up and put you in a lineup like that." What if a person had picked him out of the lineup? I might have hurt somebody. I would have just had to lose my job if that happened.

In my opinion, officers feel threatened by these people who are rising up and are "against the police." Police are saying all lives matter. I have a little of this feeling, too. I think Black Lives Matter raises our social conscience. They point out things that need to be heard. Black Lives Matter definitely was needed in Ferguson, but it's needed, not just for the police. It's needed for everything: the gang bangers, the drug dealers, the people who are out here shooting black people. I credit them with the push [that led] to our department turnaround, which we needed.

But I have a 3-year-old who got shot yesterday. He got grazed in the back. Where is Black Lives Matter for him? If black lives matter, go to the drug dealers, go to the gang bangers—they are the ones taking black lives. Get up in their faces like you got up in ours [during a demonstration], calling our mothers names, taking their children up to the police and saying, "See that police officer. He might kill you one day."

We [The National Organization of Black Law Enforcement Officers] were working on black lives matter before Black Lives Matter was even thinking about black lives matter. Change has to come from somebody inside. The change has to be from the inside out. What NOBLE does, it takes the voice of the community inside law enforcement. We show that law enforcement does not have to be oppressive. NOBLE started because the white organizations weren't giving the community a voice. Injustice does still exist, not just on the police side. Justice for the black community has still not come to fruition. But we're much better with being forthright now.

7.

A CULTURE OF CRIMINALITY

As I moved up the ranks in the Bureau, I worked with scores of police departments and state law enforcement agencies while managing hundreds of officers who were assigned to me as part of ATF operations. We routinely used local officers in our efforts to assist cities and states implementing violent crime initiatives. In Baltimore, I worked with the Baltimore Police Department and the city's Baltimore City Housing Department police, chasing guns and drugs. In Maryland, I oversaw officers from state police and cops in 39 other counties. In Seattle, I coordinated cops in Washington state, Oregon, Alaska, Idaho, Hawaii, and the US territory of Guam. While acting special agent in charge in Denver, I managed police officers in Denver, Aurora, Grand Junction, and Colorado Springs in Colorado; Bozeman, Billings, and Helena in Montana; Phoenix in Arizona; and Albuquerque in New Mexico. Finally, I was the person in charge of the Newark Field Division. New Jersey has 466 police departments, and coordinating our operations with them had me hopping from Newark to Jersey City to Camden to Trenton to Atlantic City to Mt. Olive to Paterson and even to New York City.

Throughout my assignments there was one law enforcement organization I avoided—the New Orleans Police Department. I was fortunate. In those early days of my career, pretty much all my colleagues in ATF, the FBI, and the other federal law enforcement agencies had quietly agreed that New Orleans had one of the most corrupt city governments and one of the most crooked law enforcement agencies in the country. We dreaded the idea of working with that department. The history of police malfeasance and violence in the Big Easy is long and stunning.

In 1983, for example, a female police officer climbed into the back of an ambulance and beat a suspect as he was being taken to the hospital. In another incident during the same period, officers went on a week-long rampage after a police officer was killed. They killed four people and beat and tortured 50 others. Officers broadcast threats over a police radio as a man suspected of the killing was being transported to the hospital. Police radio officers could be heard on the radio, saying, "Kill the son of a bitch" and "Is he dead yet?" The man later died of massive skull fractures. An autopsy determined he had been stomped to death. The city paid more than $4 million to settle lawsuits stemming from that case—but not one officer was disciplined.

Meanwhile, the deputy head of the department that investigates gambling, prostitution, narcotics, and alcohol offenses was convicted of robbing bars and strip clubs in the French Quarter, even grabbing fist-fuls of money from cash registers during raids.

The chief of detectives was dismissed for working after hours for a Las Vegas–based gambling company and for operating an unlicensed private security business that was accused of cheating a visiting movie crew. The commander who enforced the department's internal rules was accused of roughing up a motorist during a routine traffic stop. The lieutenant who headed the robbery division was charged with shooting at his son. Another officer was charged with kidnapping and first-degree murder. And in a shameless episode, an independent investigation revealed police officers were keeping recovered stolen cars instead of returning them to their owners. The department decided not to take disciplinary action against the offenders but would get the cars back to their owners.

New Orleans's police department is not alone in its history of misconduct. Departments across the nation have similar stories. In the

1990s, more than 70 Los Angeles police officers from one division were implicated in a litany of offenses, including unprovoked shootings and beatings, planting false evidence, stealing and dealing narcotics, bank robbery, and perjury. Only 24 officers were found to have committed any wrongdoing; 12 garnered suspensions of various lengths, 7 were forced to resign or retire, and a mere 5 were fired. As a result of their actions, 106 prior criminal convictions were overturned and the city paid $125 million to settle 140 civil lawsuits.

In 2014, in my hometown of Philadelphia, six officers were arrested on an array of charges, including conspiracy, robbery, extortion, kidnapping, and drug dealing. The officers allegedly pocketed $500,000 in drugs, cash, and personal property, including Rolex watches and designer suits. The head of the police department called it the worst case of police corruption in his 40 years in law enforcement. The officers were later acquitted of the charges.

Corruption exists no matter what the size of the department. In Bakersfield, California, a department with less than 500 officers, two detectives were found guilty of accepting bribes and routinely taking drugs and cash from dealers during traffic stops.

Still, New Orleans's story is the most glaring example of the unethical and violent behavior and bad practices that plague many of the nation's police departments. It's a glimpse into how far a department can sink into a culture of brutality and corruption.

In New Orleans's long history of bad cops, there are three names that exemplify the department's level of depravity: Police Officers Len Davis and Antoinette Frank, and the Danziger Bridge.

One of the department's most heinous crimes began on the night of October 11, 1994. Kim Marie Groves, a 32-year-old mother of three who lived with her mother in a working-class, though drug-infested, neighborhood of New Orleans's Ninth Ward, saw an injustice she felt she could not ignore. The next day, she went to the New Orleans Police

Department to file a complaint. She told Internal Affairs investigators she had seen two officers punching a 17-year-old friend of her son in the stomach and hitting him in the back of the head with a gun while yelling, "Where is it at?" By the time the beating ended, the kid was bloody, bruised, and dizzy from a concussion.

One of the cops was Officer Len Davis. She recognized him because they both had attended a training school for security guards. During that time, numerous New Orleans cops worked part-time jobs as bouncers and security officers to supplement their meager pay.

Davis had a track record for brutality. Between 1987 and 1992, he had received 20 citizens' complaints and was suspended six times—numbers that were cause for concern in most departments, but not NOPD. Instead, in 1993, Davis had been awarded the police department's second-highest honor, the Medal of Merit.

Two and a half hours after Groves went to the Internal Affairs office with her complaint, Davis knew about it. And he didn't like it. "Be looking for something to come down," he told his patrol partner, Officer Sammie Williams. Almost immediately afterwards, Davis had begun searching for a way to have Groves murdered.

At 10 p.m. the following night, Davis contacted a local drug dealer, Paul "Cool" Hardy. A tape catches Davis dialing and mumbling, "I can get P to come do that whore now and then we handle the 30"—*30* referring to the police code for a homicide. When they speak, Davis tells Hardy when and where he wants Groves killed.

"All right, I'm on my way," Hardy responds.

At approximately 10 p.m., Groves said good night to two people on the corner of Alabo and North Villere streets. She was one block from home and her three children, 12-year-old twin boys and a 16-year-old daughter. Davis was monitoring Groves from his police cruiser.

He telephoned Hardy again, described Groves, and gave final instructions: "A black coat, with faded jeans, with big bleach stains on the front of 'em, and the bitch [is] brown-skinned with light brown eyes. I got the phone on and the radio. After it's done, go straight uptown and call me."

At 10:50 p.m., Hardy got out of a 1991 champagne-colored Nissan Maxima. His two accomplices remained in the car. It was a clear night, about 80 degrees. He walked over to Groves, raised his 9mm to the left side of her head, and fired. Groves's children rushed outside and found their mother lying in a pool of blood, her eyes moving from side to side, and then very suddenly they stopped. She was gone.

Less than 48 hours after Groves visited Internal Affairs, she was dead.

Davis greeted the news of her death with an exultant cry, "Yeah! Rock, rock-a-bye." The shooter, Hardy, was happy to do a $300 favor for his friend. He and Davis had been partners in crime for at least the past year. Davis led a group of corrupt cops who protected the drug dealers who worked for Hardy. The cops would warn Hardy and his crew of any police plans that might interrupt their drug-trafficking operations. Davis's help gave Hardy a leg up on rival drug dealers in the turf wars that drug trafficking fueled.

FBI agents had gotten wind of Davis's drug operation even before Groves's murder and had set up a sting to bring him down. The agents pretended to be drug traffickers, and approached Davis for protection of a phony cocaine storage facility they had set up as bait. Davis agreed. When FBI agents, acting as drug dealers, told Davis they needed more protection, he supplied nine more cops. When the officers showed up to provide 24-hour protection for 280 kilos of cocaine, they were dressed in their police uniforms and were legitimate, reflecting the blatant corruption among New Orleans police. Davis was convicted of murder and sentenced to death. He is still awaiting execution at federal prison in Terre Haute, Indiana. Even as the city was reeling from the news of Davis's arrest and trial, things went from bad to worse. Worse was named Antoinette Frank.

Everything about Antoinette Frank said she shouldn't be a cop. During her application in 1993, there were several warning signs. First, she was caught lying on several sections of her application. In one instance, she claimed that the reason her employment ended at a Walmart store was because she had transferred to another Walmart. When police did a background check, they found she had been fired from the first store, which would make her ineligible under Walmart's rules to work at any other Walmart stores.

Frank also scored so poorly on two of the police department's psychological evaluations, the psychologist who reviewed her results recommended a psychiatric interview. Dr. Philip Scurria, a board-certified psychiatrist, evaluated Frank on 14 characteristics needed to be a police officer. She rated unacceptable or below average in most categories. In his report, Scurria concluded, "I do not feel...that the applicant is suitable for the job of police officer."

Depressed over her faltering job prospects, Frank briefly disappeared. She left a suicide note addressed to her panicked father, who filed a missing-persons report with the police department. But she turned up the next day.

When I was in charge at the Bureau's Office of Personnel Security, I analyzed police applicants throughout the hiring process. Our applicants went through similar screenings, written tests, psychological examinations, oral panel interviews (as many as 8–10 people), polygraph examinations, and full-scope background investigations. In many departments throughout the United States, an applicant need only fail one of these checks to be eliminated from contention as a police officer. Any applicant who had failed as many checks during the hiring process as Frank would have not been brought aboard at the Bureau.

Despite the lies on her job application, the psychologist's and psychiatrist's warnings, a suicide note, and a confusing missing-persons report, Frank was hired by the department less than three weeks later. Her hiring was indicative of the department's lax standards. In 1993, the NOPD was chronically shorthanded, and it was losing officers faster than they could be replaced. Part of the problem was money. Its officers were dramatically underpaid, much lower than in similar-sized cities. A 1992 study showed that New Orleans police, whose starting salary was $17,000 a year and who had to furnish their own uniforms and side-arms, were the 319th-lowest paid of 322 departments it examined.

Additionally, Frank was a black woman, and some police officials thought having more African-Americans on the force would ease the city's long-standing racial tensions. Frank was hired on February 7, 1993. Although she graduated near the top of her academy class, many of her fellow officers thought she had no idea what police work really entailed and lacked the decisiveness to be a good cop. At times, they thought, she veered into irrational behavior. Less than 10 months out of the academy, her superiors wanted to send her back for further training.

Frank had been on the job for a little over a year and a half when she was called to investigate a shooting involving Rogers LaCaze, a known 18-year-old petty drug dealer, and his friend, Nemiah Miller. LaCaze told police a 19-year-old known as "Freaky D" just came up and started blasting away. LaCaze was injured in the hand. Miller was shot and killed. LaCaze's mother, Alice Chaney, said she had evicted her son from the house a year earlier for selling dope. The shooting, she said, was most assuredly a result of a drug deal gone bad, she told police.

Frank, however, became smitten by LaCaze's "bad boy" persona, even though he was only 18 and she was 24. After LaCaze got out of the hospital for his gunshot wound, he began receiving regular visits from Frank. She eventually took him shopping for new clothes. She bought him a pager and a cell phone. She rented him a Cadillac. Other police officers saw her hanging out with LaCaze. He drove Frank's personal vehicle and once was seen moving her police car at the scene of an accident she was investigating. On another occasion, LaCaze went with her on a complaint call, where she introduced him as a "trainee." No one, however, reported to higher-ups the cozy relationship between a police officer sworn to uphold the law and a known drug dealer. In a department as corrupt as New Orleans's was then, who would care? Ultimately, Frank and LaCaze began pulling over motorists while in her police squad car, and then robbing them.

Sometime around 2:30 a.m., on March 4, 1995, Richard Pennington, New Orleans's new reform police superintendent, was awakened by a call from the department about a particularly gruesome murder at a Vietnamese restaurant in New Orleans East. The Kim Anh Restaurant, run by the Vu family, had been robbed and the owner's 17-year-old son and 24-year-old daughter had been murdered. A New Orleans cop who was moonlighting at the restaurant was also killed. Pennington had been on the job less than six months. He already had his hands full with the scandals involving Len Davis and other bad cops throughout the department. Now, one of his men had been murdered. He needed to be there.

Pennington pulled on his uniform quickly and a police car met him at his door and sped him to the scene. By the time he arrived, forensics and detectives were busy working the crime scene. Outside, police cars, officers, and technicians crowded the tan concrete and gravel parking lot. Sergeant Eddie Rantz was supervising the investigation. He could be seen inside the restaurant talking to witnesses just past the wall of windows that made up the storefront. At one of the tables was Officer Antoinette Frank, who was explaining to Rantz how she had been in the kitchen getting something to drink when she heard the shooting. She said she tried to push all the employees out through the back door, but the boy and his sister wouldn't leave. She told Rantz that she drove from the restaurant to the 7th District station to report the shooting and then returned to the scene—and that's why she was there when other police arrived.

Her explanation raised numerous questions. Frank had a cell phone and a police radio with her. Why didn't she call it in instead of driving to the station? Why did she leave civilians behind at a murder scene, including a wounded police officer? None of it made sense. But then, one of the Vietnamese workers, so frightened that she initially could only speak in her native language, regained her composure. She sat at one of the restaurant tables talking with Sergeant Rantz, tears in her eyes. Then it all became clear. Frank wasn't a witness. She was the killer.

Rantz, sick to his stomach by now, walked out the glass front door into the parking lot and found Superintendent Pennington. "We're about to book this motherfucker with three counts of first-degree murder," he told the chief.

Rantz had put it all together. Shortly after midnight, Frank and LaCaze had come to the restaurant with the intention of robbing it. Frank knew the restaurant and the owners well. She had moonlighted there often as a security guard. She had been brought into the sideline job by fellow Officer Ronald Williams. Williams was on security duty at the restaurant that night. Frank knew he would be there.

One of the owners, Chau Vu, had gone to pay Williams when she noticed Frank and LaCaze approaching the restaurant. The two had been at the restaurant twice earlier in the night to eat. After Frank's last visit, Chau could not find the front door key after manually locking the door. With Frank returning for a third time, she sensed that something was very wrong. Chau ran to the kitchen to hide the money in the microwave. Frank entered the front door using the key that she had stolen from the restaurant earlier, and quickly walked past Williams, pushing Chau, Chau's brother Quoc, and a restaurant employee into the doorway of the kitchen.

Williams started to follow, but LaCaze slipped in behind him and shot him in the head, severing his spinal cord and instantly paralyzing him. As Frank, distracted by the gunshots, went back into the dining room, Chau, Quoc, and the employee hid in the rear of a large walk-in cooler in the kitchen with the lights out. They did not know the whereabouts of their other sister and brother, Ha and Cuong. The two had been sweeping the dining room floors when Frank entered the restaurant.

From inside the cooler, they heard more shots. LaCaze had shot Williams in the head again, mortally wounding him. Chau could see Frank looking for something in the kitchen where the Vus usually kept their money. Frank and LaCaze were shouting at Ha and Cuong, demanding the restaurant's money, but they did not know where Chau had hidden it. Frank pistol-whipped 17-year-old Cuong when he hesitated. Finally, Frank got the money out of the microwave, then shot 24-year-old Ha three times as she knelt pleading for her life. Then, she shot Cuong six times.

After Frank and LaCaze left the premises, Quoc emerged from the cooler and ran out the back door of the restaurant to a nearby friend's home to call 911. Frank dropped off LaCaze at a nearby apartment complex. He had taken Williams's weapon with him. She heard the 911 call on her portable police radio, saying that an officer was down at the Kim Anh restaurant. She knew she and LaCaze had left witnesses alive. So, she borrowed a patrol car and rushed to the scene. Posing as a responding officer, she intended to kill Chau and Quoc.

Parking in the rear, Frank entered through the back door of the restaurant and made her way through the kitchen to the dining room where Chau waited for help at the front door. Police showed up almost simultaneously, and Chau bolted through the restaurant's front door to the safety of the arriving officers. After finally gaining her composure, Chau fingered Frank as the person who had murdered two siblings and stolen the money. LaCaze was arrested shortly afterward at his apartment. He and Frank were later convicted and sentenced to death.

Corruption within the department abated briefly, then came Hurricane Katrina, and, by far, the most brutal and pervasive case of police corruption in the city's history.

On September 4, 2005, six days after the hurricane hit the city, five New Orleans police officers, none in uniform, drove in a Budget rental truck to the Danziger Bridge. The bridge carries thousands of cars and trucks daily along seven lanes of US Route 90, locally known as the Chef Menteur Highway. Today, however, it was closed, as was so much of New Orleans immediately following Hurricane Katrina.

Leonard Bartholomew, and his wife, Susan Bartholomew, their teenage daughter, Lesha, and some friends had just walked back from a grocery store and were then sheltering behind a concrete barrier. Like tens of thousands of New Orleans residents, they had been left homeless by the storm. Armed with assault rifles, including AK-47s, the cops lined up along the bridge "like at a firing range," one witness recalled, and began shooting at the Bartholomew family.

As the officers opened fire, James Brissette, 17, a family friend, was killed immediately. Four others were wounded. Susan Bartholomew's arm was partially shot off and later required amputation. Her husband was shot in the back, head, and foot. Lesha Bartholomew was shot four times. Jose Holmes Jr., a friend of Brissette's, was shot in the stomach, hand, and jaw.

When two brothers, Ronald and Lance Madison, tried to escape, they were pursued down the bridge by officers in an unmarked state police vehicle. One officer fired his shotgun from the back of the car at the men. Ronald Madison, who was developmentally disabled, was shot seven times—five times in the back. One officer stomped him before he died.

Homicide detective Arthur Kaufman was made the lead investigator on the case. Instead of investigating the crime, Kaufman told the officers to conceal evidence in the shootings to make the event appear justified. He also fabricated information for his official reports to help cover up the crime. Lieutenant Michael Lohman encouraged the officers to make up a cover story about what happened and to plant a firearm near the scene.

It took nearly two years for investigators to figure out what really happened on Danziger Bridge. The police officers involved in the shooting were taken into custody on January 2, 2007. Sergeant Robert Gisevius, Sergeant Kenneth Bowen, and Officer Anthony Villavaso were charged with the first-degree murder of one victim. Officer Robert Faulcon was charged with the first-degree murder of another. Officers Michael Hunter, Ignatius Hills, and Robert Barrios were indicted on charges of attempted murder relating to the other four victims. In

August 2008, however, the charges were dismissed by District Court Judge Raymond Bigelow, due to prosecutorial misconduct. Two weeks later, the Civil Rights Division of the US Department of Justice and the FBI began investigating the case. Ultimately, the five officers involved in the shooting pleaded guilty and were sentenced to prison. The city paid $13 million to settle claims against it in the incident.

Another resident, Henry Glover, was also killed by a New Orleans police officer during the turbulent days after the hurricane. His body was found in a burned car. The officer who shot him, David Warren, was initially found guilty of manslaughter and civil rights violations for use of excessive force. The officer who aided Warren by burning the body, Greg McRae, was found guilty and sentenced to 17 years in prison, far longer than Warren's 3 years. Much later, New Orleans police captain Jeffrey Winn was fired. He testified in court that he told McRae to burn the body because he didn't want it decomposing around his police officers. A number of other officers were reassigned for concealing details concerning Glover's killing.

Katrina-related misconduct didn't stop there; 91 officers resigned or retired for abandoning their posts during the hurricane and another 228 were investigated.

All the madness finally caused the Department of Justice to launch a 10-month investigation of the department in 2011 as the number of fatal police shootings and other crimes committed by police continued unabated. The report based on the investigation chronicled a pattern of unconstitutional conduct, rampant use of excessive force, and unwarranted stops and searches that I found stunning. It also found widespread discrimination based on race, ethnicity, and sexual orientation. A year later, under pressure to clean up its act, the city and the department entered into the most extensive federal consent decree in the nation's history.

8.

CULTURE VERSUS STRATEGY

New Orleans's history of malfeasance is accompanied by successive efforts by ambitious mayors and earnest police superintendents to rein in the city's runaway police department. Those efforts serve as an object lesson in the difficulties of reforming police departments, particularly those with extremely caustic cop cultures, like New Orleans's. It provides a window into aberrant behavior and bad policing practices that plague all too many departments. It also sheds light on needed changes, such as:

- establishing core principles
- implementing broader and more extensive and effective training
- putting in place better use-of-force standards and de-escalation procedures
- looking for better candidates in recruitment and hiring
- sustaining citizen involvement and community interaction
- requiring officer accountability

As heads of law enforcement, civic leaders, and community members try to revamp their departments, they must do so across a landscape of seemingly intractable poverty and neglect that fuels crime in the neighborhoods most in need of police protection and at the same time most affected by police misconduct. At issue are problems that have very little to do with police. Police chiefs or sheriffs are confronted with underprivileged neighborhoods, lacking in jobs, quality education, transportation, decent housing, and parks and recreation activities. The absence of those core community elements drives crime and pervasive violence. The paucity of money and opportunities gives rise to alternative criminal economies and desperate people who engage in dangerous behavior—drug dealing, burglaries, purse snatching, armed robberies, and theft of anything that's not nailed down. The strong prey on the weak. Despair and confusion create despondency; frayed nerves and absence of self-worth lead to anger, abuse, assault, and murder. Just look around. We don't have drive-by shootings, street corner drug sales, or high murder rates in affluent neighborhoods. The working poor are hit the hardest.

New Orleans is no different. Despite the city's endearing image of fun and frolic, of Bourbon Street, Mardi Gras, the Essence Festival, the Bayou Football Classic, and the city's incredibly rich musical culture, it is a town where too many of its residents remain locked in poverty's crushing embrace. The overwhelming majority of them are African-American. Nearly 40 percent of the children in New Orleans live in poverty, 17 percentage points higher than the national average, even though 82 percent live in a house where at least one person is employed. Their parents are working, but they are earning poverty wages. Ten years after Hurricane Katrina, the black household income dropped to the point of wiping out the black middle class. The median income for white families is $60,553; the median income for black families is $25,102. That is a $35,451 difference, more than the amount most black families earn. Consequently, New Orleans, like cities with similar income disparities— Baltimore, St. Louis, Kansas City, Memphis, Milwaukee, Atlanta, and Detroit—struggles annually with unacceptable rates of murder, robbery, rape, and assault.

The first serious effort to reform New Orleans's police department was headed by Police Superintendent Richard Pennington. Pennington was a striking figure at 6-foot-4 and 240 pounds, with the pedigree that New Orleans needed. He had served in the Air Force during the Vietnam War after graduating from high school. He began his career in 1968 as an officer in the Metropolitan Police Department in Washington, D.C. His first police partner was Donald Graham, who later became publisher of the *Washington Post*. He quickly rose through the ranks while earning a bachelor's degree in criminal justice from American University and a master's degree in counseling from the University of the District of Columbia.

He was number two in charge in D.C. when New Orleans chose him to head its beleaguered department. So, he packed up his home, his amateur camera gear, and his Harley-Davidson motorcycle, and moved to New Orleans with his new wife. Ironically, on the same day then-Mayor Marc Morial was proudly introducing Pennington as the possible savior for the city's troubled police department, New Orleans police officer Len Davis was having Kim Groves killed.

When Pennington took over the police department, New Orleans was in the midst of breaking a city record for murders, and gaining the dubious title of the nation's "murder capital." Police corruption was rampant, and citizens wouldn't report rotten cops for fear they'd end up like Groves.

To reform the department, Pennington's first order of business was to get rid of as many corrupt cops as possible. This was an important first step. Five years later, 458 officers in a department of 1,630 officers were gone; including 85 who had been arrested, 100 who had been fired, and 200 who were being disciplined. The remaining officers who left the department retired.

To regain public trust, Pennington disbanded the Internal Affairs Unit and reassigned its officers. In its place, he created the Public Integrity Bureau to conduct those investigations. He staffed it with different personnel, including two FBI agents, and a relatively new officer on the force named Michael Harrison would be key to the department's future.

By adding former FBI agents, Pennington sent a message to the rank and file that old loyalties would not help when officers came under review. The new Public Integrity Bureau was located outside of headquarters to encourage more citizens to go in and file complaints. The unit also began running undercover sting and surveillance operations on police officers. More people began coming forward as word spread that the police—at least some police—could be trusted.

To break up the cronyism that had fostered misconduct and criminality, Pennington moved all 250 detectives, including those in robbery and homicide, out of headquarters and into the eight police districts and placed them under command of the district captains. He began using computerized statistics to identify problem areas and the crimes committed there, and he established substations at three of the most crime-ridden public housing complexes in the city and staffed them with a total of 50 officers.

Ultimately, crime decreased. New Orleans had recorded 425 murders in 1994, the year Pennington took over. Five years later, the city had 162 murders, a 62 percent drop.

Pennington also turned his attention to recruiting. During his first visit to the police training academy, he discovered 12 of 17 recruits had arrest or criminal records on charges ranging from drunk driving to rape. Today, people with similar records or other negative marks—including delinquent child-support records, bad driving records, dishonorable discharges from the military, excessive debt, or a history of consorting with criminals—cannot join the force.

The new rules also applied to the officers on the force, leading to an exodus of questionable and criminal cops.

To attract and maintain a better caliber of police officers, Pennington sought salary increases. He raised starting salaries from $17,000 to $26,000 annually, with a bump to $30,000 after the first year. If you give some people a gun and not enough money, the officers will pay themselves. Many departments with high levels of corruption have low salaries, as officers subsidize their income through illegality, such as bribes and kickbacks. The raise in pay allowed Pennington to limit officers' off-duty work hours to 20 a week. Limiting off-duty jobs helped keep officers from working in places like nightclubs that can attract a criminal element. Corruption and bad practices largely disappeared until Pennington left in 2002 to run the Atlanta Police Department, following an unsuccessful bid for mayor of New Orleans. In his absence, the department gradually slid back into some of its corrupt practices.

Police Superintendent Michael Harrison is the latest department head tasked with turning NOPD around. He was only on the job three years when Pennington took charge. The news of Officer Davis's arrest and the changes the new chief put in place set off a small tsunami through an already fractured department.

Now it was Harrison's job to take on a corrupt criminal culture. "Morale was rock-bottom," he told me. "I had watched the new chief [Pennington] and learned some things. When dealing with a department during rocky times, I learned how to deal with controversy and stay poised even when you're making unpopular decisions that upset the status quo."

He is being prodded forward by a US Justice Department consent decree that found the department was routinely violating its citizens' constitutional rights. Some officers beat suspects as a matter of course, even those in handcuffs. There were incidents in which officers unnecessarily assaulted mentally ill suspects. Officer-involved shootings or in-custody deaths were investigated inadequately or not at all. The mishandling of investigations was so bad that the department thought it looked intentionally botched.

I met Harrison in the summer of 2017 when we appeared together in New Orleans on a panel discussing police and use of deadly force. He is an immediately likable man—warm, smart, dedicated. He was born in the Ninth Ward, but moved back and forth between the Ninth Ward and New Orleans East when his parents split up. The two communities were dramatically different. The Ninth Ward was gritty New Orleans—gumbo, music, tiny homes with pralines cooking next door, shootings and stabbings and having fun all at once. New Orleans East encompassed suburban-style homes and lawns and sedate communities before its decline in the 1980s. Harrison graduated from high school, joined the Air Force National Guard, got married, and bumped around before he joined the police force. At that point, he and his family moved to Algiers, the second-oldest neighborhood in New Orleans and the only Orleans Parish community on the west bank of the Mississippi River. Historically, the community has been known for poverty and crime, much of it rooted in some of the neighborhood's public housing projects—Fischer Projects, DeGaulle Manor, and Christopher Homes. But, like everything in New Orleans, Algiers has another side. It is also famous for Super Sunday, an all-day Mardi Gras event held there since Harrison was a toddler. Each year since 1970, hundreds of residents line up along Whitney and Newton streets on the third Sunday in March to watch the parade of approximately 40 Mardi Gras "Indian tribes," black men and women adorned in elaborate, impressive costumes of jewels and pink, gold, blue, and green feathers.

Harrison joined the NOPD in 1991, four years after graduating from high school. He quickly advanced through the ranks. He became a detective in 1995, a sergeant in 1999, a supervisor in the Public Integrity Bureau in 2000, the Seventh Police District assistant commander nine years later, and, from 2011 to 2012, he was commander of the division that oversaw drugs, vice, criminal intelligence, and gang enforcement. He was named to head the department in 2014.

His ascension was most likely accelerated, Harrison told me, by his penchant for knowledge. After he received a bachelor's degree in criminal justice, he earned a master's degree in the same subject from Loyola University. He also busied himself with management training at the School of Police Staff and Command, the Senior Management Institute for

Police, and the FBI's National Executive Institute, among others. Deeply religious, Harrison is an elder at his church, City of Love Church.

Harrison's job is complicated by the fact that he is being asked to be a transformational leader in the same police department in which he grew up. Over the past 26 years, Harrison had to survive a cesspool of police malfeasance in an often lawless law enforcement agency. To be a good officer, Harrison had to swim through a river of foul cops and illegality and somehow come out on the other side clean. He is not an outsider, as Pennington was when he came in with the same mandate. Harrison began seeing the levels of corruption among his fellow officers from the moment he joined the department as a rookie.

"I admit that I've seen us in our darkest hours," Harrison told me. "I saw things that I shouldn't have seen. It was crazy. Officers were doing bad things and good officers who saw them doing bad couldn't say anything, or they'd be punished and ostracized. Those good officers were pushed aside. They weren't the ones who got promoted. It was the bad guys who got promoted, and you had a lot of good officers who were being swayed by the dark side."

Harrison has started his efforts by holding fast to a set of principles and personal commandments for a department that had come off the rails again. When I asked him about reform, he listed what his department is doing: The department must be open and clear to the public. To that end, it has vigorously embraced body cameras; to the tune of 800 cameras at a cost of $8 million. Every patrol officer who encounters the public is assigned one that must be turned on when the officer is engaged with the public. Additionally, the department has developed guidelines for a nine-day release of all video to the public after it has been reviewed internally.

The department has created a web page to provide residents and others with a plethora of information, including a list of all police calls and responses over a 24-hour period, a map of all criminal activity in the city, the city's annual crime data, a daily internal NOPD administrative major offense log that documents major offenses or events occurring over a 24-hour period, a copy of all press releases, and the Justice Department's consent decree.

Harrison told me that listening to residents and being responsible are vital. He said that's all part of his efforts to encourage community support and involvement. "I'm as much the police chief for the residents of New Orleans as I am for the department," he said. Consequently, he and his officers, from top-level commanders to regular beat cops, are often asked to meet with residents to hear their concerns, whether it be abandoned buildings, lack of recreational facilities for children, drug dealers, or neighborhood toughs.

Additionally, the department has expanded its web pages to include information many residents need or want. The website now offers information about financial assistance for crime victims, enrollment in a Citizens Police Academy that spotlights the various functions of the police, and sections where residents can file online complaints against an officer or give commendations, request barricades in their neighborhood for special events, and view a list of registered sex offenders in a radius they define and then track their records.

With all this in mind, there is a catchphrase that has been circulating around management discussions for years: "Culture eats strategy for breakfast." It is a shorthand way of saying that no matter what strategy you may have to change an organization, unless you address the culture of the group—how people perceive their jobs and responsibilities, workers' ingrained performance routines, current staff allegiances, and how and why they work—your strategy will fail every time. Nowhere is that truer than within law enforcement and nowhere in law enforcement was it more true than New Orleans.

In a department with a history of abuse, Harrison struggles to instill in his officers the idea that people come first. He has a saying: "A negative outcome doesn't have to be a negative experience," probably a message he picked up from one of his many management classes. But his logic is clear. When a motorist receives a traffic ticket or a person is jailed for a crime, for the civilian that is a negative outcome. Nothing will change that part of the police encounter. But how the officers handle the incident determines whether it is a negative experience. Was the person handled with dignity and respect? Was he given clear and concise commands and information during the encounter? Did the officer listen to the complainant's concern? Did the police response make the situation worse or better? Did the officers treat the people who pay their salaries with respect?

So, when President Donald Trump seemed to endorse aggressive and violent police conduct shortly after becoming president during a speech to police officers in Brentwood, New York, Harrison made his point clear. "The president's comments stand in stark contrast to our department's commitment to constitutional policing and community engagement," he said in a public statement. "Any unreasonable or unnecessary application of force against any citizen erodes trust at a time when we need support from our local communities the most."

Why, I asked Harrison, was it important for him to make a public statement attacking the president? He easily could have said nothing. Others in law enforcement, including the 23,000-member International Association of Chiefs of Police, had already taken the president to task for his comments on use of force. It wasn't enough, he said. He needed to send a very clear message to a lot of people. "It was a message for the president," he told me. "It was a message to the members of our department, to my police chief colleagues around the country, to any potential applicants who want to join the New Orleans Police Department, and, most of all, to the men and women who work here to know that we are committed to ethical policing. It was important to show our community the importance of our transformation. We will be hard on crime and be soft on citizens."

It's one thing to say a department needs a culture change. It's another to change that culture. Harrison has begun by moving quickly against the code of silence that is almost sacrosanct among law enforcement and hinders the ability to root out bad cops and bad practices. Less than a year after taking the job, he fired three cops and suspended one after an officer's bodycam video showed one of them striking an intoxicated, handcuffed man several times while he was seated inside a station house in New Orleans's famous French Quarter. The incident was discovered during the daily review of officers' body-worn cameras. The patrolman who hit the man was fired, along with two officers who witnessed the event and lied about it when they were questioned. The third officer was questioned and admitted that he saw the abuse. He was suspended because he didn't report what happened immediately, as required by department policy.

"When officers do something wrong, and when the officers who don't tell find themselves in bad [or worse] shape, the culture starts to change," Harrison said. "But it takes some executive decisions on the front end. We have put in a system now where sergeants [patrol officers' first line of supervision] can be held liable for their officers. Trust me, when officers see sergeants getting demoted or fired, they pay attention. You must have a strong disciplinary process. You have to be fair. You have to show equity in promotion and discipline. There have to be systems of accountability—punishment for bad behavior and reward for outstanding service.

"It's difficult because, over time, officers develop relationships. It's just natural. They're friends. One person becomes the godparent to the other person's child. An officer loans another one money to pay his mortgage. But everybody has to understand that our individual actions affect the entire community—the police community and the citizen community. It shapes everybody's perception."

One of the initiatives Harrison has launched to eliminate police malfeasance is a homegrown effort called Ethical Policing Is Courageous (EPIC). It requires police officers to police fellow officers in the field. He wants officers to stop fellow cops before their conduct escalates into something they would regret. "I saw things going on when I was a patrol-man, but I didn't report it," he said. "I don't want that to happen now. When my officers see a fellow officer about to go down a path, about to do something that we would all regret, I want his partner to stop him. I want him to intervene. We have eight hours of instruction on this every year. In the past, bad things happened and good officers weren't empowered to intervene. Don't just stand there. Intervene."

Three days after New Orleans Mayor Mitch Landrieu named Harrison the new police superintendent, Harrison reshuffled his top command staff. Harrison named a new deputy chief of the Investigations and Support Bureau, which oversees the evidence and crime lab divisions as well as major criminal investigations into murders, rapes, and gangs. He demoted two former ranking supervisors and named a new commander of the Compliance Division, to oversee new policies, including performance standards, crime analysis, and body-worn cameras. Harrison told the media it represented his "commitment to strengthen and rebuild the department."

He told me later that was his highest priority when he took the job. "You have to have the right leadership team to change. We grew up in this department. I had to find people who were willing to be ridiculed by the people they grew up with in the department. That is the most critical aspect of being a transformational police chief."

Harrison has been aided by a change in the personnel rules approved by the Civil Service Commission and pushed through by the New Orleans mayor that gives him greater flexibility in hiring, evaluating, promoting, and rewarding employees. Within two years, he had promoted 41 officers to the position of sergeant and 37 sergeants to the position of lieutenant, and had made even more high-level changes.

With all of Harrison's efforts, crime has gone down. The independent monitors who oversee the police department's progress under the Justice Department's consent decree recently completed two annual surveys: one that judges how New Orleans residents see the department and a second to see how officers view their leadership and the department's direction. Sixty-four percent of New Orleans citizens said they think the department is more competent than it was a year ago, up from just over 50 percent earlier. Just as important, 79 percent of the officers in the department said they approve of the department's leadership and believe that it is headed in the right direction.

I asked Harrison how a chief knows he has at least turned the corner in reform. "There are a number of things," he said. "First, crime will be going down. If crime is going down, citizen satisfaction is going up. If citizen satisfaction is going up, that means officer job performance is going up. We have to be able to say we no longer need federal oversight and we can prove that we no longer need to be under a consent decree. We need to continue to get high marks from the citizens who are giving us favorable satisfaction reviews. We've got to increase our staffing back to the original numbers of about 1,500 police officers. We're down to 1,165 police officers right now. We want to make sure that we are seven minutes or less in response to an emergency call. We are updating our equipment on a consistent basis so that officers can do their jobs.

"But one of the biggest things is for the city not to put the entire burden of reducing crime on policing. We all know that lack of jobs, poor education, poor parenting, no cultural activities and recreation, and failing faith-based institutions lead to crime. Crime starts and feeds on the lack of all these things, and that part has nothing to do with police presence. I think we have changed the conversation with many of our politicians, so they know that we need to do our job, but they have a job to do, too."

Harrison is a case study for how departments across the nation should be looking at our profession differently. We must consider law enforcement models far beyond what we have traditionally made part of our processes.

For instance, what types of early warning systems are in place in departments to identify officers who may go rogue? Should police officers and sheriff's deputies be tested for their psychiatric stability every five years on the job? Traditionally, officers are given a psychological evaluation only once in their careers, during the hiring process. Dealing with the worst of our society on a daily basis can take its toll. Some handle it better than others. Statistics show that police officers commit suicide at a rate that is twice that of the nation's average. How can we do more to support the officers and the communities they serve?

Should there be statewide or national hiring standards? Should there be a consistent age for police hires? In some states you can be a cop at 21 and in others you have to be 25. Some departments require associate's degrees, others require bachelor's degrees, and, for others, a high school diploma is sufficient. These are just a few of the important questions facing law enforcement in the world of 21st-century policing.

Chris Magnus

Chief, Tucson Police Department

I did not let people know I was gay when I first started as a police officer. I doubt I would have been successful coming up through the ranks as a gay man. Based on the environment, it was super unlikely. I heard the language. I knew what other cops thought about gay men. Even today, it's still very difficult. Police departments are not easy places for folks who do not fit a very traditional portrait of policing.

There are arrests that I've made that I think back on and sort of wince. I did not police the way, today as a police chief, I expect my officers to police. My use of force was questionable at times. I grew up arresting everybody who looked at me the wrong way. I took a hard line. I was involved in way too many fights and I made way too many arrests. Lansing, Michigan, had a lot of disorderly offenses on the books that gave cops a wide latitude to arrest people. We had failure to obey; hindering, obstructing, opposing, and providing false information. We used all of that often as justification to search people. You can always find a reason to arrest somebody. At the time, I didn't know better. I thought that's how you do police work.

There are two kinds of police chiefs. There are people who see their job as holding down the fort, crisis management, keeping the trains running on time. I know a great many of these folks. They are professional people. They see their job as maintaining a status quo approach to policing and their agency.

Second, there are people in varying ranks who have been looking for an opportunity to do something different. They are often held back or not really given an opportunity. They get pushback against change. People react with fear, anger, and there's a lot of passive-aggressive behavior. Officers who want change must figure out who are their allies. There's trial and error in figuring out which people are going to partner with you. Police officers know police chiefs come and go. They don't know how long a chief will be around. If they go along with his plans for change, they may be offending people they've got to work with throughout their careers.

Ultimately, cops are pragmatic, and if chiefs can show them how change works better and how it makes things better for them, officers will ultimately go along with it. Chiefs have to show how new use-of-force techniques and models keep officers out of civil and criminal liability, and keep them out of trouble with their bosses. The average cop is far more concerned about what their sergeant thinks [about their performance] than what I say as chief. Chiefs must get their sergeants to engage and help officers understand, "If you're going to be successful [in this police department], you have to be engaging with the community." We have to get more sophisticated about what we're expecting from our officers, [the behavior] we're encouraging and what we're rewarding.

There is a photograph of me holding the Black Lives Matter sign in Richmond (California). I moved from Lansing to a nearly all-white community in Fargo to a city that was 85 percent people of color, low income, high levels of violence, and high levels of mistrust of the police. We had built a very broad relationship with the community and with different neighborhood groups. There had been a whole series of very ugly marches in Oakland and Berkeley following the shooting of Michael Brown.

In Richmond, we heard there was going to be a demonstration. We prepared for potential problems, but what we did was, my entire command staff just went out and talked to people who were in the march. Between us, we knew the majority of the folks who were there. If I didn't know somebody, my deputy chiefs or captains did. It is harder to be hostile toward police you've gotten to know and have built a relationship with over the years. We approached it along the lines of building bridges and opening lines of communication.

One of my captains said to me, "Chief, people have been out here for a long time, and they are getting hungry." So, we went out and got pizza and gave it to the people. People had their kids with them. We still had some people looking at us like, "Fuck the police," but at the same time people were taking pictures with us. One woman asked to take a selfie with me. She held up her sign and we took a picture. I did not in a million years expect it to get the attention that it did. Of course, black lives do matter.

It is unfortunate that there are people who see this continuum of black lives matter and police lives matter as being on either end of the equation. It's such a false equivalency. It's not a matter of one being on one end of the spectrum and another being on the opposite end. There's nothing that says people who care about the past and the future of people of color—and [who] realize that we have a lot of bad history and that it takes a toll in many ways and that there are still a lot of bigoted attitudes—are antipolice.

We can acknowledge that and it's not saying what police do is not important, or that police officers' lives are not important. There is nothing that says addressing the first means you're not committed to the second. The great majority of the black community want a good relationship with the police. They have a lot of respect for what cops do. Are there people who are not helpful in their behavior and rhetoric? Yes, there are. But most black people, in no way are they antipolice or anti–law enforcement.

Richmond was a community where we were taking as many as two guns off the street a day. There are a lot of communities where guns are part of the fabric. Here in Tucson, people would argue that guns are part of a way of life. It's fair to say that, in Richmond, it was very hard to avoid guns, particularly because of gang activity and a sense of personal danger. A lot of folks, their whole word is a small and dangerous place. Carrying a gun for them is as much a defensive act as anything else. When I got to Richmond, it was a very, very violent city; a lot of homicides and a lot of shootings. [Richmond, a city of 115,000, had 38 homicides the year Magnus took charge. With 1,078 violent crimes the year before, it was considered one of the 10 most crime-ridden cities in the United States, with a per-capita murder rate that earned it the reputation of the Bay Area murder capital.]

We could have been shooting people every day, but we tried to create a culture that said, "You're a professional police officer and committed to the idea that life is sacred. The people you might be arresting, they're the sons and daughters of somebody in that neighborhood. You want to be a little more thoughtful. You want to be more selective in your use of force." Our goal was to train officers so they understood that they had multiple tools and strategies to deal with dangerous individuals, other than just shooting people. We really focused on scenario-based training. We looked at providing them with de-escalation training.

On a daily basis, my officers were involved in foot chases with people who were armed. I would never encourage my officers to put themselves in harm's way, but there are different ways to pursue somebody. You can box people in. You can slow something down, so you're not just reacting out of panic and fear. These are issues related to training. You need training and then more training to reinforce the training.

There's value in a weird way of coming from the perspective of being a gay man. I know what it's like to be discriminated against, to be treated in a way that's very unkind and bigoted and mean-spirited. I don't claim to know what it's like to be black or Hispanic, but it gives me a glimpse into other people's experience.

9.

A MURDER IN CHICAGO

The day I flew into Chicago, most of the East Coast was still enjoying unseasonably warm fall weather. It was 50 and 60 degrees back home in Pennsylvania. Chicago, instead, was living up to its reputation. It was cold and wet and windy as hell. The next day would bring snow. Aside from my numerous flights in and out of the Windy City as an ATF agent, I had not spent much time there professionally. I was in Chicago now to understand the dynamics of police and race in a city that had registered more murders the previous year than the nation's two largest cities, New York and Los Angeles, combined. I was set to talk with Chicago Police Superintendent Eddie Johnson; activists like Father Michael Pfleger, who has been wrestling with the city's violence for 40 years; and Arne Duncan, former CEO of Chicago's public schools and secretary of education under President Barack Obama. And I was there for Laquan McDonald.

Of all the police shootings of African-Americans, McDonald's is one of the most telling I've found about police misconduct and bias. It shows the extent to which police, with the tacit approval of public officials, will lie to protect each other. McDonald was a mentally unstable 17-year-old black boy, shot and killed by a police officer just two months after the shooting of Michael Brown in Ferguson, Missouri. Nine of the 16 bullets that hit him were in his back; nearly all the shots were delivered while he was on the ground and at least 10 feet away from the officers.

Chicago police officers and city officials engaged in a massive, one-year cover-up to hide how McDonald was killed. Once revealed, it led to the murder indictment of one officer, conspiracy charges against three others, the firing of the police chief, voters' removal of the county prosecutor, and political fallout that even now threatens to derail the career of the city's mayor, Rahm Emanuel.

Despite all the media attention paid to crime in Chicago, it is not America's most dangerous city. St. Louis, Memphis, and Baltimore vie annually for that dubious distinction. Detroit is not far behind, nor is Newark. Even the nation's capital is worse. Chicago didn't even rank in the top 10 as of the writing of this book.

It may not be as dangerous as the others, but it feels dangerous. It's not because of the blocks and blocks of derelict buildings, like parts of Baltimore and St. Louis. Chicago has one of the nation's most attractive skylines, an extensive and inviting system of public parks, a gorgeous and accessible waterfront dotted with public beaches and friendly bike and running paths that stretch along every neighborhood bordering Lake Michigan. However, what I noticed in Chicago is the sense that people seem to be consciously and unconsciously mentally navigating their way through a minefield of violence. It is tucked inside casual conversations. It lies among things said and unsaid, how daily activities are altered, how neighborhoods are avoided, and how interactions with strangers must be carefully negotiated.

My introduction to Chicagoans' unique everyday conversation began almost immediately upon arrival. As usual, I texted a ride-sharing service for my trip from the airport to my downtown hotel. A courteous African-American woman named Cynthia pulled up. Cynthia was in her mid-30s. She works full-time as a middle school teacher at a Chicago public school. Big smile, smartly dressed, nice personality. She eased her Toyota Prius away from O'Hare International, nosed it into highway traffic, and we began the usual passenger-to-driver banter to fill the silence. At one point, she asked me what had brought me to town. I answered. Then began one of the many stories I would hear over the next few days about people's personal encounters with the city's crime.

"*Pop, pop, pop*—they shot into my house," Cynthia said. "Somebody was shooting at somebody on the corner. I heard it from inside. *Pop, pop, pop*, and now I've got bullet holes in my house. Those bullet holes remind me every day to be careful. It's like that in a lot of places. Everybody in my family knows the drill. You hear gunshots, you hit the floor."

"Maybe you should move," I said.

"Nope, not me," she replied. "That's what they want me to do. That's part of the problem. They want us to move. People are selling their houses cheap, and white people are snapping them up. Then, because it will be mostly white, the neighborhood is going to change, and things are going to get better. Next thing you know, you'll see white women jogging, pushing a stroller with a Labradoodle running on the side. Nope. I'm not selling my house. I'm going to get through it."

Later, I would slide into the back seat of another ride-share, this time with Martin, an African-American man in his mid-40s. I had just concluded an appointment on 79th Street on Chicago's South Side and was heading back downtown. Martin wore eyeglasses and sported a thick black beard. A black wool cap was pulled down over his ears against the cold. We headed north on the Dan Ryan Expressway, and just before the turn down the Stevenson Expressway toward the city's famous Lakeshore Drive, Martin got talkative. When he's not working this job, Martin told me, he is a bus driver for the Chicago Transit Authority. The agency operates all the city's rapid transit. Martin brushes up against the city's danger in both jobs. As a ride-share driver, he hears the gunshots often as he ferries people through the city's 77 neighborhoods. They are discomforting, but he's not afraid. He *is* fearful when he drives the bus.

"When you're driving a bus, you don't know what to expect," he said. "All kinds of people are on the bus—kids, old people, gang members,

professional people, crooks. They get on the bus, they are cussing, hol-
lering, mad. We don't have metal detectors. So, someone could be carrying a gun. I don't know. I can look at them and think I know, but I don't.
So, I have to be careful.

"I have to watch the road and watch the inside of the bus at the same
time. I've got to watch my back. Right now, it's so crazy. If a person gets
on the bus and doesn't put in the fare, if I ask them and they still don't
pay the fare, I'm not going to ask them again. I'm going to let it go,
because I don't know what's going on. I don't know who I'm talking to,
and I'm not trying to get shot."

Another ride-sharing driver, Carlos, picked me up late at night when
I needed a ride from a location on 87th Street. Carlos was in his 40s,
balding with eyeglasses. He looked like a college professor but worked
during the day as a state social worker. For him, the problems that plague
Chicago's poor children are immediate—overburdened, underemployed
parents; limited child health care; nearly nonexistent mental health care;
parental abuse and neglect; abandonment; foster homes; uneducated
children; high dropout rates; juvenile delinquency; drugs; and gangs.

I was coming from The Rink Fitness Factory, a Chicago landmark
known to locals as The Rink on 87th Street. I went there to see what my
friend Saletta said would be a uniquely Chicago experience and to speak
to some longtime Chicago residents. Saletta had managed a rival skating
rink on 76th Street when she lived there. She'd moved to Chicago from
northern California and moved away three years later.

"My daughter was born in July and I moved the next May, because
the shootings increase in the summer and I didn't want to be around for
that," she said adamantly. "That's not a place where I want to raise my
child. It's too hard. I don't want to have to be conscious of every step
I take all the time. I have a friend, I actually hired him to work with
me at the rink. He says in the summer, he sleeps on the floor because
they shoot in the alley behind his apartment and he's afraid of a bullet

coming through the window. So, he moved his mattress to the floor, so a bullet wouldn't come through the window and hit him."

I had heard a similar story before I ever made it to Chicago. In preparation for the trip, I had reached out to Dimitri Roberts, a CNN contributor. Roberts had also been a police officer in Chicago. We'd never met or appeared together, but I thought I'd touch base with him to get some advice on who to talk with and what to look for while I was in his hometown. Roberts told me a story about what forced him out of Chicago.

"As you know, being a cop can be dangerous, but you get used to certain things. You're around a lot of things—poverty, drugs, people who are mad and depressed and confused. You learn how to calm yourself in the middle of craziness. Anyway, I was in my apartment one night washing dishes after dinner. My daughter was helping Daddy; she was about 8 then. We lived in the Bronzeville neighborhood. We're washing dishes and talking and suddenly I hear gunshots in the distance. *Pop...pop, pop, pop, pop.* I turned and my daughter was on the floor. Her friends had told her to hit the floor when she heard gunshots. It was at that moment that I decided to move out of Chicago."

Saletta was right. The Rink was unique. It was adult skate night, and hundreds of black men and women in their 40s, 50s, 60s, and even in their 70s, bounced and danced on roller skates to R&B and funk from across the ages—James Brown, New Jack Swing, Little Anthony and the Imperials, Michael Jackson, and Diana Ross and the Supremes. The manager of the rink said it's not unusual to see 300 people there at 10 a.m. on a weekday, showing off their skating moves as they glide across the expansive wooden floor. They may be third- and fourth-shift postal workers; Chicago Transit drivers; schoolteachers; college professors; hospital workers, from the nurses to the nutritionists to the janitors; Drug Enforcement Administration agents.

Tim is an aircraft mechanic for a major airline. He has achieved it all—nice car, family, and house. He earns twice the annual salary of most people in Chicago. As a kid, he and his friends spent most weekends at this roller rink. It was their weekend refuge. It kept them safe from the pitfalls that awaited black boys and teenagers in Chicago's streets. Skating has since become a tradition—recreation and exercise. The problems on the street that he was trying to avoid as a youth still exist, he said, and, in some ways, he is still running from them. Tim and his girlfriend had recently sent their 13-year-old daughter to live with relatives in Florida. Tim told me he didn't want her to become another Hadiya Pendleton.

Hadiya Pendleton was an honors student at Dr. Martin Luther King Jr. College Preparatory High School. She played on the school volleyball team and was a majorette in the marching band.

On January 29, 2013, she and her friends, all honors students, gathered in a nearby park after school exams. Hadiya had returned to Chicago from Washington, D.C., just a week earlier, after performing in the second presidential inaugural parade for one of her heroes, Barack Obama. Smart, driven, and talented, Hadiya appeared headed for a life of promise.

When it began to rain, she and her friends huddled under a shelter. As they stood there laughing, joking, and gossiping, a teenager jumped a fence and ran toward the group, firing. The shooter then jumped into a car and sped off. Police later arrested Michael Ward, 18, and Kenneth Williams, 20, as they were heading to a strip club. They told officers it was a mistake. They thought Pendleton and her friends were members of a rival gang. Pendleton was struck in the back and died on the scene. She was 15 years old. Tim said he didn't want his daughter to go out like that.

It was seriously cold, maybe 18 degrees, when I stepped outside of the rink for my ride back to the hotel. Carlos was waiting for me. I confirmed that I was his passenger, and eased into the back seat. The warmth washed over me. Carlos and I were silent for a while. No banter, no music, no sound, except for the whir of the wheels along the highway as we sped north.

"You don't look like a skater," he said, though in truth, I could have fit right into the crowd.

"No, I'm here working on a book and talking to people about crime and police in Chicago," I said.

He didn't say anything. I was relieved. It was nearly midnight, the end of a long day, and I was talked out. The car got quiet again. Neither of us spoke for miles.

Then, for some reason, Carlos kind of blurted out, "It's bad out here, real bad." I could see a pensive look in the mirror. "I have been in neighborhoods to pick up people or to drop them off and I can hear people shooting. You can hear the gunfire, but you don't know where it's coming from. Everybody is a little scared. That's why some drivers won't go into certain neighborhoods. I go to them, but some guys won't."

"Why? They worried about being robbed?" I asked. "You guys don't carry cash. What are they going to steal?"

"It's not that so much," he said. "You don't want to get hit by a stray bullet, and people are so desperate—you just don't know."

I had had enough talk of fear and violence for one day. I didn't want to be callous, but I really didn't want to hear any more. I got quiet. He didn't speak. The silence returned. I leaned back and closed my eyes.

Few American cities exemplify the paradox of the strained yet interdependent relationship between police and communities of color as Chicago does. In Chicago, and other cities, police and their poorer black and brown communities maintain an anxious relationship in which residents most in need of police assistance request help, while simultaneously fearing which officers will show up and what kind of "help" they will receive.

Will they get the Chicago police officers who saved the life of a

9-year-old girl by performing the Heimlich maneuver after her grand-mother called to report that the child was choking on a toy truck she had swallowed? Or will they get the officers who shot and killed a 19-year-old, mentally ill Northern Illinois University student and, as police declared, "accidentally" shot the 55-year-old grandmother who lived next door after the student's father dialed 911 for help? Will they get the two Chicago officers who rescued eight people in response to shots fired in the notorious West Englewood neighborhood? Or will they get Chicago Police Officer Jason Van Dyke, who murdered Laquan McDonald?

The two entities—police and people of color—are distrustful of one another, defensive, and insular, yet remain uneasy partners in a struggle against the same problem—the assorted violence that plagues and confounds them.

Chicago has been awash in violent crime for years. A series of highly public mass gang shootings in one neighborhood led to the area being dubbed "Terror Town." In 2016, however, the city's rate of violence hit a 19-year high. That year, there were 762 murders, a 50 percent increase over the previous year, and 3,550 shooting incidents in which 4,331 people were shot.

Gang-related shootings account for just over half those shootings, but everybody knows the true culprits behind those frightening numbers are the grinding poverty and lack of opportunities that sap souls, suck the life out of already weary bones, and ultimately trigger crime. The police, public officials, and residents told me the real bad guys are high unemployment and low-wage jobs, broken families whose children drift into gangs for lack of other companionship and guidance, an educational system that doesn't educate and leaves high school dropouts and near-illiterates in its wake.

The combination has fueled an alternative economy of drug deals, robbery, and a pervasive gang culture—so broad that it can reach out and touch anybody and so vicious that members marched a 9-year-old into an alley and murdered him in retaliation against a rival gang member. It has given rise to boarded-up and abandoned buildings and economically barren neighborhoods, where residents shop at tiny corner markets where the merchandise and the merchants are secure behind Plexiglas walls for fear desperate shoppers will walk away with the chips or the dishwashing liquid or a jar of peanut butter.

In Chicago, the correlation between crime and poverty is clear and dramatic. In some cities, like Atlanta, quiet desperation and the associated criminality can be obscured by seemingly calm, tree-filled neighborhoods, divided by gently sloping streets. In Los Angeles, the near-constant warm weather and ubiquitous palm trees blur the reality of security bars on doors and windows, and neighbors fearful that some-one may walk away with all they own while they're away at a low-paying job. It says vacation, not crime.

Not Chicago.

Take the neighborhoods of Washington Park and Hyde Park. Each is adjacent to Washington Park on the city's South Side. They are sepa-rated east and west by the park's eight-block width. To the east is the Hyde Park community, an economically vibrant, racially mixed neigh-borhood. It is home to the University of Chicago and the Museum of Science and Industry. Stores and shops abound. Over on 53rd Street, there are fashionable eateries like Nando's, Chipotle, and Roti. A Star-bucks, a microbrewery, and a Baskin-Robbins also line the street, which is anchored by a Target. Atop Target is a new, 20-story apartment build-ing. Another new high-rise stands a block away on 51st Street. A Hyatt Hotel is close by. A short walk away you'll come upon a movie theater and an LA Fitness franchise. On nearby Hyde Park Boulevard you'll find a Whole Foods market, a Michaels store, and a Marshall's. On 55th Street are Medici and other boutique restaurants. On 57th Street is another Starbucks.

The median individual income for its 25,700 residents is $39,243, about $12,000 more than for the average city resident. Ninety-five percent of its residents have a high school diploma, unemployment is

7 percent, and about 15 percent of residents live below the poverty line, just a tick above the national average. Over the past 10 years, there have been 16 murders in Hyde Park.

Just to the west is the Washington Park neighborhood, a high-crime community stretched over 1.57 barren miles of abandoned buildings and little industry. There is the Grand Boulevard Plaza. Inside are Lim's Beauty Supply, bordered by MK Jewelry. Not far away are Wayne's Bar-B-Q and Cajun, Hair Experts, Boost, JJ Fish, and City Nails. Al's Italian Beef, the New Grand Chinese Kitchen, a check-cashing facility called Check Changers, Payless Shoes, Family Dollar, Liberty Tax Service, and Cricket. Hardly high-end.

The median income for Washington Park's 11,717 residents is $13,087, less than half of what the average Chicagoan earns. Unemployment is 23 percent; two of every five people officially live in poverty and nearly one in three residents does not have a high school diploma. Washington Park has racked up 71 murders over a decade, even though it has less than half the residents of Hyde Park.

The relationship between crime and poverty is obvious in all the city's tough neighborhoods. To the south is the troubled Englewood neighborhood, formerly home to NBA star Anthony Davis, superstar singer and actress Jennifer Hudson, renowned sculptor Richard Hunt, and magazine publisher Jamie Foster Brown and her journalist sister Stella Foster. Clearly, some people make it out. Most people, however, do not.

The average individual income in Englewood is $11,993. Forty-two percent of residents live in poverty; 21 percent are unemployed. There have been over 190 murders there in the past 10 years. In Fuller Park, the average individual income is $9,016. Fifty-six percent of residents live in poverty; 40 percent are unemployed, 34 percent have earned no high school diploma. Englewood has one of the highest murder rates in the nation.

Chicago's municipal leaders know the statistics. They recognize the correlation between poverty and crime. Like heads of police departments across the nation, Chicago Police Department Superintendent Eddie Johnson will tell you those disparities fuel the city's crime and violence. Society's failure to address core issues of education and unemployment makes his job that much more difficult.

"We can't just police our way out of this," Johnson told me. "In these impoverished neighborhoods, we have to invest in them and show them hope and give them a path to take care of themselves and their families. We have a program within the police department in which we identify would-be perpetrators of murders or the victims. We find them partners who can offer them resources. We get them training, housing, resources. Three out of five of these individuals take us up on the offer. When we are able to provide a guy who has been on the wrong side of the law a real opportunity, so they can find employment and get a paycheck, you talk about pride? I've seen it. It's a beautiful thing. I know, the majority of these guys want to get out. They take us up on it, so they can get out of that lifestyle."

Father Michael Pfleger, a Catholic priest, echoes this concern. Known among the people in his South Side neighborhood as "Father Mike," Pfleger is the spiritual leader of St. Sabina Church and a longtime community activist. His church is in the heart of a low-income black neighborhood on Chicago's South Side. A Chicago native, he has been working on issues of violence, economic and educational opportunities, health, crime, a faulty criminal justice system, and homelessness for over 40 years. He has led campaigns against the sale of drug paraphernalia, against billboards for alcohol and tobacco use that targeted children in black and brown neighborhoods, against music that glorified violence and disrespected women, against easy access to guns and their unrelenting violence.

Father Mike is unorthodox. He and his congregants once went out onto the streets and paid prostitutes for their time, so they could talk about how they could turn their lives around. He adopted and raised two black boys to give them a better life. He took in a third black boy, Jarvis

Franklin, as a foster child. Franklin was killed by gang crossfire in 1998 just a few blocks from Pfleger's church. Pfleger had just finished performing a wedding when people ran and told him about Jarvis. Pfleger held the boy's bloody head and prayed. Jarvis died a few days later.

I was scheduled to meet Pfleger at his church later in the week, but I was inadvertently introduced to him earlier. On my first night in Chicago, I was invited to attend a panel discussion not far from downtown for some of the city's business leaders. The question before the panel that night was how to turn the tide of Chicago's murders. Pfleger and other panel members were trying to convince people in the business community to offer real training and jobs to folks from the toughest neighborhoods, most with criminal backgrounds.

"Help us open doors for these young brothers and sisters to get opportunities," Pfleger pleaded before a crowd of about 100 men and women. "We need a job for them to go to. They feel like they are disposable, because they've been treated like they're disposable. We have whole communities that are not in post-traumatic stress, they're in present-traumatic stress. [They're] in communities where people are in trauma every single day because of poverty, because of violence, because of abandonment. The common thread is always double-digit unemployment, underperforming schools, lack of economic investment. . . .

"There is a tremendous lack of opportunities for youth. Our young men—people between the ages of 17 to 28—believe they are throwaways and have been treated like they've been thrown away. If you feel like nobody values you, then you believe you have no value and you act like your life has no value. . . . There was this African-American brother who had a summer job, and then the program ended, and I saw him on the corner selling drugs. I said, 'What are you doing?' He said, 'You know what I'm doing. I've gotta take care of my baby and my grandmother. If I could find a job, I would walk away from all this today.' If we could get 2,000 companies to just hire one of these guys, we could make a big difference."

Cities and business leaders have long heard that plea from community activists and the men and women in those poor communities. The response has mostly been either minimal investment or the promise to fix the core problems sometime in the future. Crime, however, is right now.

The death of Laquan McDonald is a metaphor for Chicago's and America's neglect of its most vulnerable population and its refusal to prioritize its resources to help them. Like too many young black and Latino males, McDonald was born into a world of poverty, dysfunction, and neglect. He was shuttled among five homes in the first five years of his life. He was abused and neglected so much that, by the age of 11, he confessed, he turned to daily marijuana use, because it kept him calm, he told a juvenile court clinician. Smoking marijuana helped him suppress the anger, the feelings of abandonment, and allowed him to "keep a smile on my face," he'd said. By age 13, he had been placed in hospitals for psychiatric treatment three times and diagnosed with post-traumatic stress disorder and other serious conditions. He admitted that he had no coping skills, so to hide from the real word, he used drugs, instead of the medication prescribed him. "I like how high I be," he told one counselor. "Everything be funny."

McDonald was born in September 1997, the child of an unwed 15-year-old mother and an absentee father. His mother had been taken into protective custody months earlier because of her guardian's drug use. So, McDonald was born a second-generation ward of the state. He was taken from his mother at age 3 just before Christmas 2000 by the Illinois Department of Children and Family Services because, agency reports said, his mother didn't provide him with proper supervision. Officials noted burns on his 8-month-old sister that the agency said happened because his mother was high at the time. He and his sister were moved into the home of his great-grandmother, Goldie Hunter.

Hunter was a retired laborer and widow with a seventh-grade education. She lived on Chicago's rough-and-tumble West Side in a six-bedroom, subsidized house in the 1100 block of North Laramie Street, in Chicago's Austin neighborhood. Goldie Hunter was the matriarch of the family. She managed to care for and help raise at least 12 children, some of them her own and some the children of others, including McDonald's mother, Tina Hunter. Two years later, McDonald was returned to his mother, but it was soon clear that something was wrong. According to a March 2003 day-care report, "Laquan was punching and hitting himself on the face." Three months later, McDonald returned to protective custody after reports that his mother's boyfriend was abusing him. The boy's bruises showed that the boyfriend was punching him and hitting him with a belt. A report noted that McDonald also said, "The boyfriend abused his mother." McDonald was returned to his great-grandmother, but before that, the state twice placed him in foster homes outside the family. McDonald said that during one of those placements he was beaten and sexually abused. He said he was whipped with an extension cord and barely fed in one foster home, according to one report. He returned to his great-grandmother at age 6 and remained with her until her death at age 78, on August 9, 2013.

McDonald, angry and confused, began getting in trouble as early as the fourth grade, when he threw a chair at a teacher and threatened to kill her. In 2011, he had 10 school suspensions and drifted into selling marijuana to support his habit. He also began an affiliation, he said, with two gangs—the New Breeds and the Four Corner Hustlers. "It was the hood I was in," he told a counselor two summers before his death. He said his childhood friends had joined gangs and it looked like they were "having fun." He told the counselor he got into a few gang-related fights with "sticks and bottles," but never a gun or a knife. By the time he was 10, it was clear that his great-grandmother couldn't keep up with him, and it wasn't long before police in his Austin neighborhood took notice.

His great-grandmother told court officials he would "normally get arrested two or three days a week." She did not believe the police were "picking on him," she said. In fact, she noted, officers let him go with several reprimands. Seven of his police arrests between 2012 and 2014 resulted in juvenile court cases, nearly all involving possession of small amounts of drugs. He was placed on long periods of intensive probation, often with electronic monitoring, mandatory school attendance, community service, outpatient mental health services, drug treatment, and in-home therapy. On his last marijuana arrest, he spent four months in juvenile detention before being released in May 2014. Just days before his 17th birthday and a month before his death, McDonald took the initiative to attend Sullivan House High School, a school for at-risk students and high school dropouts between the ages of 16 and 21. Instructors said he was apparently trying to turn his life around. He was quick to smile and hug his teachers, school officials said, and he regularly made A's and B's. Most importantly, he never got into any trouble there, they said. On October 24, he was scheduled for a hearing, and, with a good report, might be released from probation.

Instead, shortly before 10 p.m. on October 20, 2014, police were called to investigate reports of a man carrying a knife at 4100 South Pulaski Road. It was McDonald. The caller said the man had been breaking into vehicles in a trucking yard at 41st Street and Kildare Avenue. When officers arrived on the scene, they confronted McDonald. Police said he used a knife with a three-inch blade to slice the tire on a patrol vehicle and damage its windshield. McDonald walked away from police after numerous verbal instructions from the officers to drop the knife. At that point, responding officers requested taser backup, according to radio recordings. The police may have suspected what was ultimately proven in the autopsy: McDonald had taken PCP, a powerful hallucinogen.

PCP, according to Drugs.com, "often causes users to feel detached, distant, and estranged from their surroundings. Numbness of the extremities, slurred speech, and loss of coordination may be accompanied by a sense of strength and invulnerability. A blank stare, rapid and involuntary eye movements, and an exaggerated gait are among the more observable effects. Auditory hallucinations, image distortion, severe mood disorders, and amnesia may also occur. In some users, PCP may cause acute anxiety and a feeling of impending doom; in others, paranoia and violent hostility, and in some, it may produce a psychosis indistinguishable from schizophrenia. Many believe PCP to be one of the most dangerous drugs of abuse." Let me just tell you this: PCP is a cop's worst nightmare. I wrestled with more suspects on PCP than I care to recall. One is too many. They are impervious to pain and have super-human strength. It's dangerous, and the best strategy is to steer clear of PCP users until adequate backup reaches the scene. The officers were wise to give McDonald a wide berth.

Other patrol cars and several officers were already on the scene when Jason Van Dyke and his partner, Joseph Walsh, arrived in a police cruiser. So far, none of the officers had unholstered their guns. None feared for their life. Walsh and Van Dyke exited their vehicle, guns drawn, and within 10 seconds, Van Dyke began firing at McDonald. McDonald was at least 10 feet away from him. Van Dyke's first shot spun McDonald to the ground. He lay there and never made another move. Van Dyke then proceeded to fire 15 more shots over 15 seconds until his 9mm semiautomatic pistol was empty. Count it off: *1 Mississippi, 2 Mississippi, 3 Mississippi, 4 Mississippi, 5 Mississippi, 6 Mississippi, 7 Mississippi, 8 Mississippi, 9 Mississippi, 10 Mississippi, 11 Mississippi, 12 Mississippi, 13 Mississippi, 14 Mississippi, 15 Mississippi.*

When it was over, the first responding officer said that he did not see the need to use force. No other officers fired their weapons. Walsh and Van Dyke were the only officers to pull their guns. McDonald was taken to Mount Sinai Hospital, where he was pronounced dead at 10:42 p.m. His death marked the end of a brief, troubled life, and the beginning of a city's lesson into the depths that police and public officials would go to hide the truth behind his murder.

10.

THE COVER-UP

Initially, Laquan McDonald's death was hardly a blip on the radar screen of the Chicago Police Department and most residents of the city. And why would it be? Chicago's police department had been synonymous with racism, brutality, and corruption for so long that few current residents can remember when there wasn't a police scandal. By the late 1950s, police officers' practice of collecting bribes from motorists and pedestrians, and "presents" and other "gifts" from retail merchants around Christmas, had gone on so long that Chicago residents had come to expect this from their officers. A friend told me that when he attended Northwestern University in the late 1960s, everyone knew, if you were driving into the city, to wrap a $20 bill, bribe money, around your driver's license in case a Chicago cop stopped you.

Still, Chicagoans were surprised to learn in 1960 that several of their officers were helping a professional burglar sneak into and rob homes of wealthy North Side residents during what became known as the Summerdale Scandal. The eight officers acted as lookouts for burglar Richard Morrison during the break-ins and helped haul away the loot in their squad cars. Ironically, it was the cops' idea to forge the partnership. Morrison said that when they approached him with the proposition, they told him, "We like nice things, too."

1970s and 1980s

Those offenses were minuscule affairs compared to the crimes Chicago cop Jon Burge and others committed, starting 12 years later. From 1972 to 1991, Burge, a Chicago police detective, and other officers whose help he enlisted, tortured hundreds of African-American and Latino men accused of crimes until they gave false confessions. Scores of his victims went to prison, including at least four men who were sentenced to death. Burge and the officers used vicious beatings, Russian roulette, and other violent methods. They burned suspects with radiators and cigarettes and shocked their testicles with electric cattle prods to coerce confessions. When the extent of their crimes began to be revealed years later, then–Illinois Governor George Ryan in 2000 declared a moratorium on all executions in the state, because it was unclear whether many of the black men on death row were there because they were guilty or because Chicago police had tortured them into giving false confessions. Ryan later pardoned four of Burge's victims on death row and commuted the sentences of 167 inmates slated to be executed.

Burge and his men acted with impunity. City officials, police, and prosecutors all knew by the mid-1970s of Burge's torture tactics, but they were allowed to continue until he was fired in 1993. Ironically, Burge was never tried in court for torture because the statute of limitations had expired. Instead, he was convicted in 2010 on charges of obstruction of justice and perjury in relation to testimony in a 1989 civil suit against him for damages for alleged torture. He was sentenced to four and a half years in federal prison on January 21, 2011, and was out in October of that year.

The case of Andrew Wilson is just one example of what happened during Burge's reign of terror. In 1982, Wilson was arrested on a February morning for the murder of two police officers. At the end of the day, he was taken by police and admitted to Mercy Hospital and Medical Center with lacerations on various parts of his head, including his face, chest bruises, and thigh burns. More than a dozen injuries were documented as having been caused while Wilson was in police custody. A doctor who saw Wilson sent a memo to Richard M. Daley, then the prosecuting attorney for Chicago and surrounding Cook County. He asked Daley's office to investigate what he saw as a clear case of police brutality.

"I examined Mr. Andrew Wilson on Feb. 15 & 16, 1982," the doctor wrote. "He had multiple bruises, swellings and abrasions on his face and head. His right eye was battered and had a superficial laceration. Andrew Wilson had several linear blisters on his right thigh, right cheek and anterior chest which were consistent with radiator burns. He stated he'd been cuffed to a radiator and pushed into it. He also stated that electrical shocks had been administered to his gums, lips and genitals. All these injuries occurred prior to his arrival at the jail. There must be a thorough investigation of this alleged brutality."

Daley, son of the former longtime mayor Richard J. Daley, would be elected the 43rd and longest-serving mayor in Chicago's history; he ignored the doctor's report. Instead, Daley's prosecutors convicted Wilson and his brother, Jackie, of the murders, and Andrew Wilson was sentenced to death. In 1987, the Illinois Supreme Court overturned the convictions, ruling that Wilson was forced to confess involuntarily after being beaten by police. An internal police report that had been suppressed for years revealed an earlier police review that found criminal suspects were subjected to systematic brutality by Burge and his men at headquarters for 12 years, and that their commanders had knowledge of the abuses.

Scores of people came forward to tell of their torture at the hands of Burge and other police officers. Gregory Banks filed a civil suit in 1991 for $16 million in damages against Burge, three other cops, and the city of Chicago. He said he had falsely confessed to murder in 1983 after he was tortured by officers who placed a plastic bag over his head and put a gun in his mouth. While he was being tortured, he said, he saw 11 other men being beaten, burned, and getting electric shocks. Marcus Wiggins filed a lawsuit against Burge and the city, alleging that, when he was 13, he had been subjected to electric shock and forced to give a false confession. Another lawsuit described 23 incidents against black and Latino suspects between 1972 and 1985, and more than 150 Illinois state prisoners filed suit against the city, saying Burge had tortured them as well into making false confessions.

Legal wrangling and fallout from the Burge scandal continued until 2015. Ultimately, the city paid more than $57 million to his victims and spent another $50 million on defense of the officers.

1990s

Through the years, cases of police corruption continued unabated. In 1996, seven officers from the Austin District on Chicago's West Side were charged with shaking down drug dealers for cash and narcotics. A year later, three cops in the Auburn Gresham District were charged with similar offenses, and the police superintendent resigned after it was discovered that, in violation of department rules, he was buddies with a convicted felon.

In a case that would lay bare the city's underlying bias, police charged two African-American boys, ages 7 and 8, with the rape and murder of an 11-year-old girl, Ryan Harris. It was 1998. Police claimed the boys had confessed to striking her with a rock, then raping her with a tubular object and suffocating her with her underwear by stuffing it in her mouth. The boys, and, by extension, their parents and Chicago's mostly black South Side communities were vilified by prosecutors, police, and politicians as "depraved" and "monsters." A month after their arrest, however, police found semen on the girl's underwear. They couldn't have done it. Boys aged 7 and 8 don't produce semen. The real murderer was a man named Floyd Durr, a sexual predator who had preyed on girls and teenagers in the area. He pleaded guilty and received a life sentence, plus 30 years. Prosecutors said his IQ was so low he was not eligible for the death penalty.

The following year, an unarmed black man and an unarmed black woman were shot and killed by police in the same week in separate and suspicious incidents. What was so striking was not the circumstances, but who they were in the community. Robert Russ was an honors student and a star football player for prestigious Northwestern University in nearby Evanston, Illinois. LaTanya Haggerty was a 26-year-old computer analyst. Russ was 22 years old and two weeks from graduation when he was shot. He had been chased by police and his car had come to a stop. He was unarmed inside the vehicle. A Chicago jury awarded Russ's 4-year-old son $9.6 million after finding that the officer who shot him acted "willfully and wantonly" in causing his death.

Following a high-speed chase of a car in which Haggerty was a passenger, she was shot by a female officer who said she saw an object in the car that appeared to be a gun. There was no gun. According to the department's investigation, the officers ignored a sergeant's order to end the high-speed chase. The officers failed to get immediate medical help for Haggerty after she was shot. Three officers fired their guns without justification, the department said, and three officers gave false information to investigators about the incident. Haggerty's family was awarded $18 million.

2000s

The number of cases of corruption and malfeasance against Chicago's cops picked up in 2001. In April of that year, Chicago police officer Joseph Miedzianowski was convicted of racketeering and conspiracy to distribute drugs. He was later sentenced to life without the possibility of parole. Miedzianowski used his position as head of the Chicago

Gangs Unit for most of his 22 years on the force to organize four different gangs in the Humboldt Park neighborhood and begin trafficking in crack cocaine. He shook down rival drug dealers while using his contacts to provide protection and reveal the identities of undercover police officers to gang members. In all, 24 people were convicted with him, including the leaders of the four street gangs, Miedzianowski's mistress, and his former police partner.

Six months after Miedzianowski was convicted, Chicago Police Deputy Superintendent William Hanhardt, one of the highest-ranking officers in the police department, pleaded guilty to running a nationwide jewel-theft ring. For over 20 years, he and his gang stole over $5 million in diamonds and other gems. Hanhardt, a member of the department for 33 years, was sentenced to 12 years in federal prison. Two months later, Chicago Police Sergeant Eddie Hicks was dragged into court and indicted for operating a gang that included another Chicago police sergeant and two civilian members of the police department. They raided known drug houses and took the money and drugs. They kept the cash and resold the drugs to other dealers.

During their capers, Hicks and his accomplices used counterfeit police department badges, phony search warrants, unmarked cars from the police department, and license plates from other police cars. When they finished a heist, they would return to the police station at 51st Street and Wentworth and divvy up the spoils. Hicks was awaiting trial after fleeing and being recaptured in 2017.

In 2007, the Chicago Police Department was engulfed in scandal after a surveillance camera at a local bar recorded drunken, off-duty police officer Anthony Abbate savagely beating female bartender Karolina Obrycka. Obrycka sued Abbate for assault and the city's police for attempting to cover up the attack. Initially, Chicago police officers ignored the tape's existence and failed to mention in their police report that Abbate was a city cop. Additionally, Obrycka's attorney presented evidence, including hundreds of phone calls between Abbate and other cops in the hours after the incident in which they plotted to cover up the attack. Abbate was eventually found guilty of felony battery and lost his job. He was sentenced to two years of probation and anger management classes. In 2012, a federal grand jury sided with Obrycka and said the Chicago Police Department had tried to cover up his crime and awarded her $850,000.

In the most recent case, Cook County prosecutors threw out the convictions of 15 African-American men in November 2017 in the first mass exoneration in the history of Chicago's courts. The men had been framed on a plethora of phony charges by a group of drug-dealing Chicago cops led by a name infamous in African-American neighbor-hoods on the city's South Side, Sergeant Ronald Watts. Convictions of five other people had been thrown out the previous day, bringing to 20 the total number of black men cleared of wrongful convictions. Two of the men had spent more than 27 years in prison for murders they didn't commit.

For years, Watts had been forcing residents and drug dealers in one South Chicago neighborhood to pay him "protection" money. If they didn't, he would concoct bogus cases against them and send them to prison. Residents complained to the police department and in court, but judges, prosecutors, and police Internal Affairs investigators all believed the testimony of Watts and his corrupt cops. Watts was finally caught when he tried to rob a federal agent acting as a drug courier. The arrest resulted in a relatively minor charge and Watts, the man who had sent scores of men to prison for hundreds of years on phony charges, was sentenced to a mere 22 months in custody. He was out years before his victims were exonerated. Attorneys estimate there may be as many as 500 convictions tainted by Watts. Ironically, seven of the officers who allegedly framed the men with Watts were still on the department and working the streets on the day the men's cases were thrown out.

Even with such a long history of police malfeasance and racism, the shooting of Laquan McDonald would ultimately stun even the most hardened Chicago residents. Initially, there was no reason to believe that McDonald's death wouldn't be business as usual for the city. Chicago police were known for shooting people. From 2010 to 2014, they shot and killed 70 suspects, more than any other city in the nation. Overall, they shot 242 people during that period, an average of nearly one every week. It seemed unlikely that officers would be charged criminally in the McDonald case, based on the city's history. Chicago's Independent Police Review Authority, which had been set up in 2007 to provide a firmer hand in resolving police use-of-force cases, had investigated more than 400 police shootings by 2015—fatal and nonfatal shootings. Every shooting except for two was ruled justified, including the shooting of Calvin Cross.

Cross and a friend, Ryan Cornell, were two blocks from Cross's house in the West Pullman neighborhood in 2011 when a police cruiser slowed nearby. Cross had just returned to Chicago from a Job Corps work assignment in southern Illinois, where he had earned a certificate for bricklaying. He had signed up for the Job Corps program, his mother said, because he had learned that his girlfriend was pregnant with a boy, and he needed a skill to support them. The officers in the cruiser—Mohammed Ali, Macario Chavez, and Matilde Ocampo—were members of the Mobile Strike Force Unit, charged with making gun and drug arrests in high-crime areas.

The officers claimed in their report after the incident that they stopped Cross because they saw him "making movements with his hands and body" that suggested he had a gun. The officers ordered Cross and Cornell to show their hands. Cornell, who had been stopped numerous times by the police, did. Cross started walking faster and then bolted across a field. In their final report, two of the officers said that Cross fired three shots as he broke into a sprint. "I saw him bring the weapon towards us," one of the officers said later, "and I saw a muzzle light, shooting out at least three times." That was impossible. Cross didn't have a gun. A six-cylinder Smith & Wesson revolver was found more than 30 feet away from his dead body, but it was fully loaded. It had not been fired. In fact, it couldn't have been fired. It was so caked with dirt and grime, an Illinois State Police lab said, that it was inoperable. Additionally, there were no fingerprints on the gun, and Cross had no gunpowder residue on his hands. The only shell casings found at the scene belonged to the police officers.

When Cross ran, Chavez opened fire with the department-issued assault rifle he kept strapped to his chest. Ocampo let loose with his 9mm pistol, as did Ali. When they did, it was clear in that moment that Cross's black life did not matter.

There was another way to take him into custody without taking his life. He was running away, so he wasn't a threat. His friend, who knew his family and where he lived, was already in custody. Cross could have been apprehended that night or the next morning. Nor did the officers care about other black lives in the neighborhood as their torrent of gunfire tore into trees and parked cars, and, fortunately, no people.

Cross's mother heard the shooting from inside her home and wondered what was going on. She had no idea her 19-year-old son was being killed by police. The officers stopped shooting for a moment and found a wounded Cross lying among bushes in a vacant lot. When he moved slightly but failed to show his hands, the police said, Chavez fired three more times with his assault rifle, emptying his clip with shots 26, 27, and 28. Chavez then switched to his 9mm Beretta and fired three more times. Ali also reloaded and fired at Cross as he lay prone. In all, the three officers fired 45 times. The medical examiner reported that the shot that killed Cross struck him in the face, between his nose and his right eye. After examining all the facts in the incident, the Independent Police Review Authority's investigation concluded that the officers were justified in killing Cross, because "the officers were reasonable in their fear" that Cross "posed a threat."

There was no reason to believe that what happened in the Cross shooting wouldn't be repeated in the death of Laquan McDonald. But there was something quirky about the McDonald shooting almost from the start. The official story of the shooting that night, first by the police officers' union representative and in further official police department reports and explanations, was that Van Dyke fired after McDonald, brandishing his knife, lunged at Van Dyke. The officer then fired in self-defense, police said. According to the official report, Van Dyke told investigators, "[McDonald] was swinging the knife in an aggressive, exaggerated manner." Van Dyke ordered McDonald to "drop the knife" multiple times. McDonald ignored Van Dyke's verbal instruction to drop the knife and continued to advance toward Van Dyke. When McDonald got to within 15 feet of Van Dyke, McDonald looked toward Van Dyke. McDonald raised the knife across his chest and over his shoulder, pointing the knife at Van Dyke.

According to the police's internal investigation report, "Van Dyke believed McDonald was attacking Van Dyke with the knife and attempting to kill Van Dyke. In defense of his life, Van Dyke backpedaled and fired his handgun at McDonald to stop the attack. McDonald fell to the ground, but continued to move and continued to grasp the knife, refusing to let go of it. Van Dyke continued to fire his weapon at McDonald as McDonald was on the ground as McDonald appeared to be attempting to get up, all while continuing to point the knife at Van Dyke. The slide on Van Dyke's pistol locked in the rearward position, indicating the weapon was empty. Van Dyke performed a tactical reload of his pistol with a new magazine and then assessed the situation. McDonald was no longer moving, and the threat had been mitigated."

Van Dyke's partner, Joseph Walsh, repeated the story in his statement to investigators. "When McDonald got to within 12 to 15 feet of the officers," Walsh said, "he swung the knife toward the officers in an aggressive manner...Van Dyke continued firing his weapon at McDonald. McDonald continued moving on the ground, attempting to get up, while still armed with the knife." Officer Daphne Sebastian said she "heard the officers repeatedly order McDonald to 'Drop the knife!'

McDonald ignored the verbal directions and continued to advance on the officers, waving the knife." Officer Janet Mondragon said, "McDonald got closer and closer to the officers, continuing to wave the knife." Officer Arturo Becerra said "as he approached the scene of this incident, he observed a black male subject, now known as Laquan McDonald, in the middle of the street, flailing his arms."

Officer Dora Fontaine said, "McDonald ignored the verbal direction and, instead, raised his right arm toward officer Van Dyke, as if attacking Van Dyke." Officer Ricardo Viramontes said he "heard Officer Jason Van Dyke repeatedly order McDonald to 'Drop the knife!' McDonald ignored the verbal direction and turned toward Van Dyke and his partner, Officer Joseph Walsh. At this time, Van Dyke fired multiple shots from his handgun. McDonald fell to the ground but continued to move, attempting to get back up, with the knife still in his hand. Van Dyke fired his weapon at McDonald continuously, until McDonald was no longer moving." The officers said that, at most, Van Dyke fired seven or eight shots. The official police statement said McDonald was struck once in the chest.

If all their statements were true, many wondered, why did the city offer McDonald's mother and his 15-year-old sister $5 million just six months after his death? Yes, a settlement was in line with the city's normal procedure. Chicago had spent more than $500 million settling wrongful death and police abuse cases filed against the police since 2004, the vast majority of which the department ruled as justified. But city attorneys had taken the unusual step of offering the family money before the family's attorneys had even filed a lawsuit. And why did the 47-member Chicago City Council, with Mayor Rahm Emanuel presiding, unanimously approve the payment in a mere 36 seconds without a single word of public discussion or debate?

The answer was simple: Because the city council, the police department, and a handful of other city officials knew the real story. They knew how damaging the police officer's dashcam footage of the event was, showing what had really happened that night. Whether they had seen the video or just been briefed about it, as the mayor said he was before he proffered the settlement, they knew it exposed the previous descriptions of McDonald's death as egregious lies. So, they remained quiet and rubber-stamped the settlement, and by their silence and approval of hush money to McDonald's mother and sister, they had become participants in a cover-up to keep the truth hidden from the people of Chicago. Bit by bit, however, the tale police had woven, and city officials had tried to keep from becoming public, began to unravel. Its undoing began a little over two weeks after McDonald's death.

On November 7, 2014, McDonald's mother, Tina Hunter, hired attorneys Jeffrey J. Neslund and Michael D. Robbins to investigate her son's death. Neslund and Robbins were already handling the case of two African-American brothers and their sister who had been wounded by a Chicago cop who fired 11 shots into their back door on New Year's Day at the beginning of the year. Robbins claimed that Hunter heard about his firm "by word of mouth," but that is highly unlikely. It's more probable that someone the attorneys knew sought her out and set up the meeting. Hunter signed an agreement to give the attorneys 40 percent of any settlement or judgment they obtained for her.

Initially, Robbins was skeptical: "I didn't think there was a case, if he had lunged at a police officer," the attorney said. Neslund issued subpoenas to the police department for all police videos, reports, and all records and audio dispatches related to the shooting. Once the materials started coming in, Robbins said, "We knew there was something wrong with the official explanation." First, the attorneys saw the autopsy report. McDonald hadn't been hit once by the seven or eight shots police on the scene said he fired. Instead, McDonald's body was riddled with 16 bullets. He had been shot in the left neck, the left chest, the right chest, the back of his left elbow, the back of his right arm, his left wrist, the front of his right hip, the rear of his left shoulder, the rear of his left elbow, his right shoulder, the back of his right arm, the back of his right wrist, the back of his right hand, his right buttocks, the back of his right thigh, and there was a graze wound on the top of his head.

By December, the media began talking to each other of a possible police dashcam video of the shooting. Chicago police officers are required by department regulation to turn on the cameras on their dashboard for such stops. The same month, Mayor Rahm Emanuel's administration knew the shooting could pose a problem. On December 8, Scott Ando, then the head of the Independent Police Review Authority, sent an email to Janey Rountree, deputy chief of staff for public safety, linking to a press release in which two local watchdogs suggested video might contradict the police union's claims that the officer's life was in danger. By the beginning of 2015, rumors of what was in the police reports and on the video began to filter out of the police department. Craig Futterman, a University of Chicago law professor who studies police accountability, said he was tipped off about the existence of a video from a source inside the department. He said his source told him, "This is really horrific. This looked to at least some people in the department that it may be an execution. That people hadn't seen anything like this, and that there was a videotape of what occurred—that video of the shooting was caught on police in-car cameras, and that those videos would show the truth. That there was a situation that appeared to be under control, and there wasn't any immediate risk of human life, and that an officer then just got out of his car and shot Laquan when he was cornered between a construction fence in a pretty deserted area, and then after being on the ground the same officer unloaded his gun multiple times."

In February 2015, activist and writer Jamie Kalven wrote the first article casting widespread doubt on the police account. Kalven, an author and freelance journalist, had received a copy of McDonald's autopsy and published an article in the online magazine *Slate*, confirming that McDonald had been shot 16 times. Meanwhile, Neslund and Robbins continued working behind the scenes to reach a settlement. On March 3, they requested the videos and other police records with a promise to keep the material confidential until the deal was finalized. They were pushing to bring the deal to a close. Based on what they already knew about what had happened, they believed Van Dyke could be indicted at any minute. A criminal case could delay for years any settlement the family might get in the future.

Three days later, Neslund and Robbins sent a letter to the city outlining the reason the city needed to pay McDonald's family. They made it clear that they now knew what the city and the police were hiding. Aside from the fact that McDonald was shot 16 times, they noted, "This horrific and shocking event was witnessed by a number of civilian witnesses as well as police officers. More importantly, the entire shooting was captured by the dashcam video of a responding unit…Contrary to the false statements the City allowed the [police union] spokesman to spin to the media, the dashcam confirms that Mr. McDonald did not 'lunge' toward the police. This case will undoubtedly bring a microscope of national attention to the shooting itself as well as the City's pattern, practice and procedures in rubber-stamping fatal police shootings of African-Americans as 'justified.' This particular shooting can be fairly characterized as a gratuitous execution as well as a hate crime." The lawyers argued that a public trial "would show a 'code of silence' to cover up wrongdoing in the police department. We hereby demand $16,000,000.00 to resolve all claims on behalf of the estate of Laquan McDonald," they wrote, $1 million for every bullet he took. The lawyers insisted on a response within seven days.

Ten days later, they met with city attorney Thomas Platt and City Hall's chief lawyer, Stephen Patton. As they negotiated on behalf of McDonald's mother and sister, Neslund and Robbins compared settlements in other police shootings, including the 2011 shooting of Flint Farmer, part of which was caught on video. Flint Farmer, 29, was unarmed when he was shot and killed by then-Officer Gildardo Sierra in June 2011. It was Sierra's second fatal shooting and third shooting. Sierra fired at Farmer 16 times, hitting him with seven shots, three of them in his back. Despite video suggesting that Sierra stood over Farmer as he shot him in the back, Cook County State's Attorney Anita Alvarez declined to charge Sierra criminally. She said the officer reasonably mistook a cell phone for a gun pointed at him on a dark South Side street. Even though Alvarez's office never bothered to question Sierra about the incident, she said she did not think her office could show that the shooting was unreasonable. Alvarez was still the state's attorney when McDonald was shot, and by now she had seen the video of the McDonald shooting, but had not brought charges. Farmer's family filed suit against the city and was awarded more than $4 million.

Neslund and Robbins also discussed the shooting of Rekia Boyd. Boyd, 22, was in an alley laughing and having fun with friends when Officer Dante Servin came out to complain about the noise. Servin, who was off duty, got into a heated argument with one of the men in the alley, pulled his weapon, and fired five shots into the crowd. He claimed he thought someone had pulled a gun. No one in the group was armed. Boyd was hit in the head and killed. Servin was found not guilty of involuntary manslaughter by Cook County Judge Dennis Porter in a bench trial. Boyd's family was awarded more than $4 million in a subsequent settlement.

The meeting ended and in a follow-up letter a few days later, Neslund and Robbins noted, "None of the cases discussed involve a graphic video which depicts, in vivid detail, a 17-year-old being shot multiple times as he lay helpless on the street."

In a letter to Platt dated March 23, 2015, Robbins reprimands city officials for sharing with the police department information in their letters and then goes on to say they have found that police falsified citizens' accounts of the shooting. "One witness whom the police reports alleged did not see the shooting in fact told multiple police officers that he saw the shooting, and it was 'like an execution,'" the attorney said.

"Civilian witnesses have told us that they were held against their will for hours, intensively questioned by detectives, during which they were repeatedly pressured by police to change their statements. When the witnesses refused to do so, the investigating officers simply fabricated civilian accounts in the reports." Robbins wrote that if the city won't settle soon, he and Neslund will sue. .

By April, the parties were close to an agreement. They swapped settlement proposals and Robbins objected to the city's requirement that the dashcam video be kept secret until criminal charges were concluded, if they were ever filed. The pace of the agreement quickened as Platt agreed to drop a section that said releasing records could interfere with the criminal investigation, but Robbins and Neslund, on a gentlemen's agreement, had no intention of releasing the video. On April 8, the city and McDonald's mother agreed on $5 million. Five days later, as the mayor's chief attorney, Patton urged the Chicago City Council Finance Committee to approve the deal. "Attorneys for the estate will argue that Mr. McDonald did not pose any immediate threat of death or great bodily harm to Officer A and that instead McDonald, as I mentioned before, was walking away from police when he was shot, and they will argue that the videotape supports their version of events," he said. "This is kind of a unique case where we had the original two officers who arrived at the scene follow Mr. McDonald for some number of blocks and manner of minutes and never saw fit to discharge their weapons."

Two days later, the full City Council approved the agreement 47–0. McDonald's mother, Tina Hunter, was to receive 45 percent of the money, $2.25 million, in monthly payments for 20 years. Her attorneys were to receive 40 percent of her share, $900,000. McDonald's sister was to get 55 percent of the settlement, $2.75 million, in monthly payments until 2060. Neslund and Robbins received a third of her share, $916,667. The nature of the McDonald settlement, the rumors about the shooting, and just plain sense signaled the media and anyone who had been paying attention that a police dashcam video existed of McDonald's death. The media, activists, and community leaders, particularly those in African-American communities, clamored for its release. The city's corporation counsel, Stephen Patton, refused. Instead, he promised to release the potentially incendiary video at the "appropriate time," but not while an "active federal and state criminal investigation" was ongoing.

In response, *Chicago Tribune* reporter Brandon Smith filed a Freedom of Information Act request with the police department in May, asking to see all video related to the shooting. He also asked the attorneys for McDonald's family to share with him the copy they had received from the police. They were under no legal obligation to keep it secret. They refused. Though it was not in writing, they had promised the city they wouldn't release it until the city had filed criminal charges. McDonald's mother, they said, supported their decision not to release the only true depiction of what happened the night her son was killed. The police department stonewalled Smith and the *Chicago Tribune* for months over the videotape before denying their request altogether on August 4. Smith and his newspaper filed a lawsuit for release of the video the next day. They ultimately received a court date, and attorneys for the city and for the *Tribune* made their arguments before Cook County Judge Franklin Valderrama. Valderrama had been appointed to his seat by the governor in 2007, then reappointed in 2011, and again in June 2014. He was widely respected as fair and impartial. As the courtroom drama played out, activists, civic leaders, and many Chicago residents grew increasingly impatient with State's Attorney Anita Alvarez. Alvarez, who had refused to indict cops in several other high-profile shootings, had failed to bring charges against Van Dyke, more than a year after the McDonald shooting. Even now, she continuously told the media, her office was still investigating McDonald's death.

Thursday, November 19, 2015, was unseasonably warm for usually frigid Chicago. Temperatures rose to 44 degrees and the sun was out most of the day. Usually by this time of the year, the city was blanketed with six inches of snow and locals were bundled under layers of clothing to protect themselves against the cold. Those in the media, the police department, and at City Hall awoke anxious that day. Judge Valderrama was scheduled to announce his decision on whether to order the city to release the police dashcam video. Mayor Rahm Emanuel and his administration had tried desperately to keep the video hidden. Emanuel had known what was on it for months. In private conversations, he called the shooting "profoundly hideous... It's a shock to your conscience of what happened, and it should not have happened." Still, he fought its release at every turn. He wanted the tape concealed for fear that it might damage his run for reelection. It could also hurt the court's ability to empanel an unbiased jury in any criminal trial. Possibly a bigger concern was the turmoil that could engulf the city once it got out. So far, he had succeeded in keeping it under wraps. On the day before the ruling, Emanuel and his staff were reading statements for release, whichever way the decision went. His staff carefully edited and reedited the text, looking for the most precise language. When the judged handed down his ruling that morning, an aide in the city's Law Department dashed off a hurried email to Emanuel's office. "We lost," it said.

Valderrama ordered the city to release the video by November 24, just two days before Thanksgiving. His announcement sent people across the city into a frenzy. The police department went on high alert. It began marshaling its forces. Plainclothes officers were asked to wear their uniforms to maintain a larger police presence on the street through the week of the video release. They began mapping out strategies for the demonstrations that were sure to come. Mayor Emanuel began reaching out to religious leaders, asking them to carry a message of nonviolence to their members and others. One of them was the Reverend Michael Pfleger of St. Sabina's, the prominent antiviolence activist on the South

Side. The mayor wondered if, when the video was released, Pfleger would be a voice for peace. Or would he call for civil disobedience?

"I never, ever, ever believe in violence being the response," Pfleger said. "Of course, I was going to call for peace. I'm a follower of Dr. [Martin Luther] King. I believe in the power of nonviolence. Civil disobedience, yes. But nonviolence. If we respond with violence, then we are no better than the perpetrators we're angry with. There should be no violence."

Community activist Andrew Holmes said he and other leaders also planned to spread a message of peace and keep riots from breaking out. Chicago should be an "example city," he said. Still, Pfleger and others did not back away from calling for protests. Pfleger urged his parish members during his homily the Sunday before the video release to lead the protest, drawing on the legacy of civil disobedience during the 1960s civil rights movement.

"If you really want to make a statement, Black Friday is coming up. The number one business day," he said. "Don't shop on Black Friday, and go down to Michigan Avenue and sit down in the street and block the street on Michigan Avenue with civil disobedience peacefully, and say, 'Business as usual can't go on while our children are dying.'"

With each day prior to the deadline for release of the video, the tension mounted, even as far away as the White House in Washington, D.C. On the weekend before the release, President Barack Obama's aides emailed Emanuel's staff to ask for more information on the case. Emanuel had served as Obama's chief of staff before running for mayor of Chicago. Elias Alcantara, the White House's senior associate director for intergovernmental affairs, sent an email that said, "We've been tracking the media coverage of the Laquan McDonald case and would like an update. Do any of you have a minute to jump on the phone and provide an update on the situation? Hoping to get an update to the team here later this afternoon."

"Yes," David Spielfogel responded. Spielfogel was Emanuel's senior adviser. "Can update you later when I'm out of meetings. Around 3 your time?" Melissa Green, the head of Emanuel's Washington office, followed up by noting that the chief of staff to Attorney General Loretta Lynch had also been briefed. Meanwhile, Emanuel's senior aides prepared the mayor for a Monday conference call with religious and community leaders, emails show. Various drafts of both the invitation and the script from which Emanuel would read during the call were sent around.

On Tuesday, November 24, Officer Van Dyke was charged with first-degree murder. Hours later, the city released the police dashcam video of the shooting. The timing of the charges confirmed the suspicions in the minds of many that the state's attorney had had no intention of filing charges, and only did so now that her hand was forced by the footage. I got a call from CNN shortly after the video was released. Producers sent me a copy of the video and asked me to analyze the contents for an upcoming show. I had not seen the video previously, but I had followed the accounts of what police said happened that night. When I saw the footage, I was stunned. I thought I had seen the worst when I saw the video of a North Charleston, South Carolina, police officer shoot a fleeing Walter Scott in the back after a traffic stop and then place a taser near his body. After seeing the McDonald dashcam video, I was angry, furious. Somebody needed to go to jail, and not just Van Dyke. I've been a use-of-force trainer with ATF and for numerous police departments, and, as I told my CNN anchor, this shooting was inconsistent with any use-of-force training standards that I had ever been exposed to.

The footage laid bare all the lies told by numerous police officers and their superiors about the incident. McDonald wasn't walking toward the police when he was shot. Instead, he was walking away from them. He was not swinging a knife wildly or flailing his arms. He did not raise his arm with the knife across his chest or point it toward Van Dyke. He didn't make any threatening moves toward Van Dyke. Van Dyke did not "fall back" and start shooting in fear for his life. No, McDonald didn't move to get up after he was shot. He didn't raise the knife toward Van Dyke. Instead the video showed that Van Dyke fired 6 seconds after getting out of his cruiser with his gun drawn and moving directly toward McDonald. It showed McDonald being shot and immediately collapsing onto the street. It showed that 14 seconds passed from the time Van Dyke fired the first shot to the final shot, and, for 13 of those seconds, McDonald was lying on the ground.

Mayor Emanuel gave a statement in response to the video.

"We hold our police officers to a high standard," he said. "Obviously, in this case, Jason Van Dyke violated both the standards of professionalism that comes with being a police officer, but also basic moral standards that bind our community together. Jason Van Dyke will be judged through the court of law. That's exactly how it should be."

Considering all that had transpired over the previous year, Emanuel's words rang hollow. The next day, demonstrators—black, white, Hispanic, young, old, Christians, Jews, Muslims, Buddhists, atheists, college students, high school dropouts, scientists, day laborers, college professors, fast food workers, lawyers, defendants, health care workers, janitors, business owners, and retail employees—poured into the streets. They blocked LaSalle Street in front of City Hall, demanding that Emanuel and the state's attorney resign and the police chief be fired. They lined up along Michigan Avenue, the city's "Magnificent Mile," and blocked traffic with chants, shouts, and raised clenched fists. Stunned shoppers and tourists gawked as the demonstrators lined downtown streets, armed with a sea of signs. Six women demonstrated together, each carrying a billboard with a lighted letter of McDonald's first name, L-A-Q-U-A-N. Other signs read, "Black Boys Matter," "Fire Rahm," "No More KKKiller Cops," "Justice for Laquan McDonald; Arrest Rahm Now," "Stop Police Terror," "16 Shots," and "I Am Laquan." Protestors locked arms and blocked traffic on Randolph Street, at Harrison and State streets, and at the intersection of Franklin Street and Wacker Drive. They waded onto a major freeway and temporarily halted startled motorists. Some unleashed their anger toward individual officers, cursing them and shouting angrily into their faces.

Twitter lit up:

Johnetta Elzie
I never thought I could see anything worse than the footage of Walter Scott's murder. I was very wrong.

Pej Vahdat
I'm absolutely disgusted. RIP #LaquanMcDonald my thoughts and prayers are with his family. But that does nothing. This has to stop.

Lauren Houston
If you do not have your eyes open and cannot see the police brutality and murders going on, then God help you.

Meira Gebel
Outraged, hurt and astounded at the news of the death of #Laquan-McDonald. Currently standing in solidarity with #Chicago and humanity...
    2:00 AM—Nov 25, 2015 Calabasas, CA

Andrea Zopp
I was a prosecutor for 13 years, this investigation did not need to take 13 months #LaquanMcDonald

Shaun King
Average investigation length when a police officer has been killed in 2015 before an arrest is made = 38 hours. #LaquanMcDonald = 400 days

Demonstrations, large and small, would continue for days that would stretch into months, into March 2016, and sporadically through the second anniversary of the shooting. The political fallout was immediate. A week after the video footage of the shooting was released, Emanuel fired Chicago Police Superintendent Garry McCarthy.

"At the end of the day, [city residents] didn't like the results, and somebody had to take the fall, and somebody had to take the hit," McCarthy would say later about his firing.

Five days later, then–US Attorney General Loretta Lynch announced that the Justice Department would launch an investigation into Chicago's policing. A week after the video's release, Emanuel announced the creation of the Task Force on Police Accountability. It would study the processes, oversight, and training at the police department, and make recommendations, he explained. A day later, Van Dyke was indicted on six counts of first-degree murder and one count of official misconduct. By then, Emanuel's approval ratings had plummeted into the teens. The state's attorney would ultimately be voted out of office.

By the end of 2015, many speculated that things could not get much worse for Chicago's residents and law enforcement. They were wrong. By this time the following year, the city would be ravaged by a wave of violence and murder nearly unprecedented in the city's history and residents' relationship with police, particularly among the African-Americans and Hispanics who needed them most, would be frayed almost beyond repair.

11.

DAMAGE CONTROL

Eddie Johnson, like every other officer in the Chicago Police Department, was watching anxiously to see who would be their next boss. Mayor Rahm Emanuel had thrown former Police Superintendent Garry McCarthy under the bus in the wake of the protests and demonstrations following the release of the Laquan McDonald video, the video that Emanuel had used all his powers to keep secret for over a year. With the video out, somebody had to go, and it was McCarthy. Now, the department needed a new leader. Johnson, a 27-year department veteran, had a little more at stake than most. He had been deputy chief in charge of all patrol units in the nation's second-largest police department for the past four years. A new superintendent might want his own person in that spot. So, Johnson nervously awaited the outcome with the rest of the department.

The first step in finding the new head of the department fell to the Chicago Police Board, nine people Emanuel had personally selected. It was their task to sift through 39 people nationwide who applied for the job and come up with a handful of the best candidates from which the mayor would select the top cop. For the next three months, they would conduct dozens of interviews and pore over hundreds of pages of essays and papers from candidates explaining their qualifications and their goals for the department. They carefully investigated the applicants' competence and character. John J. Escalante was serving in the first months of 2016 as the interim superintendent after McCarthy was dismissed. He applied for the permanent position, but was turned down. Johnson had been rooting for him to become the first Latino to head the department. It would be a difficult job, no matter who got it. Murders and violent crime had spiked dramatically and begun to wash over parts of the city. The cover-up and subsequent release of the video of the McDonald shooting had created a huge gulf between black and white Chicagoans and the police. In response, police had begun to hunker down, refusing, in some cases, cops said, to do their jobs.

The choice to head a police department is always contentious in large cities. It almost always comes down to this question: Does the city need more of the same or something new? Some want a chief who will maintain the status quo, a person with deep roots in the city who understands the city's unique communities and will ensure that the system continues to function largely as it has in the past. Others want a change agent, an outsider not bound by loyalties, who will institute new policies that will be fairer and more inclusive. No matter which desire prevails, the final choice inevitably will rankle some or all the city's constituencies.

African-Americans and Latinos want a leader who will bring more fairness to policing, who is sensitive to the challenges of the city's poorer neighborhoods, and who wants to end the historical animus and distrust that characterize the relationship between their communities and the police. White residents principally want to feel safe from crime. Issues of fairness, respect, and courtesy traditionally have not been a problem for them. They want a police department that is accessible and responsive, and will protect them from things that are dangerous, unfamiliar, and uncomfortable. Commercial and civic leaders want someone who understands the importance of protecting the city's business interests and the role police and crime rates play in the city's image as a place for businesses and families interested in relocating.

The Chicago Police Board announced its three finalists in March

2016 with a press conference at the public library named in honor of the city's former black mayor, Harold Washington. The media gathered, as did other stakeholders, academics, community activists, business leaders, politicians, and curious citizens. The board's members sat behind a banquet table covered by a black cloth, each identified by the white placards placed neatly in front of them. The board's president and a former federal prosecutor, Lori Lightfoot, made clear the group's priority as she addressed the audience.

"Things have to change from the inside out," she told the audience. "The next superintendent must demonstrate leadership in a way that welcomes and demands accountability. Accountability has to be the rule of the day for the Chicago Police Department, and that has to happen regardless of who is chosen as superintendent." Lightfoot and the other members noted all its candidates—two African-American men and a white woman—had handled police misconduct and police shooting incidents and were best equipped to rebuild the community's trust in the police department and fight crime.

It was an impressive bunch.

Eugene Williams, a deputy chief with the Chicago Police Department, was a 36-year department veteran and had been a finalist for the job in 2011. He commanded the bureau that oversaw training and accountability. Williams had worked his way up through the ranks. He had been a homicide detective, a beat officer, a narcotics and gang investigator, and had held various command posts for the past 15 years. He had served as chief of patrol, overseeing beat patrols in the department's 22 police districts. While he was head of the Austin patrol district on the West Side, the crime-ridden community where Laquan McDonald had lived, the area went six months without a homicide. He was considered a favorite among many African-American ministers in the city. Williams had made it clear that if he got the job, there would be change. He outlined how he had been instrumental in pushing the department's new accountability measures for dashboard cameras and their audio components. Officers had repeatedly violated these policies for years without consequences, he said, and, in some cases, had intentionally damaged the dashcam video and audio. The McDonald shooting, he said, was an example of the problem: "For this lack of integrity, we have never seriously disciplined any department member. As a result, we have not had video and audio in several of the high-profile police-involved shootings or other allegations of misconduct."

Anne Kirkpatrick had been the chief of the police department in Spokane, Washington, until she retired in 2012. If selected, she would be the department's first woman superintendent. Kirkpatrick was then an instructor with the FBI's Law Enforcement Executive Development Association in the Seattle area. Originally from Tennessee, Kirkpatrick began her law enforcement career in 1982 as an officer in the Memphis Police Department. She worked there three years before leaving to attend law school in Seattle. After earning a law degree in 1989, she joined the police department in Redmond, Washington, a suburb of Seattle. She was later hired as police chief at two small Washington communities before being named in 2016 to head the department in Spokane, the state's second-largest city. She arrived in Spokane while the city was wrestling with its own use-of-force controversy. Spokane police officers had been accused of beating and hog-tying janitor Otto Zehm months earlier during a confrontation at a convenience store. Zehm died on the scene three minutes after the officers put a mask over his face that was not attached to oxygen. Initially, police had reported he lunged at an officer, but surveillance video released months later, as in the McDonald case, showed him backpedaling away.

Perhaps the most widely known of the three was Cedric Alexander, the public safety director in charge of the police department for DeKalb County, Georgia, just outside of Atlanta. Alexander had appeared often as a commentator on CNN and other news programs in discussions about police and tensions with African-American communities. In many ways, Alexander seemed like the ideal candidate. He had nearly 40 years of law enforcement experience, with at least three police departments, and experience working in homeland security posts. He had served on President Barack Obama's Task Force on 21st Century Policing. As president of the National Organization of Black Law Enforcement Executives, he was on the ground during police controversies in Baltimore and Ferguson. He had worked as an assistant professor of psychiatry at the University of Rochester Medical Center. As head of the Rochester (New York) Police Department, he had developed training programs to help police learn how to engage people suffering from mental illness. He had also worked on homeland security issues for the state of New York and for the Transportation Security Administration in Dallas. Alexander's leadership in DeKalb, however, was clouded by four questionable police shootings in the past two years. In one instance, a white DeKalb officer had fatally shot a naked, unarmed black man in 2014.

I knew all three finalists. I had worked with Eugene Williams on subcommittees as a member of the National Organization for Black Law Enforcement Executives (NOBLE) for years. Whenever I needed something out of Chicago, I called Gene. I worked with Anne Kirkpatrick when she was police chief in Redmond, Washington, and I was second in charge of ATF in Seattle. Anne and I would see each other frequently when I represented ATF at the police chiefs' association meetings. Alexander and I worked together at NOBLE and CNN. We had been involved in more than a dozen joint interviews, talking about police-related matters in Baltimore, Ferguson, Tulsa, Minneapolis, Baton Rouge, Charleston, and New York. I even knew McCarthy from my days running the ATF office for New Jersey, while he was commanding the Newark Police Department, the state's largest.

The mayor took his board's three choices under advisement and began his own deliberations. He met with each one, and, at one point,

Alexander told friends he was all but assured the job. Two weeks after the police board's press conference to announce the finalists, Emanuel called a press conference of his own to present the city's new police supervisor to the public. Surprisingly, none of the initial candidates stood by his side. He had rejected all three candidates. Instead, standing next to him was Eddie Johnson, who had not even applied for the job.

"I believe Eddie Johnson has everything that the city needs," Emanuel told a stunned crowd. "I happen to believe at this moment—this time—at this critical juncture, he has the command, the character, and the capability to lead. I think Eddie Johnson is the right man at the right time."

I'm sure the finalists were stunned by Emanuel's decision. I've been through the process of applying for executive positions. It is a grueling process, involving hours of writing essays and gathering all sorts of documentation, and hours of interviews with numerous department heads. For Emanuel to then give the job to someone who had not undergone that process must have been extremely disappointing, and, to some degree, an insult to all the applicants.

Many read Johnson's hiring as a bow by the mayor to the desires of black and Latino aldermen. The previous superintendent had come from the police department in Newark, New Jersey. They argued that another outsider would take too long to learn the machinations of the department and the intricacies of a diverse city of 2.7 million with a unique character. Others were concerned that an outsider might exacerbate already sinking morale among the rank-and-file officers. Latino alderman George Cardenas and other council members who made up the African-American and Latino coalition gave their approval.

"Eddie Johnson fits the bill, according to the people I'm talking to," Cardenas said.

Emanuel said he believed Johnson could rebuild officer morale while being a "bridge to the community," as police engaged in an all-out battle

to tamp down the city's violence. Williams, some noted, could have filled
that role, and he at least said he wanted the job. Still, the mayor, undaunted,
said Johnson was his choice. He'd been impressed with Johnson since his
days as South Side commander. He praised Johnson's integrity, recalling
a meeting with command staff in which Johnson exercised leadership by
saying he would wear a body camera and expected other top officials to do
the same. Emanuel's selection of Johnson temporarily threw the selection
process into disarray. Even though the mayor wanted him, he couldn't be
made the permanent head of the department because he had not applied
for the job. He could only be made the interim chief. The board would
have to begin the hiring process all over again, this time with Johnson as
the preferred candidate. Two weeks later, April 13, 2016, the city council
made it permanent, approving Johnson's appointment 50–0.

In my meeting with Johnson, I found him thoughtful, deliberate,
but forceful and very clear about where he wants to go and how he wants
to get there. His first year—2016—was eventful. In that year, Johnson
was wrestling with the worst violence in Chicago in nearly 20 years.
Murders had increased by 40 percent over the previous year to the highest number in Chicago in the past 20 years, all while having undergone a
kidney transplant. In May alone, there were 66 murders, with 318 shooting incidents in which 397 people were shot. Nearly half the victims
were children. Almost all of them were black. Many of the victims were
innocent bystanders, caught in the crossfire of immature, untethered
gang members killing rivals in retaliation for the most minute slights,
particularly on social media. One said something on Facebook the other
didn't like, or another claimed on Instagram that he was standing on the
other's turf and dared him to come meet him. Another "punked" a rival
on Snapchat and the offended party went looking for him.

According to the University of Chicago Crime Lab, one of every five
teenagers wounded or killed by gunfire in Chicago was not the intended
victim. For Johnson, it came to a head with the shooting of Nykea Aldridge,

the cousin of NBA superstar Dwyane Wade. Aldridge was pushing her infant child in a stroller on the city's South Side near Dulles School of Excellence, where she was attempting to register some of her four children. Two brothers, one 26, the other 22, started shooting after one of them "exchanged looks" with a man. The man was dropping off women he had picked up in the suburbs and driven into the city. The brothers knew the guy was not from the neighborhood and thought he might be armed. They chased the man down the street, firing at him as they ran. They missed him, but two bullets struck Aldridge, one in the head and another in the arm. She died 45 minutes later at the hospital. To the media, a relative of a famous native son had been killed and the death automatically set it apart from the hundreds of others who'd been shot that year.

Superintendent Johnson knew what everybody else knew: that a handful of "shooters," gang members police had identified, were behind the murderous crime wave, but people who knew them—ministers, church members, parents, community activists, friends, neighbors, social organizations—wouldn't help police bring them to justice. Consequently, they were free to continue their reign of terror. He was pissed off. There was no other way to describe it.

"I'm so sick of every weekend talking about the murders that happen in the street," he said at a press conference. "And the frustrating part is I've told you all countless times, we have 1,400 individuals who are driving the gun violence in this city. This isn't a mystery. We've gotten very good at predicting who will be the victims or perpetrators of gun violence. These guys choose that lifestyle, [and] they continue it, because we continuously show them there's no consequence.

"They're going to keep doing it until we show them we're serious. I don't need to preach about the incentive for other leaders to do something about this problem...I feel bad for the Wade family," he said, glaring at reporters. "I feel bad for the Aldridge family. But I feel bad for all of the families in Chicago who have lost someone unnecessarily because of this silly gun violence that we're experiencing. These streets belong to the rest of Chicago, not to [gang members]."

As the death toll rose, the pressure mounted for Johnson to turn things around. At the same time, Johnson was struggling with a mandate to heal a history of crimes and hurts that police had inflicted on black and Latino communities that now had been rubbed especially raw by the police shooting of Laquan McDonald and the subsequent year-long cover-up.

"Laquan McDonald shattered a lot of trust we had in black and white communities," he told me. "People felt police wouldn't hold themselves accountable. In the black neighborhoods, they felt police didn't give them the respect they deserved. Some in the white community felt it was excessive, and it damaged trust among them, but not to the extent that it did in the African-American community. It really tore at the hearts of some black people."

Johnson knows how those hearts were broken. As a young black boy growing up in Cabrini-Green, he experienced police from the other side of the badge. The collection of low-income, high-rise apartment units on Chicago's North Side was Johnson's home until age 9, when his family moved to a better neighborhood on the city's South Side. The city began emptying out and demolishing the units in 1995 and completed the task in 2011. At one point, it was home to 15,000 people, crammed into 3,607 apartments. It was considered the most notorious housing project in the nation. Poverty, neglect, and desperation mashed together to produce a dangerous no-man's-land of drugs, prostitution, robbery, theft, and violence. Johnson can recall as a boy asking permission to pass by adults in the midst of drug transactions on the buildings' public stairwells on his way to school. Police were a constant in the neighborhood. "There were certain officers we knew to stay away from. I avoided mistreatment, but I know it's not the same for everyone," he said.

To win back lost trust and engender trust where it had not existed before, Johnson is trying to instill a new attitude about police in Latino and African-American neighborhoods. "To do so, we have to engage in non–law enforcement settings," he said. "That's particularly true of the young people. If they only see us when we're arresting someone or getting physical, that shapes their perspective."

The Englewood neighborhood was an example of early success. "This past Halloween (2017), we had 500 kids show up for the haunted house in our police station in Englewood. That's never happened in my entire career as a police officer, and I have been here 29 years. That says to me that we are breaking down the mistrust, not just with kids but with their parents."

Additionally, murders declined in the neighborhood significantly, in part due to greater support for law enforcement efforts from residents.

————

Johnson's other strategic move is to change the culture of the police department. He calls it a "heavy lift."

Anyone who has read the Justice Department report following its examination of Chicago's police department clearly understands what *heavy lift* means. Following the release of the Laquan McDonald video, the Justice Department launched an investigation of the department. The report painted an unflattering picture of an organization replete with poorly trained, reckless police officers, functioning in a cowboy culture where individual officers are largely unaccountable to anyone but themselves and their own rules.

The report said police were routinely verbally and physically abusive, mostly against African-Americans and Latinos. Police used their guns and badges to bully residents, including children. They handed out their version of street justice by beating people and tasering them indiscriminately. In one instance, a female suspect was handcuffed and sprawled on the ground. One officer ordered the other to "taser that bitch 10 times." Their record of shooting and killing suspects with impunity was well-documented.

Racism was at the core of much of Chicago's police culture, something the mayor readily admitted. "The question isn't 'Do we have racism?'" Emanuel said. "We do. The question is 'What are you going to do about it?'"

Police misconduct was protected by supervisors and fellow officers, and when it was documented, it largely went unpunished, the report said. The department and its abuses were shrouded in a "code of silence" that the mayor and the union acknowledged, the report said. It cited numerous incidents in which police not only failed to report misconduct by fellow officers, but blatantly lied, even when they knew there was visual evidence, such as video footage, that contradicted their sworn statements. The report cited numerous incidents in which police lies were unmasked by citizen videos. It said officers routinely used the same catchphrases in describing defendants to justify their unnecessary and unlawful use of violence.

When blacks and Latinos complained, they were largely ignored. White residents had a different experience. An analysis of complaints against Chicago police officers showed a great disparity in response by the department, depending on the race or ethnicity of the person complaining about the abuse. When the complainants were white, the likelihood of action against the officer was six times greater than it was when the complainants were Latinos and three times greater than it was when the complainants were African-Americans.

The training, as described in the report, was dismal. The Justice Department investigators looked at the department's training equipment, manuals, tapes, and programs, and they concluded, "[The Chicago Police Department] and the City of Chicago have not provided [adequate] training to CPD officers for many years, to the disservice not only of those officers but to the public they serve. Officers at all ranks, from new recruits to the superintendent, agree the training is inadequate."

After reading the report, I agree. The report was the worst I have ever seen.

As an example, it noted that one class on the use of deadly force had officers viewing video made 35 years prior, long before key Supreme Court decisions altered the standards used to evaluate the reasonableness of use of force. A training official said the police department is using lawsuits to "measure training effectiveness," because the lack of quality training is resulting in civil lawsuits. Another officer said, "Our coworkers are going to die because of no training."

After recruits finish training at the police academy, they are assigned to what's called "field training officers," or FTOs, who are supposed to mentor them through their rookie months of active policing. One ranking supervisor called the program a "hot mess," another official described it simply as "terrible," and a third said the FTOs are simply "warm butts in a seat" who do not provide any real training. The training facility, built in 1976, and the equipment used there are outdated and in disrepair, making trainings difficult and potentially dangerous.

Johnson's goal is to develop a wide range of progressive policies: new use-of-force rules; more scenario-based, use-of-force training rooted in de-escalation; annual psychological and physical examinations to help officers perform better and to give them a pathway to help in their high-pressure job; and a program to match criminals with jobs and help get them off the street.

"One of the fundamental things we're doing is far more training," Johnson told me. "Our officers are starving for [on-the-job] training. We get training and the training wanes. Next year, we will start providing 16 hours of training every year for every officer. By 2021, they'll be getting 40 hours a year to keep them fresh on best practices and mandatory training on use of force. They want it. We've also done a terrible job of protecting our officers' mental health. We are in the process of revamping that to include either annual or biannual mental health screenings.

We owe it to them to unpack some of that stuff. We have to make it normal for officers to seek mental health therapy."

Johnson added, "There will be quick action when officers violate policy. It's the first time in the history [of the department that we've done this]. In the old days it would take us weeks, if not months, to do something with the officers-involved incidents. Now, if they provide me with evidence that policy has been violated, I will take action within 48 hours.

"If it turns out the incidents were because of training, then we will handle it and get more training. If it's egregious conduct, we will deal with it accordingly. My message to officers is you either change or you find something else to do."

12.

THE JOURNEY FORWARD

All new police chiefs claim the department and police procedures will be different under their leadership. Unfortunately, that is rarely true in major police departments. It wouldn't take long for the public to find out whether Police Superintendent Eddie Johnson would follow through on his bold pronouncements on accountability. Just four months from assuming office, Johnson received his first test. In July 2016, a black teenager named Paul O'Neal carjacked a Jaguar convertible and led police on a high-speed chase that ended with him being shot and killed in the rear of a house in a residential neighborhood. In response, Johnson did something nobody had ever done. Johnson stripped police powers from three of the officers involved in the shooting within 48 hours and placed them under investigation. More importantly, Johnson released the police dashcam and bodycam videos of the shooting to the public within eight days. Those actions were unprecedented. They stunned many in the city, particularly following previous efforts to conceal the footage from other shootings, including Laquan McDonald's. The media and the public applauded the department for how quickly it had released the videos. Some inside the department, however, weren't quite as pleased. Some officers grumbled behind closed doors that Johnson had left their fellow cops dangling, that the early release of the footage allowed the public to prejudge the officers before all the facts were in.

"I had to explain that releasing the video is not indicting the officers," Johnson told me. "The video is not going to change, no matter when we release it. It will be the same footage. It's better to be transparent than not."

The department took heat for what was caught on the body camera. Johnson was even shouted down by outraged demonstrators as he tried to hold a press conference a few days later. Many were outraged, and, after seeing the footage, it was understandable. The video showed one officer on foot turning and recklessly firing numerous shots at the speeding car, with complete disregard for bystanders. Other officers also fired at the car, all in disregard of Chicago police policy clearly stating that officers are not to fire into a fleeing car unless the officers' or others' lives are in danger. Too much can go wrong when firing at a moving vehicle. Officers could accidentally shoot bystanders. They could accidentally shoot someone else in the car who is not involved in a crime. They could kill or disable the driver who could then lose control of the vehicle and injure or kill someone in an accident. Nobody should have to be maimed or die for a stolen car.

During the chase, the video showed O'Neal hitting two of the police cruisers, jumping out of the vehicle, and running into a backyard. One officer was helped by another to crawl over a fence into the backyard. Bad move. If the suspect had been armed, the officer was now alone and vulnerable in a closed environment. O'Neal wasn't going anywhere. Other officers were on the way. They should have waited for backup. If the other officers didn't get to O'Neal at that moment, they would get to him shortly. It's a car. It's a crime, but it isn't worth the officer's or the thief's life.

Police heard gunshots, but there was no video footage of the shooting because the officer who went over the fence and fired the shot did not have his body camera engaged, a violation of policy that Deputy Chief Eugene Williams said repeatedly happened among cops when he submitted his application to head the department. Based on the video released, only one officer had his body camera operating during the foot chase, which ended with O'Neal being shot in the back. As O'Neal lay facedown, handcuffed, and dying, one of the officers asked, "He shot at us, right?" He hadn't. O'Neal was unarmed, and no weapon was ever found. The medical examiner ruled his death a homicide.

Five months later, Johnson would be tested again. On the second day of 2017, off-duty officer Lowell Houser was arguing with his neighbor, Jose Nieves. Nieves, 38, and Houser, 57, had engaged in verbal skirmishes before. The Nieves family claimed Houser, a 28-year veteran of the department, had threatened to shoot Nieves before, and the family had complained to the Chicago police. There was a police record of their previous troubles. This time, Nieves was in the process of moving a sofa into his apartment, which, for some reason, annoyed Houser. During the argument that ensued, Houser pulled out a gun and shot Nieves several times. Nieves died. Johnson, dressed in blue jeans, a hoodie, and with a ski cap pulled down over his ears, hurried to the scene. It was a hell of a way to start the year. Johnson declined to make a statement to the media, which arrived on the scene after hearing of the incident over their police scanners. He told them that, for now, he had more questions than answers. Apparently, he found some answers relatively quickly. Less than 48 hours after the incident, Johnson had again stripped the officer of his police powers.

Within three weeks, Houser was charged with murder. It was a dramatic turnaround in procedure for a department in which officers rarely faced criminal charges in shootings. The city had almost always cleared them of wrongdoing, even when the evidence clearly suggested misconduct. Perhaps it was no longer business as usual, some thought.

Father Michael Pfleger has his doubts. He certainly has earned that right. Pfleger is an icon in Chicago. In the 40 years he has spent working on issues of violence and crime, poverty, education, addiction, alcoholism, domestic abuse, unemployment, abandonment, and incarceration, he has seen Chicago police superintendents come and go. He knows Johnson well enough to call him by his first name, and he's skeptical that things are changing, because, for him, there is a fundamental flaw in the system.

"I tell Eddie all the time that he's a great cop," Pfleger said as we sat in a secluded room at St. Sabina. "He's a good guy, but it doesn't trickle down. I see officers on the street and the way they talk to the brothers. It's 'motherfucker this' and 'motherfucker that.' [Better policing] has to ripple down to the sergeants and the beat cops. When I see a cop saying 'motherfucker this' and 'motherfucker that,' I challenge him. I say, 'Every cop he sees from now on, he's taking out what he feels about you. You are creating this relationship in him.'

"We have to see fundamental change. I talk to police officers all the time. Here's what happens. The black cop is in the police car with a white cop who's been around. The white cop says to the black cop, 'This is how we do it out here.' When the black cop says, 'We don't have to do it that way,' the white cop says, 'If you want to make it here, this is how we are.' Then you see something like the Laquan McDonald video. When we all finally got to see what really happened to Laquan McDonald, I felt extremely angry. It actually validated for the world what people of color had been saying for years. I was angry that no one in the line of authority in dozens of offices and roles had the courage to do the right thing. Now, we've seen video after video after video and police get off free. The culture of racism in the police department is rampant, and until police start going to prison, that's not going to change. There has to be a change in the attitude of police. Until that happens, I don't think we have a chance to change anything in the community."

Pfleger said that with deep regret, because he believes in that change, so much so that he organizes days for gang members and cops to get together at his church to learn that each is human, with strengths and weaknesses, aspirations and doubts, and families they love and who love them.

"We take 12 brothers from four different gangs, get 12 guys from the police, and they play basketball. Then, we go to the basement, close the doors, and, respectfully, we say, 'Let's hear each other.' We do some role-playing where I'm the cop and you're the brother on the corner and we change it back and forth. It's enlightening for both groups. I want to see it change. I want to see trust between the two communities because it would be helpful, but we don't have it now. The young people who know most of the information are reluctant. They are treated poorly by the police. So, they don't trust the police, and you don't give private information to people you don't trust. They say, 'If I talk, and I tell you what happened, now you're dropping my name on the street and my house is getting shot up.' And I've seen that happen. I agree that both people have to come together, but it's 60 percent on the shoulders of the police."

Pfleger, 69, is an oddity—a blue-eyed, blond-haired, 1960s-style activist who has spent his adult life working on issues related to African-Americans. He grew up just 10 minutes from where we were sitting in a traditionally homogenous white neighborhood. He got his first taste of the real world in the summer after his freshman year in high school, when he volunteered with a Native American population in Arizona for two weeks.

"One day, it was really hot, and about 10 of us went to get ice cream. The guy at the store said, 'You can come in, you're white. They can't. They're Indians.' I called my mom and said, 'How can this be going on? This is America.' She said, 'Welcome to America.'"

In August 1966, he heard that a man named Martin Luther King Jr. was coming to Chicago's Marquette Park. Pfleger had read about him and wanted to see the man who was creating so much commotion. He and a friend rode their bikes to see. King was in Chicago to march for houses and apartments to be rented to African-Americans. The marchers were met with a hail of bricks and rocks. One brought King to his knees. The experience changed Pfleger's life.

"I had never seen that kind of violence and rage," he said. "I saw all these white folks calling racist names, throwing rocks and bottles, and trying to turn over police cars. Some of them were families of some of my friends, people who went to my church, to my school. And King was not responding. He's saying, 'Brothers and sisters, we have to live together.' I'm riding my bike home that day and I said, 'There's something about this man. Either he is crazy, or he has a power that I want to know about.'"

Pfleger finished high school and attended college, "because I learned how much King valued education." His plan was to complete his studies at the seminary and work with King.

"Then King got killed, and my whole life fell apart," he said.

He moved to the West Side of Chicago and lived with a black family in the projects. He got involved with the Black Panthers, a black nationalist organization that promoted self-defense and started the free breakfast program that children enjoy in schools today. The organization was targeted by J. Edgar Hoover and the FBI. "Back then, nobody in the neighborhood was doing more to help the community than the Panthers. Not the churches, nobody."

He was named as the spiritual leader of St. Sabina in 1981 at age 31. Since that time, he has dealt with scores of issues, but none as troubling and intractable as the pervasive violence that has consumed parts of Chicago and so many other cities. In too many cases, it has been his job to try to hold together the survivors in its wake. He has worked to steer teens and young men and women away from the fates that consumed their siblings and friends. He has nurtured surviving families through the grief that leads to divorce, alcoholism, suicide attempts, and depression. He has watched as impoverished parents organize car washes to come up with enough money to bury their children, and then, years later, do the same thing all over again. And he's presided over the funeral services of far too many young men whose lives were ended by a bullet, including the black boy he took in as a foster child. Pfleger held the child's head in his lap as the blood oozed from his neck wound. All that pain has left a scar.

"To me there is no greater symbol of evil than seeing a child in a casket," he told me. "That has nothing to do with God. It's pure evil. It angers me, and it breaks me down at the same time."

As we talked, there was a knock on the door. An assistant came in and ushered him away. He returned about 15 minutes later. "Sorry about that," he said upon his return. "Somebody had turned in a gun to the church a few days ago, and a police officer had stopped by to pick it up. We have a give-back program. Bring a gun in, no questions asked. We hand them over to the police."

While Superintendent Johnson spends much of his time arresting black men, Pfleger is trying to save them from death, drugs, and the prison system. He works daily with "the brothers," the young black men society has thrown away and left isolated and distanced from the world they see passing them by. Many have records. Almost everybody has done something wrong. Pfleger and the people who help him are trying to bring them into the world of possibilities that most of us take for granted. If he is successful, for many it will be the very first time. While Pfleger believes in redemption, there are no free passes. A few years ago, his church began issuing rewards for information leading to the arrest and conviction of people involved in murders.

"We put out a bounty of $5,000 on their heads," he said. "I hate the prison system, but if you shoot and kill somebody, you should not be able to go home and eat McDonald's and watch television." So far, the church has paid out nearly $150,000.

As far as Pfleger and so many others are concerned, ultimately the answer to the insane, senseless crime embedded in cities like Chicago, Memphis, Baltimore, and Detroit lies at the feet of a society that out of racism and greed deserted communities of color. "We have consciously abandoned whole communities, and then we put police in to keep order, to keep them locked in those communities, to keep the natives quiet. Each of the areas has a common thread—double-digit unemployment, under-performing schools, more abandoned buildings boarded up. Individuals come back from incarceration and they can't get jobs. There is a lack of economic investment and easy access to guns. (Phleger says he knows of two incidents where bags of guns were dropped off in black neighborhoods with a note for people to defend themselves.) It's immoral."

"And if you look at the disparity in every major issue—unemployment, education, jobs, social services—race is always one of the primary factors. I was giving a talk one time to two white wealthy Northwest suburbs. And this lady asked me, 'What do you think it is going to take for society to stop this?' I said, 'I'll talk with you afterwards.' When it was over, I said to her privately that in the last week, 12 black youth had been shot and killed. 'When 12 white youth become shot and killed in the week, you'll see an end to this.'"

Could Pfleger be right? Could that be it? Could it be that we're coming back to that same discussion that we've been wrestling with openly for four years and unconsciously for more than 300—black lives don't matter?

Pfleger thinks so, and so does former US Secretary of Education Arne Duncan. He has returned to Chicago to join with Pfleger to try to rescue those most in need and, in the process, help all of us.

"If even half of those 762 people who got killed in Chicago were the same color as me, and not the color of the police superintendent, the number of murders in Chicago wouldn't be allowed to happen," Duncan told me. "It's impossible to say black and brown lives matter as much as white lives, when you look at who is getting killed in Chicago. If they were white, this would stop now."

They leave us all with a warning. If we won't reach out to address the core issues fueling crime because it's the right thing to do, because we believe that all lives matter, we might want to do something because our lives matter.

"Violence has car keys," Pfleger said. "I suggest people get involved before it knocks on your door. Just like drugs. It's coming to your door. It's coming for your child."

Philip Banks

Former Chief, New York City Police Department

Do black lives matter? No, they don't matter. They matter to me, but absolutely, they do not matter. Point to any institution and tell me where black lives matter in any form or fashion. They don't matter in law enforcement. They don't matter in education. They don't matter in health care. People do not care about black lives. This system does not care about black lives. When the crack epidemic hit [black neighborhoods], our total response was incarcerating people at record levels. It devastated black communities. Now you have the opioid epidemic. Police officers are now trained in how to administer an antidote for overdoses. If the opioid epidemic was in the black community, those officers would not be trained to treat addicts, and if the crack epidemic had happened in white communities, those [special drug] laws would have not been enacted. The truth is, you can't have a society that has inflicted so much harm on a group of people and then expect them to perform like everybody else.

I grew up in Brooklyn and Queens, but I claim Queens as my home. My father was a police officer, but it wasn't like he wore cop on his sleeve. It wasn't like, "Oh, my father is a cop, we have to do the straight and narrow." Instead, it was "You are going to act right, because I raised you right." The biggest thing he cared about was education. I don't ever remember getting a beating from my father, except when it was about school. When we got that beating, it was a vicious beating. It didn't fit his personality. When I came out of college, I interviewed for a bunch of jobs. The starting salaries for most of them were a lot less than what the civil service jobs were paying. So, I took the bus driver's test, I took the police officer's test. My plan was to go to grad school and get a degree in finance. When I got into the police department, it became very interesting to me, so I decided to stay.

I get enjoyment out of somebody asking me for a favor and me being able to do it for them. Don't ask me why, but I enjoy that. As a police officer, I had the ability as a 22-, 23-, 24-year-old person to have a million positive impacts a day. That was a high for me. At that point in your career, you have a bigger impact on people's day-to-day life at this stage than in other professions and even in any part of your career as a police officer. That got me. So, throughout my whole career, it has been customer service, customer service, customer service. It could be the smallest thing. You have a lady who comes into the precinct, and she's having a problem with the landlord. She's called the police. For me to take two minutes to understand what her problem is and tell her what she should do to solve her problem, to me, that is special.

What police do not understand is that every issue is a police issue when you are living in certain communities. I don't care if it's the garbage not being picked up, or that they are able to call somebody back and solve a noise complaint. In those communities, there is not an issue that isn't a police issue. That's not true in wealthy communities, but police are the all-and-everything in those other communities. That's part of the problem with law enforcement. That's why the progress hasn't been made [toward creating trust between police and minority communities]. Police are looking at themselves differently from the way the community is [looking at them].

From a political point of view, every law enforcement agency will say they have defined goals and measurement of whether they are being successful. For law enforcement, we're dealing with how many arrests we make; how much crime has decreased. That becomes your only metric of success. That's your gold standard. Your measurement of success, however, may not be sufficient or accurate. The only thing [police] don't put in the metric system is the police-community relationship, but it is the most important thing that they do. How do the police "know" the community, and how does the community "know" the police? While police look at their success as arrests and summonses, the community looks at their success as respect in their interactions. So, you have people arguing, because they have two different criteria of what makes a successful police department. The leaders in law enforcement need to understand that. That's why they've had so much trouble bridging that gap. They're talking about two different things.

That's how in the police department other things get covered up.

If you don't perform in football, they cut your ass. You're out. If you don't perform in the police department, they just shuffle you around to somewhere else. You're still a problem, but in order for you to lose your spot in law enforcement, you have to do something over and beyond. You have to throw 440 interceptions instead of 2. You have to kill somebody. If you look at officers being terminated [versus those who are not], it is such a high, high threshold. Departments ignore the early signs [that an officer is a problem]. They ignore all the off-side penalties. The reason they do that is because customer service has never been part of the mission, never been part of the fabric of law enforcement. The criteria are to make arrests; it's enforcement. If you have a business that's a monopoly, you will probably be arrogant. That's the police. Consequently, an officer who may not be suited to be in law enforcement will still be on the department because he is not violating the principles of law enforcement.

When you have true customer satisfaction, you minimize crime and you are serving the customer, which is the community, but in [police leadership's] minds, they can arrest their way to success. So, you have one police officer who sees three kids doing something wrong, and he locks them up. You could have another police officer who took the three kids home to mom and talked to everybody and said, "I don't want to see this again." The second officer may have stopped more crime in the future and saved those kids from becoming part of the criminal justice system. Right now, under the current metrics, the first guy is going to get the promotion, because he made an arrest. The other guy may get a reprimand, because arrests are a measure of productivity. So, the question is how do you keep the community safe versus just keeping crime down.

Everybody in the community has a role to play when it comes to policing—citizens, other government agencies, churches, community organizations. The problem is most people don't know what their role is or should be. Once that role is given to them, they can determine whether they are filling that role. Then and only then can they be a proper critic of the other side of that equation, which is law enforcement. In order to make a critique, you have to ask, "What did I do or didn't do to make this better?" I'm not so sure that the fault [for the current friction between black and Hispanic communities and police] has not fallen too heavily on the law enforcement side. They deserve the brunt of it, but not all of it. Police have become the default of any problem. If society is lacking something, it falls to police to handle it. When those systems fail—housing, jobs, education— they affect poor people by and large. It's a poverty issue more than anything else. But racism comes into play when the system is designed to keep certain people in poverty. When you have no hope, when you don't feel there is hope, you just say, "Fuck it," and then all those problems in some form or other lead people into the criminal justice system.

Maybe it's an unfair burden to place on police, but right now it's the hand we've been dealt. The community has a responsibility, too. For instance, in the African-American community, I don't think leaders have done enough to kill this "Snitches get stitches" code. They haven't battled it enough and it's hurting everybody. The bottom line is everybody has to be willing to expand their roles. If they aren't, they should not expect police to do anything but strictly be hard-core and just fight crime. If you look at police departments, they are dealing with lots of things that are not their traditional role. They are not mental health workers. So, why are they responsible for dealing with the mentally ill people on the streets and in people's homes? We're the police. People call us. We are not juvenile counselors. So, why should we be responsible for having positive interactions with the youth? We are not medical workers, but we are being trained to offer medical treatment to bring people out of opioid overdoses. You can't expect police to expand their roles and perform these jobs if you are not willing to expand outside of your core mind-set.

For instance, churches, just like they have ministries for different things—finance, health, education—they should have a person who is a law enforcement liaison. It is his or her responsibility to learn as much as they can about policing. They need to learn about police procedures and who are the patrol officers for their neighborhood. The liaison should establish a relationship with their precinct. They should invite an officer to their church regularly. The officer can talk about crime patterns or any other issues in the neighborhood. The person should be talking to police about concerns that the church's members have and they should be disseminating [to the congregation's information about] what a police officer is supposed to do and what they are not supposed to do. For instance, if you explain that once a police officer writes a ticket on your car, by law, the officer cannot take it back. Your people would understand that it's not personal. There is nothing the officer can do. The church needs to know the name of the police officer in the precinct who has the most complaints from the community. They need to make sure that they settle down on this guy.

The same thing with education. One of the things is that if you develop a relationship between police and the kids and the schools, it creates a different dynamic. Every school should get a police officer to adopt their school. The officers come in once a month or twice a month. There's a big assembly. The officer talks to the kids. They become more comfortable with police officers and the officers develop an affinity for the school and start seeing the kids differently. You also have to have the schools working with the police. When I was a commander, I had a problem with dismissal time. Because everybody got out of school at the same time, I didn't have enough personnel to monitor all of them. If I could have coordinated a staggered dismissal schedule with the school system in advance, I could have had my people at all the dismissals. We also needed to coordinate with the school's dismissal assistants and integrate them with our police officers. We needed to have this plan together in advance, because a lot of mischief turns into low-grade criminality.

So, here's another example of what I'm talking about. We had a bus route along a certain school that became a problem. Every time this particular bus came by the stop for the school after dismissal, it was already crowded because it had already picked up a bunch of students from other schools on the previous stops. So, every day after school, you've got this tension as five or six buses go by and every time one stops, students are pushing and shoving and shouting to get onto an already crowded bus. Now, the kids are on the bus, and they are packed in, they are noisy, hormones are raging, and if you're adult on the bus, you think they're wilding out. But they are not. They're just kids. But a lady on the bus says, the police are not doing their job. It goes back to the default position that it's a police problem. It's really a transportation problem; it's a school problem, but in the end, we become the be-all and end-all. So, what we did was coordinate with city services and have the transit authority provide three or four empty buses along that route and it eased the problem. It could have become a police problem if we hadn't expanded our role to get those empty buses to make that work. That's what I'm talking about.

I think there is an intersection between communities and police that we need to reexamine. A lot of single parents have difficulty. It's very difficult being a single parent, particularly if you are earning a low wage. You get to the point where you have given up and you see no hope. And then your kids start hitting the streets. If government and the police department are looked at as help, the person could also call the police department. As a single mom, you find your kid and they have drugs on them. What if they are hanging with gangs or the gangs are attacking them because they want them to join? Parents don't know what to do. They don't see how the police department can help. They think we are going to throw their kids in jail. Maybe we can't resolve the issue, but we can be part of the solution.

One of the challenges for police is that the people dealing with the public are often your most inexperienced workers, the people who have the least experience in policing. It's the person with one, two years on the job who is dealing with the customer. One of the problems in New York City is we haven't cultivated that training specifically for the patrol forces that are dealing with our customers every single day. The challenge for law enforcement is to take their young and inexperienced officers and be able to transform them into experienced officers quickly. Law enforcement has not done a good enough job of training. But it can't stop there. After you provide training, what do you put in place to make sure the person got the training right? Right now, in most departments there are no measures or metrics about retention or compliance. So, we've trained the officer in something, but we don't know how well the officer learned it or how well they are using it. So, when things are not working correctly, we can't say, maybe it's not training; maybe it's not follow-up training. We don't gauge compliance and retention, because if we do it and it's not accurate, then we have to do something about it. We have to get them right. We have to identify that officer who may be lacking.

13.

AT THE END OF FAILING SYSTEMS

The call came in at around 7 p.m. as a 10-96. That's the universal cop code for a mentally ill person. I'd been on several such assignments in my early days as an officer with the Arlington, Virginia, police department. I remember it was a particularly humid, muggy, summer evening when my partner and I got one of those calls. It was 1986. We rushed to the corner of Glebe Road and Walter Reed Drive. The call to the station had apparently come from one of the neighboring houses. Mental health calls are always tricky. They can be unpredictable, dangerous affairs—for the victim and the cop. Other times, I'm almost ashamed to admit, they can be, sadly, humorous distractions from otherwise taxing work. This one, fortunately, was the latter.

We found our suspect standing on the sidewalk, a man in his mid-50s, salt-and-pepper hair, unkempt, unshaven, and dressed only in a robe, socks, and slippers. On top of his head was a board, slightly larger than the mortarboards graduating students wear, that was covered with what appeared to be three or four layers of aluminum foil. Some of the foil covered his head and held the board in place. We would later learn that this was his version of a solar panel that he had designed to protect himself from the sun's deadly rays. We stopped the car and headed over.

"Good evening, sir," I said. "What seems to be the problem?"

"Solar eclipse, solar eclipse coming," he responded hurriedly. "Got to get ready."

We looked at each other and then back at him.

"One came yesterday," he said. "Were you ready?"

Maybe the man was off his medication. Maybe he was having a psychotic episode. We were police officers. We weren't trained for this. As per procedure, we talked to him a little more and observed his behavior. He showed us his identification. He had a residence. He didn't appear violent or suicidal. So, we thanked him and left. If he had badly injured himself, we could have taken him to a hospital. If he had committed a crime, we could have taken him to jail, but we could not take him to a psychiatric facility, even if we believed his mental illness was the reason for the crime. Since the man had done neither, we bid him good evening and got back in our cruiser. There's no law against being mentally ill.

Since my days as a young cop, the issues of the homeless and the mentally ill have graduated from occasional oddities to harsh fixtures on the nation's streets. In Los Angeles, the homeless population occupies 50 downtown city blocks. The homeless population in New York City is larger than the overall population in 95 percent of America's municipalities. Our nation's capital has more homeless people per capita than any city in America. Overall, nearly 200 of every 100,000 Americans are homeless. A vast number of them are also mentally ill.

Technically, being homeless and/or mentally ill are not crimes. But in the real world, it is law enforcement—police officers, sheriff's deputies, and state troopers—who have become the default responders to calls for people in mental distress or in need of housing. When families call for help for a relative in the home who is having a psychotic episode or residents report homeless people in their communities, the 911 operators don't dispatch mental health professionals or homeless assistance experts. They send men and women with guns, handcuffs, and batons.

Newport, Rhode Island, is a striking example of the nation's use of police as surrogates for mental health professionals. In the shadow of enormous wealth, a place where tourists flock to view the outsized yachts and iconic mansions, about 40 percent of all calls to police are for people who are mentally ill or have behavioral problems. In one case, police responded to the home of a 57-year-old woman 61 times in 17 months, and, with each call, the only culprits were the demons inside the woman's mind.

Meanwhile, hospitals dump homeless patients on the street for police to deal with because they are not adequately reimbursed for treating the uninsured homeless. In addition, these people often come with mental health issues hospital officials are not prepared to address. The accusations of so-called "patient dumping" had been around for years, but weren't confirmed until 2007 when officials at Kaiser Permanente Hospital were caught on video dumping 63-year-old Carol Ann Reyes on the street. She was homeless, suffering from dementia and wearing only a hospital gown and a diaper. After failing to give her medication to treat her severe high blood pressure, the hospital had arranged for her to be driven nearly 20 miles from its facility in Bellflower, California. She was dumped in Skid Row in downtown Los Angeles, where police were left to deal with her.

Other similar cases were reported in Las Vegas and Washington, D.C. The most recent incident occurred in early 2018 when the University of Maryland Medical Center in Baltimore dumped a mentally ill woman on the street, dressed only in a hospital gown and underwear in 37-degree temperatures. A passerby, a psychotherapist, videoed the incident and called 911 for help. Dispatchers sent the police.

Because law enforcement is designated to respond to these incidents, America's jails have become holding tanks for large populations of the mentally ill and homeless.

Cook County Jail in Chicago is the most glaring example. It is the nation's largest jail. Thirty percent of its inmates are certified by doctors as severely mentally ill. Consequently, Cook County Jail is the largest supplier of mental health services in the United States. No, not just for incarcerated people, but for all of America. As jail officials deliver daily rations of food and health care, they also hand out thousands of daily doses of anti-anxiety medication, antidepressants, and antipsychotics. Doctors are on staff to provide consultation and treatment. If you are poor, and you need mental health services in Chicago, you need to get locked up, the police chief told me, because, like other cities and states, Chicago has closed many of its mental health facilities.

And because America has failed to adequately provide care for the homeless and the mentally ill, every day the police find themselves on a collision course with people they are not trained to engage, often with disastrous results. Police are not health care professionals. Even with 40 hours of crisis intervention training—offered by only a few of the nation's police departments—they cannot differentiate between bipolar disorder and schizophrenia.

We're not trained to deal with patients who are in distress. Most cops don't understand what it truly means when mentally ill people say, "Don't touch me." Unfortunately, the police response, in most cases, is to touch them, because in cop world, if people don't respond to our verbal commands, we're trained to apply limited force. But how can these people follow commands when their minds don't allow them to even adequately process the conversations and exchanges?

In too many of these encounters, the result is death. Sometimes it is the cop who is killed or injured. In most cases, it is the citizen. Here's a scary number that should give our nation pause: While black people are three times more likely than other Americans to be killed by police, the mentally ill are 16 times more likely to be killed by police. Almost half of the people who die at the hands of police annually have a disability, from schizophrenia and bipolar disorder to Down syndrome, according to a widely reported study published by the Ruderman Family Foundation, a disability advocacy organization. Officers respond to emergencies with lethal force where urgent care may be more appropriate, the report said. The result? We are unnecessarily killing mentally ill people and using cops to do it.

Fast-forward 25 years from my encounter in Arlington to a cold

December evening in Baltimore. That's when two Baltimore cops got their 10-96, even though the people who needed assistance had never asked for police. It was a Sunday night in 2011, and the family of Franklin Williams needed help. Williams was schizophrenic, and he was off his medication, as are about half of mental patients daily, experts say. The family suspected so, because Williams, 37, had begun acting the way he did when he had one of his rare psychotic episodes. He had begun to drink lots and lots of water that day. He took baths and smoked cigarettes to calm himself and quiet the voices in his head. He was strange, but not violent.

When his 65-year-old mother came home, she found that he had locked her out of the house. Williams's mother called her niece, who was a nurse. She would know what to do, she thought. The niece dialed 911 and asked the operator to send someone to the southwest Baltimore home to take Williams to a hospital. The anxious mother was expecting medical professionals, perhaps an ambulance with people familiar with schizophrenia.

Instead, she got Sergeant Don Slimmer, a 10-year veteran, and Officer Brian Rose, who had been on the force for five years. When the officers arrived, a neighbor led them through their connected row house to the backyard, so they could have access to the back of Williams's home. One officer climbed through a back window and let the other one through the back door. The officers cleared the downstairs and made their way up the stairs. They stopped in a small hallway with bedrooms on either side. The officers could see Williams in the bedroom on the left. He was slumped over in a chair. Their guns were drawn. One of the officers yelled, "Police." That startled Williams, who stood up. Williams was a big man. When he stood up, it rattled the officers. He walked toward them as they commanded, and they shot him. Williams did ultimately get to a hospital, as his family requested, but it was a shock trauma unit in an Emergency Department. His attorney, Robert Joyce, told me Williams was so badly wounded he was dead on arrival. He had been shot 11 times, once in the head, but the doctors miraculously pieced him back together after several weeks of surgeries. He is permanently disabled from the incident.

The officers claimed Williams came through the doorway armed with a knife and attempted to attack them. He hadn't. That was a cover story. The cops hadn't noticed Williams's 12-year-old nephew across the hall; he saw the shooting and testified in court about what he saw. He told jurors that Williams didn't have a knife and he didn't lunge at the officers. In fact, Williams was standing inside his room when police shot him. Joyce noted to the jury that, after being shot, Williams's body was slumped inside the doorway and all the blood was inside the room.

The jury ruled for the family and awarded it $600,000 to care for Williams. The courts later cut the award down to $200,000. The cops were found to be at fault, but while that is true, it was the city, the state, the nation, all of us who are to blame. On average, each day, one mentally ill or disabled person is killed by a law enforcement officer because these officers are being asked to do a job that they simply cannot and should not be assigned to do. People who are mentally ill and the homeless are the most glaring examples of "criminal" cop encounters because of failed systems.

———

While in the St. Louis area trying to understand what happened in Ferguson before and after the death of Michael Brown, I stopped by the office of Adolphus Pruitt, the head of the St. Louis Chapter of the NAACP, to talk about his city's issues with crime and cops, poverty and police. Pruitt is an interesting guy. He had made so much money in construction in the first half of his life, that he decided to take a stab at tackling what ails the city and African-Americans as his second career. As we talked, he slid a piece of paper to me across his desk.

"Read this and tell me what you see," Pruitt said.

It was an annual murder report from the St. Louis Police Department's statistics section. It broke down the homicides by the usual categories: race of the victim, race of the assailant, age of the victim, age of the assailant, which neighborhoods the murders had occurred in. However, this document added some more information: whether the victims and assailants had used drugs or alcohol before the incident; gang affiliation, if any; previous criminal record, etc. St. Louis doesn't have nearly the number of murders as Chicago. In 2016, it reported 188, a paltry number compared to the 762 in Chicago. But when it comes to murders based on how many people live in a city, people are being murdered in St. Louis at more than twice the rate they are in Chicago. I quickly scanned the paper and shrugged. Of 188 murder victims, 159 were black. African-Americans, who made up about half the city's population, accounted for almost 90 percent of the people who were killed.

"Yeah," I said. "I've seen this before in lots of cities. That's true in just about every major city with a large black population. African-Americans make up a disproportionate number of the murder victims."

A sly smile crossed Pruitt's lips.

"Nope, look at it again," he said. "You're missing it."

I stared down at the paper. Only 18 of the victims had been gang members and only three of the incidents were gang-related. Not it. Nearly all the shooters were the same race as the victim, a long-recognized pattern for homicides. Not it. Most of the victims were male. No news there. Forty-three of the victims and 13 of the suspects were on probation at the time of the murder. Fifteen of the murders were the results of domestic discord.

"Most of the victims have a previous criminal history," I mumbled to myself.

"You're missing it," Pruitt said. "Look at the education level."

I was stunned. Not one of the murder victims had graduated from high school. Not one. The pattern was virtually the same for the people who killed them. Of all the factors on the page, it was the number one indicator of who was getting shot and who was doing the shooting. Pruitt handed me documents for the previous year and the one before that. The numbers were virtually the same in every report. Year after year, young black men were divorced from regular society, uneducated, largely unemployable, and unable to envision a future beyond robbing, stealing, dope dealing, and killing each other, while raining havoc on the rest of the city in the process.

The relationship between education and criminality exists across America. According to the Center for Labor Market Studies at Northeastern University, only 1 out of every 35 high school graduates was in jail or prison. Conversely, 1 out of every 14 white high school dropouts was in custody and 1 out of every 4 African-American dropouts was behind bars.

To be honest, you don't need a study to tell you that. Just ask any public school teacher. Schoolteachers can look across their classrooms, some as early as the fourth grade, and identify the students who will probably end up in prison or dead. They are the ones in impoverished families who can barely pay attention in class because they are quietly traumatized by unsettled homes and tumultuous neighborhoods, kids being bounced around foster care, the ones with a parent struggling to support too many children on too little money or those without present parents or stable guardians at all.

I've witnessed it as a volunteer mentor to middle school kids through my 100 Black Men chapter. Once a week, I drive from my home to Newark where I meet with six eighth-graders at Chancellor Avenue School whom school officials have identified as "at risk." The fathers of three of the six were gunned down in the streets of Newark. The father of a fourth died four months before I met him. He barely knew his father, because the father had spent most of his adulthood in and out of jail, but when I asked the kid what he would change about the world, he said, "I wish my dad was still alive."

The six arrive at each counseling session drowsy and tired because they live in households, they explained to me, with so much activity they rarely make it to bed before 1 a.m. One suffers with obvious signs of attention deficit/hyperactivity disorder. Consequently, he is constantly missing out on activities and getting in trouble. They are not bad kids; they have bad conditions.

And if they drop through the cracks, like millions of similar children, they become a police problem, because that is who we turn to when our systems fail.

Arne Duncan, former secretary of the federal Department of Education and previous superintendent of the Chicago Public Schools system, has seen it time and time again while working with public school systems. I met Duncan during a presentation to Chicago business owners about how they could help reduce the city's soaring violent crime rate by hiring and training some of those high school dropouts. Duncan had returned to Chicago to form an organization that would put black kids lost in the shuffle on a path to employment. He is working with Police Superintendent Eddie Johnson and Catholic priest Father Michael Pfleger.

Duncan explained that decades of neglect and failure to buttress faltering families and children had stunted the development of the vast majority of the men and women with whom he worked.

"Many of our guys are in the family business," Duncan said. "This is the world they grew up in. It is violent. It is dangerous. Most of them are tired of getting shot at and tired of getting shipped off to jail. There is this terrible myth that they are making all this money selling drugs. They aren't. We discovered that the guys who are doing the shooting are making $80 a day. Most would get out of that business if we could pay them $12 or $14 an hour. Transformation isn't easy, but we can't arrest our way out of this."

––––––––

As I think about law enforcement, a lot has changed. No longer are our departments homogenous bastions of white males. Many are led by African-American and Latino men and women. Still, in many departments, the percentage of cops of color is not representative of the community's populations. The numbers are a far cry from the days when black officers stood while white officers sat, when black officers were not allowed to arrest white citizens or ride in police cars, when referring to them as "niggers" or refusing to work with them because of their color was not cause for reprimand.

Yes, a lot has changed. And change is good, but it's not necessarily progress. If black men and women continue to die disproportionately at the hands of police, as they have over the past few years, we haven't made progress. If the relationship between communities of color and law enforcement remains as toxic as ever, we haven't made progress. Additionally, it begs the question of whether African-American and Latino officers are just as complicit in the continuing problem of biased enforcement as their fellow officers. For me, it points to a fundamental issue.

The wrongs inside police departments are not about a handful of bad police officers. Instead, they reflect bad policing procedures and policies that many of our departments have come to accept as gospel. To fix the problem requires a realignment of our thinking about the role police play and how closely they as a group and as individuals are knitted into the fabric of society. Do they stand apart from societal norms or will they uphold their motto of "To Protect and Serve"? Are they to be looked at as the men and women who sweep up the refuse left by our refusal or inability to tackle societal problems, or are they partners in our efforts to provide a vibrant and supportive community for all? The decision is ours.

EPILOGUE

Sixty miles south of my home is a small municipality in New Jersey called Bordentown Township. The population is 11,367, according to the 2010 US Census. Two very important things happened there in 2016. One alarmed me; the other gave me hope. The first was the arrest of the town's former police chief, Frank Nucera Jr., who had just stepped down after years on the force. Nucera was charged by the FBI with committing a federal hate crime and violating a person's civil rights while he was chief. Nucera, I would learn, is a confirmed racist. Once, when discussing a situation where he believed an African-American had slashed the tires on a patrol cruiser, he told a fellow officer, "I wish that nigger would come back from Trenton and give me a reason to put my hands on him. I'm tired of 'em. These niggers are like ISIS. They have no value. They should line them all up and mow 'em down. I'd like to be on the firing squad. I could do it."

According to taped conversations, Nucera routinely made such statements to his officers, referring to African-Americans as "niggers," "nigs," and "moulinyans," an Italian slang for nigger. He liked to intimidate local African-Americans by positioning police dogs at the gymnasium entrance during high school basketball games or by having his officers walk the dogs through predominantly black apartment units. If his officers weren't tough enough, he'd lead by example. When a black 18-year-old and his 16-year-old girlfriend were being arrested for allegedly failing to pay a hotel bill, even as they swam in the hotel's pool, Nucera approached the male teenager from behind, grabbed his head, and slammed it into a metal doorjamb. "I'm fucking tired of them, man," he said after the incident. "I'll tell you what, it's gonna get to the point where I could shoot one of these motherfuckers. And that nigger bitch lady [the 16-year-old's aunt], she almost got it."

I have known lots of New Jersey police chiefs. I was a member of the New Jersey State Association of Chiefs of Police. I knew incompetent chiefs, corrupt chiefs in New Jersey and other states, as well. Still, I was stunned that someone as morally and intellectually bankrupt as Nucera could have headed a police department in New Jersey, or any state for that matter, in these times. It would be easy to say Nucera was a bad cop, an aberration that fortunately has been excised from the law enforcement body, but who he is and what he was speaks to the explicit or tacit approval of racism and bias by mayors, city officials, and other police officers who have worked with officers like him. Nucera had been a member of the Bordentown Police Department for years. He was promoted through the ranks to become chief. Consequently, in all those years, his racism was no secret to those who worked with him day to day. In the end, it was even rewarded. His rise to the position of chief is disheartening.

Still, as sickened as I was by Nucera, there was a wrinkle of hope: his arrest. It made me think that maybe, just maybe, we are ready to rid our departments of noxious cops, dangerous police behaviors, and bad police policies that put people in danger and do a disservice to all Americans. Nucera, it turns out, was done in by one of his own men. A white police officer in his department was so offended by his racism that he went to the FBI and agreed to secretly record his conversations. Those recordings led to his arrest.

The courageous officer's actions hint at a relatively small, but significant attitudinal shift among individual officers. That shift communicates a new attitude in law enforcement: that we recognize the role police have historically played as oppressors and occupiers of African-American communities, and we want to change that relationship.

President Barack Obama began the dialogue when he convened law enforcement from across the country to develop a guide for policing in the 21st century. Terrence Cunningham, however, as head of the International Association of Chiefs of Police in 2016, signaled to law enforcement officers everywhere that its leadership has decided it is time for a change.

"There have been times when law enforcement officers, because of the laws enacted by federal, state, and local governments, have been the face of oppression for far too many of our fellow citizens," he told his 16,000 members in San Diego. "The laws adopted by our society have required police officers to perform many unpalatable tasks, such as ensuring legalized discrimination or even denying the basic rights of citizenship to many of our fellow Americans. While this is no longer the case, this dark side of our shared history has created a multigenerational—almost inherited—mistrust between many communities of color and their law enforcement agencies. We must forge a path that allows us to move beyond our history and identify common solutions to better protect our communities. For our part, the first step in this process is for law enforcement and the IACP to acknowledge and apologize for the actions of the past and the role that our profession has played in society's historical mistreatment of communities of color."

Despite Cunningham's statement, cops like Nucera prove, unfortunately, the past is not always past. Nor does his statement soothe the pain of the families of victims of police shooting and abuse such as Walter Scott, Philando Castile, Alton Sterling, Tamir Rice, Laquan McDonald, Eric Garner, Freddie Gray, and Sandra Bland, or of Fred Watson and his children.

Still, it's refreshing to have law enforcement acknowledge past misdeeds regarding African-American and Latino communities and point toward a new direction in police behavior. Additionally, some police departments, in most cases prodded by US Justice Department consent decrees after an individual police officer's action revealed systemic abuse, are moving toward a system of law enforcement, in which police officers are judged by how many people they positively serve, rather than solely by how many arrests they make and how many summonses they issue.

What departments are discovering is that while, yes, there are bad police officers, the real problem is bad systems—inadequate training, reward, and promotion issues; lack of community engagement; and mismatched expectations between what patrol officers see as their jobs and what the communities see as the police officer's responsibility.

Organizations and groups like Black Lives Matter have pushed the conversation forward by focusing all of us on the centuries-old problem of black men and women, girls and boys being routinely disrespected, discounted, harassed, jailed, and shot down indiscriminately by police.

But if black lives matter, all of them must matter, not only the ones whose lives are snuffed out by police. If Michael Brown's life mattered, then so did Richard Jordan III, a 10-year old-who loved to play football and was slain in a drive-by shooting in Memphis, Tennessee, at 4:30 p.m. on November 13, 2017, while in a car with his family, and 1-year-old Robin Keefer, who was fatally shot four days before Richard Jordan, also in Memphis, as she played in her family's apartment, and Robin Keefer's 2-year-old sister, Laylah Washington, shot and killed five months earlier, also in another drive-by.

After years in law enforcement, cops become immune to most things. Still, I always knew that one day there would be something I encountered that would shake me—some case, some murder, some thing that would burrow into my psyche and stay with me for the rest of my life. That event would be my personal reckoning.

It came on a hot summer evening in 2006, not long before I moved to Newark. Four friends—Terrance Aeriel, 18; Natasha Aeriel, his 19-year-old sister; Dashon Harvey, 20; and Iofemi Hightower, 20—had gathered on Saturday, August 5, in the playground of Mount Vernon High School, located in a middle-class Newark suburb. At around 11:30 p.m., a group of men approached them as they played music. And then the horror began. Natasha Aeriel was shot first, collapsing from a bullet to the face near a set of bleachers. The other three were then marched behind a low wall for what would be the last seconds of lives that had hardly begun. They were forced to kneel and then shot one by one, execution-style. Natasha survived.

The incident made national news. The suspects were ultimately caught. I was in charge of the ATF's Denver Division when it happened. The news hit me harder than some, because the murders struck close to home. Three of the victims were students at Delaware State University, my alma mater, and the other one had applied to go there. Three of them were in the university's marching band, the DSU Approaching Storm, the same school band that played during halftime at my football games while the other players and I were in the locker room preparing for the second half. One of them guided prospective students around Delaware State as an ambassador for the university. They were good kids; kids with hope and purpose. It was so senseless. A gang initiation.

Shortly after I arrived in my new post in New Jersey, I was conducting a special briefing for some of my supervisors just a year after the murders. As part of the briefing, we were shown the crime scene photos. Their dead faces peered back at me from the photographs flashed across the screen, and my heart broke.

Those black lives mattered, too. They mattered to me and their families and their friends and the teachers and advisers at their schools and their next-door neighbors. I couldn't get those faces out of my head. They haunted me. In response, I set up the Horace Foundation Endowment for Criminal Justice Studies at Delaware State University, which gives scholarships to students from northern New Jersey to study criminal justice. I'm not rich, so people sometimes ask me why I started a scholarship fund. In response, I quote a song by one of my favorite artists:

Nobody can do everything, but everybody can do something.
Nobody can do everything, but everybody can do something.
Nobody can do everything, but everybody can do something.
Everybody can do something.
Everybody can do something.
Everybody can do something.

SOURCES

Aside from my many years of training in law enforcement and numerous interviews with other law enforcement officials, the research for this book encompassed an in-depth look at health care, psychology, sociology, and history in the United States. My coauthor and I spoke with heads of departments of housing as well as sociologists and social scientists.

More specifically, we found resources for Baltimore, St. Louis, and Washington, D.C. at the United States Department of Health and Human Services. We pored through mounds of information regarding police training and use-of-force policies.

We also examined the history of use of force, including the Supreme Court cases that redefined law enforcement's use of lethal procedures. Publications by the Police Executive Research Forum were invaluable, as was the published work of President Obama's task force report on 21st-century policing.

We read through tons of public records to dig up information about ticketing patterns in Ferguson and the nation's opioid crisis. We culled health department reports and cause-of-death documents to understand the correlations between health care and crime.

Finally, reportage by journalists at the *Chicago Tribune*, the *New York Times Magazine*, the *Washington Post*, and *The Guardian* provided a road map that pointed us in the right direction. The list of sources below is by no means exhaustive, but it is an example of the work that was an integral part of writing *The Black and the Blue*.

American Civil Liberties Union. "A Living Death; Life without Parole for Nonviolent Offenses." (November 2013), https://www.aclu.org/ sites/default/files/field_document/111813-lwop-complete-report .pdf.

"Baltimore: A City Defined by Falling Bodies." *Waikato Times* (Hamilton, New Zealand), May 17, 2017.

Baltimore City Health Department. "Baltimore Life Expectancy, 2013."

Baltimore City Health Department. "Baltimore Life Expectancy, 2016." https://health.baltimorecity.gov/news/news-coverage/2017-07-07 -20-year-gap-life-expectancy-between-richer-poorer-areas -baltimore-cbs.

"Black Cop Says He Was Ordered to Look at Klan Web Sites." *Washington Examiner* (March 25, 2008), http://www.washingtonexaminer .com/black-cop-says-he-was-ordered-to-look-at-klan-web-sites/ article/58827.

"The Blue Ribbon Panel on Transparency, Accountability, and Fairness in Law Enforcement." City of San Francisco (July 2016), http:// sfdistrictattorney.org/sites/default/files/Document/BRP_report .pdf.

Bosman, Julie. "Journalist Who Told Laquan McDonald's Story Faces Fight Over Sources." *New York Times* (November 26, 2017), https://www.nytimes.com/2017/11/26/us/chicago-police-shooting -journalist-laquan-mcdonald.html.

Bosman, Julie, and Mitch Smith. "As Chicago Murder Rate Spikes, Many Fear Violence Has Become Normalized." *New York Times* (December 28, 2016), https://www.nytimes.com/2016/12/28/us/ chicago-murder-rate-gun-deaths.html.

Bragg, Rick. "New Orleans Is Hopeful about Police Overhaul." *New York Times* (January 29, 1995), http://www.nytimes.com/1995/01/29/ us/new-orleans-is-hopeful-about-police-overhaul.html.

Broadwater, Luke, and Kevin Rector. "Pugh Seeks Audit of Baltimore

Police Overtime after Seven Officers Indicted." *Baltimore Sun* (March 3, 2017), http://www.baltimoresun.com/news/maryland/baltimore-city/politics/bs-md-ci-police-ot-20170303-story.html.

Capatosto, Kelly. "Two Lenses, One Goal: Understanding the Psychological and Structural Barriers People of Color Face in the Criminal Justice System." Kirwan Institute for the Study of Race and Ethnicity (November 2016), http://kirwaninstitute.osu.edu/my-product/two-lenses-one-goal/.

Center for Policing Equity. "The Science of Justice: Race, Arrests and Police Use of Force." (July 2016), http://policingequity.org/research/1687-2/.

Crepeau, Megan. "Prosecutor in Alleged Cover-Up of Laquan McDonald Shooting Moves for New Judge." *Chicago Tribune* (July 13, 2017), http://www.chicagotribune.com/news/local/breaking/ct-laquan-mcdonald-cops-judge-met-20170713-story.html.

Daly, Michael. "Inside Rahm Emanuel's Vote to Silence Laquan McDonald's Family." *Daily Beast* (December 2, 2015), https://www.thedailybeast.com/inside-rahm-emanuels-vote-to-silence-laquan-mcdonalds-family.

Davey, Monica. "Officers' Statements Differ from Video in Death of Laquan McDonald." *New York Times* (December 5, 2015), https://www.nytimes.com/2015/12/06/us/officers-statements-differ-from-video-in-death-of-laquan-mcdonald.html.

Davey, Monica, and Mitch Smith. "Anger Over Killing by Police Halts Shopping in Chicago." *New York Times* (November 27, 2015), https://www.nytimes.com/2015/11/28/us/laquan-mcdonald-jamar-clark-protests.html.

———. "Chicago Protests Mostly Peaceful after Video of Police Shooting Is Released." *New York Times* (November 24, 2015), https://www.nytimes.com/2015/11/25/us/chicago-officer-charged-in-death-of-black-teenager-official-says.html.

deCourcy Hinds, Michael. "Frank Rizzo of Philadelphia Dies at 70." *New York Times* (July 17, 1991), http://www.nytimes.com/1991/07/17/obituaries/frank-rizzo-of-philadelphia-dies-at-70.html.

"Disproportionate Minority Contact in the Juvenile Justice System." The Sentencing Project (May 2014), http://www.sentencingproject .org/publications/disproportionate-minority-contact-in-the-juvenile -justice-system/.

Final Report of the President's Task Force on 21st Century Policing (May 2015), https://ric-zai-inc.com/Publications/cops-p311-pub.pdf.

Fortin, Jacey, and Jonah Engel Bromwich. "Cleveland Officer Who Killed Tamir Rice Is Fired for Lying on Application." *New York Times* (May 31, 2017), https://www.nytimes.com/2017/05/30/us/cleveland-police -tamir-rice.html?mtrref=www.google.com&gwh=6331443FF7624A1 9A5740B33B6052B25&gwt=pay.

Gainsborough, Jenni, and Marc Mauer. "Diminishing Returns: Crime and Incarceration in the 1990s." The Sentencing Project (September 2000), https://www.prisonpolicy.org/scans/sp/DimRet.pdf.

Guarino, Mark. "Chicago Killing Costs Prosecutor Job." *Washington Post* (March 16, 2016), https://www.highbeam.com/doc/1P2 -39414280.html.

———. "Why a Dash-Cam Video of a Police Shooting Might Not Be a Smoking Gun." *Washington Post* (December 28, 2015), https:// www.washingtonpost.com/national/why-a-dash-cam-video-of -a-police-shooting-might-not-be-a-smoking-gun/2015/ 12/28/9e0f8cda-ad7e-11e5-9ab0-884d1cc4b33e_story.html?utm _term=.efab2cc1131a.

Gutowski, Christy. "Laquan McDonald's Mother Opposes Release of Son's Juvenile Records." *Chicago Tribune* (July 28, 2016), http:// www.chicagotribune.com/news/laquanmcdonald/ct-laquan -mcdonald-juvenile-court-fight-met-0729-20160728-story.html.

Gutowski, Christy, and Jeremy Gorner. "The Complicated, Short Life of Laquan McDonald." *Chicago Tribune* (December 11, 2015),

http://www.chicagotribune.com/news/local/breaking/ct-laquan
-mcdonald-trouble-met-20151211-story.html.

Harvey, Thomas, John McAnnar, Michael-John Voss, Megan Conn, Sean
Janda, and Sophia Keskey. "ArchCity Defenders: Municipal Courts
White Paper." (November 2014), http://www.archcitydefenders.org/
wp-content/uploads/2014/11/ArchCity-Defenders-Municipal
-Courts-Whitepaper.pdf.

Husain, Nausheen. "Laquan McDonald Timeline: The Shooting, the
Video and the Fallout." *Chicago Tribune* (October 20, 2017), http://
www.chicagotribune.com/news/laquanmcdonald/ct-graphics
-laquan-mcdonald-officers-fired-timeline-htmlstory.html.

"Jury Awards Nearly $600K to Man Shot 11 Times by Police." *The Daily
Record* (Maryland) (March 16, 2015).

"Justice Department Cites Cleveland Police for Excessive Use of Force."
The Christian Science Monitor (December 14, 2014).

Knickerbocker, Brad. "Justice Department Cites Cleveland Police for
Excessive Use of Force." *Christian Science Monitor* (December 4,
2014), https://www.csmonitor.com/USA/Justice/2014/1204/Justice
-Department-cites-Cleveland-police-for-excessive-use-of-force.

Kohler, Jeremy, Jennifer S. Mann, and Stephen Deer. "Municipal
Courts Are Well-Oiled Money Machine." *St. Louis Post-Dispatch*
(March 15, 2015), http://www.stltoday.com/news/local/crime-and
-courts/municipal-courts-are-well-oiled-money-machine/
article_2f45bafb-6e0d-5e9e-8fe1-0ab9a794fcdc.html.

Krogstad, Jens Manuel. "Latino Confidence in Local Police Lower Than
Among Whites." Pew Research Center (August 28, 2014), http://www
.pewresearch.org/fact-tank/2014/08/28/latino-confidence-in-local
-police-lower-than-among-whites/.

Laughland, Oliver. "Tamir Rice's Mother Calls for Apology from 'Disre-
spectful' Cleveland Police." *The Guardian* (March 3, 2015), https://
www.theguardian.com/us-news/2015/mar/03/tamir-rice-mother
-cleveland-apology.

Laughland, Oliver, Jon Swaine, and Daniel McGraw. "Cleveland Officer Who Fatally Shot Tamir Rice Will Not Face Criminal Charges."
The Guardian (December 28, 2015), https://www.theguardian.com/
us-news/2015/dec/28/tamir-rice-shooting-no-charges-cleveland
-officer-timothy-loehmann.

Levin, Sam. "Tamir Rice: Cleveland Says Family Owes $500 for EMS after
Fatal Police Shooting." *The Guardian* (February 10, 2016), https://
www.theguardian.com/us-news/2016/feb/10/tamir-rice-shooting
-cleveland-police-emergency-medical-expenses?CMP=Share
_AndroidApp_Gmail.

"The Lingering Damage of Ferguson's Racism." Editorial, *New York
Times* (September 18, 2017), https://www.nytimes.com/2017/09/19/
opinion/editorials/ferguson-racism-fred-watson.html.

Mann, Jennifer S., Jeremy Kohler, and Stephen Deere. "A Web of
Lawyers Play Different Roles in Different Courts." *St. Louis Post-
Dispatch* (March 29, 2015), http://www.stltoday.com/news/local/
crime-and-courts/a-web-of-lawyers-play-different-roles-in-different
-courts/article_b61728d1-09b0-567f-9ff4-919cf4e34649.html.

Marcus, Frances Frank. "Overhaul Is Planned for New Orleans Police."
New York Times (January 16, 1995), http://www.nytimes.com/1995/
01/16/us/overhaul-is-planned-for-new-orleans-police.html.

"New Curfew in Baltimore; Parents of Violators Face Tougher Penalties." *Washington Post* (July 28, 1994).

Oppel, Richard A., Jr. "Officer Who Killed Boy Had a Negative Firearms
Review." *New York Times* (December 3, 2014), https://www.nytimes
.com/2014/12/04/us/ohio-officer-who-killed-boy-had-a-negative
-firearms-review.html?mtrref=www.google.com&gwh=8689CEBB7
F117E6D833B9DA789961BA2&gwt=pay&assetType=nyt_now.

———. "Police Gave Boy No Aid After Shooting in Cleveland." *New York
Times* (January 8, 2015), https://www.nytimes.com/2015/01/09/us/
police-in-cleveland-boys-fatal-shooting-did-not-give-medical-aid

.html?mtrref=www.google.com&gwh=35723BBE36407A44A10A9
BA24889CAA9&gwt=pay.

Police Executive Research Forum. "Advice from Police Chiefs and Community Leaders on Building Trust: 'Ask for Help, Work Together,
and Show Respect.'" (March 2016), http://www.policeforum.org/
assets/policecommunitytrust.pdf.

———. "Defining Moments for Chiefs." (February 2015), http://www
.policeforum.org/assets/definingmoments.pdf.

———. "Guiding Principles on Use of Force." (March 2016), http://
www.policeforum.org/assets/30%20guiding%20principles.pdf.

———. "Integrating Communications, Assessment and Tactics: Training Guide for Defusing Critical Incidents." (October 2016), http://
www.policeforum.org/assets/icattrainingguide.pdf.

———. "Re-engineering Training on Police Use of Force." (August 2015),
http://www.policeforum.org/assets/reengineeringtraining1.pdf.

"Probate Court OKs Settlement Amounts for Tamir Rice Family; 12-
Year-Old's Mother to Get Largest Share of $3.69M Portion." *Dayton
Daily News* (December 3, 2016).

Rector, Kevin. "Convictions Put Under Review." *Baltimore Sun* (March
24, 2017), http://digitaledition.baltimoresun.com/tribune/article_pop
over.aspx?guid=fada9107-8d8e-4e52-938a-328555ef709c.

Rosenwald, Michael S., and Michael A. Fletcher. "Why Couldn't $130
Million Transform One of Baltimore's Poorest Places?" *Washington
Post* (May 2, 2015), https://www.washingtonpost.com/local/why
-couldnt-130-million-transform-one-of-baltimores-poorest
-places/2015/05/02/0467ab06-f034-11e4-a55f-38924fca94f9_story
.html?utm_term=.0e0212e1f139.

Stern, Laurence. "Rizzo's 'Reform.'" *Washington Post* (October 30, 1978),
https://www.washingtonpost.com/archive/politics/1978/10/30/
rizzos-reform/1e39bbe1-225d-40a8-ae87-1dc02edfd357/?utm
_term=.a00eafb55740.

Stockwell, Jamie. "Baltimore Reeling from Shootings of Six Officers." *Washington Post* (November 26, 2002), https://www.washingtonpost.com/archive/local/2002/11/26/baltimore-reeling-from-shootings-of-six-officers/b654cb7b-4007-4f38-9dab-2e0e8c4abaf2/?utm_term=.aa2f356a96ed.

Stolberg, Sheryl Gay. "Fragile Baltimore Struggles to Heal after Deadly Police Encounter." *New York Times* (October 20, 2015), https://www.nytimes.com/2015/10/21/us/a-fragile-baltimore-struggles-to-heal-itself.html.

Sun-Times Staff. "$1 Million Per Shot—How Laquan McDonald Settlement Unfolded." *Chicago Sun-Times* (June 24, 2016), https://chicago.suntimes.com/chicago-politics/1-million-per-shot-how-laquan-mcdonald-settlement-unfolded-after-that-initial-demand/.

Sutin, Phil. "New Attractions Notwithstanding, Baltimore Struggles to Overcome Murders, Bad Image." *St. Louis Post-Dispatch* (December 27, 1998), https://www.newspapers.com/newspage/139696367/.

Swaine, Jon. "Shot in the Chest by Cleveland Police—Then Handcuffed and Fined $100." *The Guardian* (December 6, 2014), https://www.theguardian.com/us-news/2014/dec/06/cleveland-police-department-shot-black-man.

Thomas, Pierre. "U.S. Launches Investigation of New Orleans Police Force." *Washington Post* (July 13, 1996), https://www.washingtonpost.com/archive/politics/1996/07/13/us-launches-investigation-of-new-orleans-police-force/ec998a1a-e0d0-4f8f-a135-f30b51177688/?utm_term=.d2cedb51a0ba.

"12 Shot, Injured at Baltimore Cookout in Drug Feud." *Deseret Morning News* (Salt Lake City) (July 27, 2009), https://www.deseretnews.com/article/705319416/12-shot-injured-at-Baltimore-cookout-in-drug-feud.html.

US Department of Health and Human Services. "Results from the 2013 National Survey on Drug Use and Health: Summary of National Findings." (November 2014), https://www.samhsa.gov/

data/sites/default/files/NSDUHresultsPDFWHTML2013/Web/ NSDUHresults2013.pdf.

US Department of Justice Civil Rights Division. "Investigation of the Baltimore Police Department." (August 10, 2015), https://www .justice.gov/crt/file/883296/download.

———. "Investigation of the Ferguson Police Department." (March 4, 2015), https://www.justice.gov/sites/default/files/crt/legacy/2015/03/ 04/ferguson_findings_3-4-15.pdf.

———. "Investigation of the New Orleans Police Department." (March 16, 2011), https://www.justice.gov/crt/file/883296/download.

US Department of Justice Civil Rights Division and US Attorney's Office, Northern District of Illinois. "Investigation of the Chicago Police Department." (January 13, 2017), https://www.justice.gov/ opa/file/925846/download.

Valentine, Paul W. "Calif. Man Picked to Head Baltimore Police." *Washington Post* (December 21, 1993), https://www.washingtonpost .com/archive/local/1993/12/21/calif-man-picked-to-head -baltimore-police/27e550a6-21da-4c39-ab5b-7b907edee12b/?utm _term=.7a7044011222.

"Voters' Views of Baltimore Crime a Likely Key to Gubernatorial Bid." *Washington Post* (December 29, 2005).

Williams, Timothy. "A Persistent Case in Ferguson Raises Doubts About Reform." *New York Times* (September 4, 2017), https://www .nytimes.com/2017/09/04/us/ferguson-watson-brown.html.

Williams, Timothy, and Mitch Smith. "Cleveland Officer Will Not Face Charges in Tamir Rice Shooting Death." *New York Times* (December 28, 2015), https://www.nytimes.com/2015/12/29/us/tamir-rice -police-shootiing-cleveland.html?mtrref=www.google.com&gwh=F F9E7FAAAC84ED7FDDA0F5A29EF14F54&gwt=pay.

Baltimore Police Department website, https://www.baltimorepolice.org/. Bureau of Justice Statistics, U.S. Department of Justice

FBI Uniform Crime Report
Gallup Polls
New Orleans Police Department, https://nola.gov/nopd/.
Philadelphia Inquirer, http://www.philly.com/.
St. Louis Police Department website, http://www.slmpd.org/.
Statistica website
US Census

ACKNOWLEDGMENTS

Thanks to all the wonderful people at Hachette Book Group. Tremendous thanks to Krishan Trotman and Mauro DiPreta. To my friend and colleague Ron Harris, you now know me better than most. You were amazing to work with. I learned so much from you and thank you for accompanying me on our journey.

To Carol Mann and Malaika Adero: You believed and we achieved.

To Louise Ballard and Lorita Holley, thank you for sharing your husbands with the world.

To James Golden, Dr. Robi Ludwig, Joey Jackson, Andre Anderson, Pastor Victor Medina, Coach Joe Purzycki, Pastor Frank Burton, Linda Spaight, Dr. Towanna Freeman, Dalton Price, Elliott Weinstein, Myron Cox, Harry Cooke, Keith Glover, Jerome Hatfield, Nathaniel Jones, Victor Williams, Florence Chung and Shannon Wilkinson, Dr. Joseph Devine, Greg McCurdy, Grayling Williams, Al Berrios, Larry Washington, Drew and Kate Lewis, Ron Rivera, Dana Nichols, James Hairston, Tracy Harris, Gerard Wilcher, Kent and Songa Montford, Robert Botelho, Brian Glynn, Joe Bryant, Delaware State University, Gerard Harris, Elena Gonzalez, Kendra Tyson, Tonya Cauley-Scott, Willi and Karla Ellison, John and Lisa Ross, the Reverend Jesse Chester and the Reverend Eddie Lake, Karen Dorough, Kelvin Crenshaw, Michael Horace, Larry Ford, Jeffrey Fulton, Justin Benaugh, Ohaji Abdallah, Kenneth Spann, Debra Bressaw and Jamsheed Arjomand, Delano Reid, Fairleigh Dickinson University, Rich and Sandra Richard, Mike and Clara Colbert, Larry Ford, Tommie Bosley, Gary Lewis, Jeanne Fox-Alston, the

Chicago Skaters, the *St. Louis Post-Dispatch*, Constance Hester, Richard Rose, Dr. Adrienne Bradford, LaTeisha Larkins, Andrew Grubin, Tricia Bayley, Delford Jimmerson, St. Sabina Catholic Church, Dr. Rock, Emmitt Jordan, Andrew Cutraro, Geraldine Harris, the International Association of Chiefs of Police, the National Organization of Black Law Enforcement Executives, Scott Tennyson, Melvin Graham, David Sherman, Clark Atlanta University, Police Executive Research Forum, Joel and Tina Willis, David Carson, Robert Cohen, Noel Greenwood, Charles Adams, James Willis, James Harris, Phillip Dixon, Lorenzo Boyd, Jake Oliver, Howard University, John Batiste, Tom Masters, Arch City Defenders, Steven Woods, Dan Satterberg, Joanne Suder, John Crawford Jr., Maxine Birdsong, Kirk Montague, Larry Washington, Rebecca Gorely, Michael Wright, Tony Rice, Luke Rommel, Van Brooks, Reverend Sammy Vaughan, Marcellus Edwards, Terry Langen, Tim Borchers Esq., Debbie Bullock, Charles Humphrey, Carolyn Williams, Jeffrey Fulton, Charles and Carol Reed, Robert Moskaitis, Joyce Breassure, Tonya Cauley-Scott, Paul Schmick, Cecilia Molinari, Sheryl Axelrod, Brian Mallory, Pamela Liflander, and the scores of people who were gracious enough to share their time and their stories.

To my family, Dawn, Courtney, and Matthew, you are the wind beneath my wings. To Mom Elaine, thank you for your love and support. Dad, rest in peace. I hope I've made you proud. And to Will and Maureen, I am eternally grateful for your support.